Michel Foucault

Key Concepts

Key Concepts

Michel Foucault

Key Concepts

Edited by Dianna Taylor

Routledge
Taylor & Francis Group

LONDON AND NEW YORK

First published in 2011 by Acumen

Published 2014 by Routledge
2 Park Square, Milton Park, Abingdon, Oxon OX14 4RN
711 Third Avenue, New York, NY 10017, USA

*Routledge is an imprint of the Taylor & Francis Group,
an informa business*

Notices
Practitioners and researchers must always rely on their own
experience and knowledge in evaluating and using any
information, methods, compounds, or experiments described
herein. In using such information or methods they should be
mindful of their own safety and the safety of others, including
parties for whom they have a professional responsibility.

To the fullest extent of the law, neither the Publisher nor the
authors, contributors, or editors, assume any liability for any
injury and/or damage to persons or property as a matter of
products liability, negligence or otherwise, or from any use or
operation of any methods, products, instructions, or ideas
contained in the material herein.

ISBN: 978-1-84465-234-1 (hardcover)
ISBN: 978-1-84465-235-8 (paperback)

British Library Cataloguing-in-Publication Data
A catalogue record for this book is available
from the British Library.

Designed and typeset in Classical Garamond and Myriad.

Contents

Contributors

Ellen K. Feder is Associate Professor of Philosophy at American University in Washington, DC. She is author of *Family Bonds: Genealogies of Race and Gender* (2007) and is writing a manuscript on ethics and the medical management of intersex.

Cressida J. Heyes is Canada Research Chair in Philosophy of Gender and Sexuality at the University of Alberta and the author of *Line Drawings: Defining Women through Feminist Practice* (2000) and *Self-Transformations: Foucault, Ethics, and Normalized Bodies* (2007).

Marcelo Hoffman is Assistant Professor of Political Science at Marian University, Wisconsin. He is the author of "Foucault's Politics and Bellicosity as a Matrix for Power Relations" (2007). His article "Containments of the Unpredictable in Arendt and Foucault" is forthcoming.

Richard A. Lynch is Instructor of Philosophy at DePauw University. His translations include *Foucault, Ewald, and Isabelle Thomas-Fogiel's Reference and Self-reference: On the "Death of Philosophy" in Contemporary Thought* (forthcoming), and his scholarly articles address Foucault, Hegel, Habermas, Bakhtin and others.

Todd May is Class of 1941 Memorial Professor of the Humanities at Clemson University, USA. He is the author of ten books of philosophy. His most recent work is *Contemporary Movements and the Thought of Jacques Ranciere: Equality in Action* (2010).

Edward McGushin is an Associate Professor of Philosophy at Saint Anselm College, New Hampshire. He is author of *Foucault's Askésis: An Introduction to the Philosophical Life* (2007).

Eduardo Mendieta is Professor of Philosophy at the State University of New York, Stony Brook. He is author of *Global Fragments: Globalizations, Latinamericanisms, and Critical Theory* (2007) and co-editor of *Pragmatism, Nation, and Race: Community in the Age of Empire* (2009).

Johanna Oksala is Senior Lecturer in Philosophy at the University of Dundee. She is the author of *Foucault on Freedom* (2005) and *How to Read Foucault* (2007) as well as numerous articles on Foucault, feminist theory and political philosophy.

Brad Elliott Stone is Associate Professor of Philosophy at Loyola Marymount University, where he is also the Director of the University Honors Program. His research interests are contemporary continental philosophy, philosophy of religion and American pragmatism.

Chloë Taylor is Assistant Professor of Philosophy at the University of Alberta. She is author of *The Culture of Confession from Augustine to Foucault* (2009) and is writing a manuscript entitled *Sex Crimes and Misdemeanours: Foucault, Feminism, and the Politics of Sexual Crime*.

Dianna Taylor is Associate Professor of Philosophy at John Carroll University, Ohio. She has written articles on Foucault and Hannah Arendt and co-edited *Feminism and the Final Foucault* (2004) and *Feminist Politics: Identity, Difference, Agency* (2007).

Karen Vintges is Lecturer in Social and Political Philosophy at the University of Amsterdam. She is the author of *Philosophy as Passion: The Thinking of Simone de Beauvoir* (1996) and several other books in both English and Dutch.

Introduction:
Power, freedom and subjectivity

Dianna Taylor

Foucault the experimenter

Michel Foucault was not a systematic thinker. He referred to himself as an "experimenter" as opposed to a "theorist" (1991a: 27);[1] eschewed the labelling of his work in terms of existing categories;[2] and asserted that "thinking differently" and self-transformation, rather than "validating what is already known", lay at the core of his philosophical work (1990b: 910). "I don't feel that it is necessary to know exactly what I am," Foucault states in a 1982 interview:

> The main interest in life and work is to become someone else that you were not in the beginning. If you knew when you began a book what you would say at the end, do you think you would have the courage to write it? What is true for writing and for a love relationship is true also for life. The game is worthwhile insofar as we don't know what will be the end.   (1988: 9)

In addition to being unsystematic, Foucault's work also challenges fundamental aspects of the Western philosophical tradition. As he sees it, philosophers have exerted much intellectual time and effort and devoted many pages to creating a dualistic and overly simplified worldview that valorizes aspects of human existence that provide us with a false sense of our own ability to gain certainty about the world, and to thereby become masters of it and ourselves. This worldview imbues us with a false and misguided sense of security that, nonetheless, because it is preferable to the threat that uncertainty appears to

1

pose, ensures the reproduction and eventual systematizing of the same faulty thinking.

A principal objective of Foucault's work is to illustrate the historical and contingent nature of what philosophy has traditionally viewed as absolute and universal. In fact, Foucault contends that the very ideas of absolute and universal knowledge and moral values are themselves historical phenomena. Foucault therefore does "not seek to identify the universal structures of all knowledge or of all possible moral action" (1984a: 46). Instead, he conducts an "ontology of the present", a type of philosophical analysis that, on the one hand, seeks to identify the conditions out of which our current forms of knowledge and morality emerged and which continue to legitimize those forms, while also, and on the other hand, endeavours to "separate out, from the contingency that has made us what we are, the possibility of no longer being, doing, and thinking what we are, do, and think" (*ibid.*). In other words, Foucault investigates how persons in the West have come to be where they currently are, shows that in so far as their current condition is the product of historical development it is not a necessary condition, and enquires into how they might be different. Foucault is specifically concerned with promoting change that counters domination and oppression and fosters what he refers to as "the work of freedom" (*ibid.*).

Some scholars consider Foucault's unsystematic, non-traditional philosophical approach to be a weakness. They contend that the critical aspects of his work undermine or even prohibit Foucault from being able to promote positive social change through his philosophy. Charles Taylor submits that while the critical aspects of Foucault's work might possess the potential to open onto new and emancipatory modes of thought and existence, the way in which Foucault conceives of the nature and function of modern power undercuts that potential. "There is no truth which can be espoused, defended, rescued *against* systems of power," Taylor writes, "[a]nd there is no escape from power into freedom" (1986: 70). Similarly, Nancy Fraser argues that Foucault might be able to identify and critique problematic aspects of contemporary society, but he cannot provide us with reasons why we ought to reject these aspects. That is, because Foucault's critique encompasses traditional moral systems, he denies himself recourse to concepts such as "freedom" and "justice", and therefore lacks the ability to generate positive alternatives (Fraser 1994). Jürgen Habermas suggests that Foucault ultimately recognized that the critical and positive aspects of his work were fundamentally contradictory and therefore returned to a more traditional philosophical approach in his later work. "Perhaps", Habermas writes, "the force of this contradiction caught up with Foucault, drawing him again into the circle of the philosophical discourse of modernity which he thought he could explode" (1986: 108).

Thinking differently about power, freedom and subjectivity

Unlike Foucault's critics, the contributors to this volume see Foucault's unconventional philosophical approach as a strength. They reject the view that the critical aspect of his philosophy eclipses its positive and emancipatory potential. Each of the three sections of the book illustrates how Foucault reconceptualizes a key philosophical concept – power, freedom and subjectivity – and provides examples of how that reconceptualization facilitates new ways of thinking and acting that are able to counter oppression and domination.

The essays in Part I of this book show that the view of Foucault's work as merely negative stems from a fundamental misreading of his conceptualization of power. Foucault argues that with the rise of the modern era, the exercise of power in the West takes new forms. In his book *Discipline and Punish*, he shows that sovereign power, which is held or possessed and then wielded repressively by one individual over another or others, became ineffective in the face of increasingly complex social, political and economic relations that developed in the latter part of the sixteenth and early part of the seventeenth centuries. For example, violent public executions (such as that of Damiens the regicide, which Foucault graphically describes in his book's opening pages) were no longer having the desired effect of displaying the king's power and thereby discouraging criminal acts and ensuring social and political order. Instead, these events were invoking the peoples' rage against the king's authority, thereby promoting social and political unrest.

Throughout his work, Foucault analyses the new, "productive" forms of power that emerge as a result of the waning of sovereign power.[3] As Ellen Feder notes in Chapter 4, power is productive in the sense that it consists of "both positive and negative, unstable valuations that can be reversed through history". As the chapters on disciplinary power and biopower show, Foucault conceives of modern power as an interactive network of shifting and changing relations among and between individuals, groups, institutions and structures; it consists of social, political, economic and, as many of the contributors to this volume show, even personal relationships (including our relationships to ourselves). "I hardly ever use the word 'power'," Foucault states, "and if I do sometimes, it is always a short cut to the expression I always use: the relationships of power" (1994: 11). Given its productive, ubiquitous, dynamic and relational character, the pernicious effects of modern power are more difficult to identify, and therefore to counter, than the sovereign's power to take his subjects' lives in overtly violent and public ways.

Like most people in the modern West, Foucault's critics "[remain] attached to a certain image of power-law, of power-sovereignty" (1990a: 90). They therefore see Foucault's contention that "power is everywhere" negating freedom and subjectivity (*ibid.*: 93). Yet this would be the case only if we continue to commit the error of Foucault's critics and insist on conceiving of power only in its sovereign, "repressive" form. "It is this [sovereign notion of power] that we must break free of," Foucault writes, "if we wish to analyze power within the concrete and historical framework of its operation" (*ibid.*: 90). Analysing the reality of the workings of modern power is crucial. Foucault argues that as long as we continue to adhere to a very limited and increasingly outdated understanding of power we cannot begin to navigate modern power relations effectively. Uncritical acceptance of anything that is presented as natural, necessary, or ineluctable is problematic from a Foucauldian perspective. Such uncritical acceptance allows power relations to devolve into static states of domination, where only a very limited range of thought and behaviour is deemed valid or acceptable, with the result that many more modes of existence are considered invalid, immoral, or deviant and thereby deserving of social sanction, legal punishment, or eradication.

Taking Foucault's analysis of the workings of modern power seriously does not destroy possibilities for freedom and subjectivity. But it does mean that these important concepts need to be reconceptualized. If, as the contributors to this volume believe, Charles Taylor and Nancy Fraser are incorrect in their respective assertions that Foucault's conceptualization of power destroys possibilities for freedom, then what does freedom in fact look like from a Foucauldian perspective? First of all, if power is not something tangible that one possesses and uses in a repressive manner against others (i.e. the king deploying his power against his subjects), then freedom does not stand in an oppositional relationship to power. As the chapters in Part II show, Foucault does not conceive of power and freedom as opposed; rather, they are mutually constitutive. "Power is exercised only over free subjects," Foucault asserts, "and only insofar as they are free" (1982a: 221). Freedom for Foucault is not a state we occupy, but rather a practice that we undertake. Specifically, it is the practice of navigating power relations in ways that keep them open and dynamic and which, in doing so, allow for the development of new, alternative modes of thought and existence. The practice of freedom functions to "[disconnect] the growth of capabilities ... from the intensification of power relations" (1984a: 48).

During an interview, Foucault explains the relationship between power and freedom, and how engaging in the practice of freedom keeps power relations dynamic:

> What does it mean to exercise power? It does not mean picking up this tape recorder and throwing it on the ground. I have the capacity to do so ... [b]ut I would not be exercising power if I did that. However, if I take this tape recorder and throw it on the ground – in order to make you mad or so that you can't repeat what I've said, or to put pressure on you so that you'll behave in such and such a way, or to intimidate you – Good, what I've done, by shaping your behavior through certain means, that is power ... [I]f ... that is to say, I'm not forcing you at all and I'm leaving you completely free – that's when I begin to exercise power. It's clear that power should not be defined as a constraining act of violence that represses individuals, forcing them to do something or preventing them from doing some other thing. But it takes place when there is a relation between two free subjects, and this relation is unbalanced, so that one can act upon the other, and the other is acted upon, or allows himself to be acted upon.   (1980g)

If Foucault throws the tape recorder to the ground to shape the behaviour of the interviewer, the interviewer can respond in any number of ways: he can appease Foucault in order to finish the interview (without the use of tape recorder); he can refuse to conduct the interview on Foucault's terms and simply terminate it; he can simply appear to complete the interview on Foucault's terms, and then write whatever he originally intended to (or even include some uncomplimentary remarks about Foucault). The point here is that although the relationship is not equal, the interviewer is free in so far as he can respond to and in turn attempt to influence Foucault's actions. The interviewer does not exist in a state of domination where no response to Foucault's actions is possible.

As mentioned previously, "effective" navigation of power relations involves critically analysing our present conditions in order to identify norms and practices that reinforce the status quo to the point where prevailing modes of thought and existence come to be seen as given, as what must be. It also entails thinking and acting in ways that do not simply reinscribe prevailing, narrowly defined terms of what it is possible and acceptable to think and do. If, as Foucault argues, power relations are continually shifting and changing, then we must continue to analyse our present critically: practices that facilitate our navigation of power relations in one context or at a certain point in time may not be effective in other situations or contexts. While the interviewer may be able to appease Foucault by agreeing to Foucault's terms, this action might not be effective in a different interview situation. Some other interviewee might, for example, lose respect for an interviewer who immediately gives in to her demands and decide to terminate the interview herself. It is no accident, then, that Foucault characterizes freedom as "ongoing work".

Just as Foucault posits a relationship between power and freedom, so does he also conceive of a relationship between power and subjectivity. In a late text, Foucault emphasizes that although he is best known as an analyst of power, subjectivity has in fact been his primary concern. "My objective", he writes, "... has been to create a history of the different modes by which, in our culture, human beings are made into subjects" (1982a: 208). What does Foucault mean when he says that human beings are "made into" subjects? As the chapters in Part III illustrate, part of what he means is that the idea of "the subject" is itself a historical construction. Foucault explicitly states that "the subject" is a "form" as opposed to a "substance" (1994: 10). Within the context of the Western philosophical tradition, "a subject" takes the form of an active agent, an individual "rational being", to use Immanuel Kant's terminology, that thinks about and acts upon the world (which takes the form of an "object") and is a bearer of political rights and moral responsibilities. This understanding of what it means to be a subject (and, therefore, the specifics of the distinction between and opposition of subject and object) is perhaps most explicit within Enlightenment thinking, but its roots may be traced as far back as the work of Plato. Foucault devoted several of his Collège de France courses to analysing the different forms that subjectivity acquired in ancient, Hellenistic and early Christian contexts (see Foucault 1999a; 2005a). In doing so, he illustrates and provides support for his argument that subjectivity is a social, cultural and historical form rather than a pre-given "substance" that is outside of and therefore distinct from sociocultural norms and values.

By illustrating the sociohistorical character of a concept that is taken within the tradition of Western philosophy to be objective and neutral, Foucault helps us to see the extent to which the idea of being a subject is implicated in power relations. Remember that, for Foucault, power is productive: certain power relations give rise to or produce the definition of subjectivity presented in the previous paragraph, relations which that definition effectively masks. Thus, while all rational beings are purported to be subjects, the reality of the situation is that the Enlightenment understanding of subjectivity excluded a wide group of people, including, for example, women and the people of lands that had been colonized by white European men.[4] Foucault further illustrates the degree to which subjectivity is implicated in relations of power when he analyses the production of different categories of subjects, as well as the processes by which we as individuals construct ourselves in, through and in opposition to those categories. Focusing on the modern era, Foucault illustrates how the emergence of the human sciences (psychology, anthropology, sociology, biology, psychiatry) during the eighteenth century both solidified the Enlightenment understanding of subjectivity and gave birth to a plethora of new subject categories: human beings have now become both the subjects and objects of their own knowledge. In Volume I of *The History of Sexuality*, for example, Foucault shows how the fields of psychology and psychiatry categorized a whole range of human behaviours as sexually deviant, thereby producing a multitude of new modes of subjectivity that allow for (if not demand) social intervention into the population intended to distinguish "normal" from "abnormal" behaviour, encouraging the former and inhibiting (or even eradicating) the latter.

But, as noted above, Foucault also makes clear that subjectivity is not simply imposed externally. We take up and occupy the subject positions that our sociohistorical context makes available to us: subjects are not only made, we make ourselves. And, as contributors to this volume show, in so far as we make ourselves, we can unmake ourselves, or make ourselves differently: we can use the norms and values of our society in new ways, work on creating totally new forms of subjectivity, or even dispense with "the subject" as a mode of existence. "Maybe the target nowadays is not to discover what we are," Foucault writes, "but to refuse what we are. We have to imagine and build up what we could be to get rid of this kind of political 'double bind,' which is the simultaneous individualization and totalization of modern power structures" (1982a: 216). By showing that subjectivity itself is a sociohistorical phenomenon, as well as by illustrating oppressive effects of prevailing notions of subjectivity, Foucault makes clear that experimenting with being other than what we currently are is not only possible but also an integral part of navigating power relations in a way that both constitutes and in turn promotes the practice of freedom.

Risky business

Armed with an accurate understanding of Foucault's conceptualization of power and, therefore, of the ways in which freedom and subjectivity are not opposed to but rather interconnected with and implicated in power relations, Foucault's emphasis on experimenting and thinking differently begins to make sense, and the positive ethical and political potential of his work begins to take shape as well. Foucault's analyses of power, freedom and subjectivity make clear that not being able to rely uncritically upon existing norms and values in order to gain access to absolute truths about ourselves and the world in which we live, or to provide us with a moral code we can uncritically follow, does not leave us either in a state of epistemological and moral nihilism, or trapped within a perpetual state of domination. Rather, as Foucault readily admits, taking his work seriously places us in an oppositional position relative to prevailing modes of thought and existence and thereby deprives us of "access to any complete and definitive knowledge" of both the world in which we live and the "limits" of our ability to know and act within that world (Foucault 1984a: 47). We are, as he puts it, "always in the position of beginning again" (*ibid.*).

Perhaps part of what troubles Foucault's critics about the position in which he leaves us is that it offers no guarantees and it requires much of us. No one tells us how to perform the work of freedom. While Foucault may offer us some "tools", we must figure out the use to which we will put those tools. We must critically analyse our present, identify oppressive norms and practices and figure out how we may counter those norms and practices: simply telling us what to think and do would undermine the emancipatory aspects of Foucault's work. Moreover, Foucault encourages us to reflect critically upon why it is that we desire someone else to tell us what to think and what to do, why we believe that we must have absolute and universal norms and standards that dictate our thoughts and actions, as well as upon the effects of that desire. What is perceived by his critics as Foucault's inability to provide norms and standards by which to think and live thus needs to be seen instead as a refusal to do so. What would it mean for us to begin to think and act differently, to "seek out in our reflection those things that have never been thought or imagined" (Foucault 1980g)? "What is good", Foucault tells us,

> is something that comes through innovation. The good does not exist … in an atemporal sky, with people who would be like the Astrologers of the Good, whose job it is to determine what is

the favorable nature of the stars. The good is defined by us, it is practiced, it is invented. And this is a collaborative work. (*Ibid.*)

Notes

1. Foucault states: "Each new work profoundly changes the terms of thinking which I had reached with the previous work. In this sense I consider myself more an experimenter than a theorist; I don't develop deductive systems to apply uniformly in different fields of research. When I write, I do it above all to change myself and not to think the same thing as before" (1991a: 27).
2. "I have never been a Freudian, I have never been a Marxist, and I have never been a structuralist" (Foucault 1990c: 22).
3. Foucault makes clear that sovereign power does not disappear completely with the rise of modernity. See Foucault (1991b).
4. Many feminists and philosophers from a diversity of racial and ethnic backgrounds have argued that to the extent that the enlightenment notion of subjectivity continues to be adhered to it continues to produce oppressive effects.

PART I

Power

PART I

Power

ONE

Foucault's theory of power

Richard A. Lynch

An important step in understanding Foucault's broader projects is to understand his view of power.[1] Foucault's analyses of power are simultaneously articulated at two levels, the empirical and the theoretical. The first level is constituted by a detailed examination of historically specific modes of power and how these modes emerged out of earlier forms. Hence, he identifies modern forms of power, such as the closely related modes he termed "disciplinary power" and "biopower", and earlier, premodern forms such as "sovereign power". Indeed, much of his work on power is devoted to the task of articulating the emergence of later modes of power from earlier ones, and his analyses of disciplinary power in particular have been especially useful for subsequent scholars.

Three very simple examples can illustrate these forms of power. First, imagine a pyramid, with a king at the top, his ministers in the middle and the king's subjects (the people) at the bottom. If the king issues an edict, then his ministers will execute the order, imposing it upon the king's subjects. Traditionally, power has been understood as "being at the top of the pyramid"; and that was all that it was understood to be. But Foucault expands (indeed, totally reconceives) what constitutes power, and shows how this traditional view can be situated within a fuller understanding. He observed that in actual fact, power arises in all kinds of relationships, and can be built up from the bottom of a pyramid (or any structure). Thus, an academic transcript, the record of a student's courses and performance, becomes an instrument of power (how many times have you been told that "this will go on your permanent record"?), but begins from observation at the bottom of the pyramid, not from an edict from the top. Each and every student has a transcript, and this record of their performance, the fact that each one is observed (and not that the school has a principal), is what influences students' behaviour. The academic transcript is an instrument of disciplinary power: it serves to make a student regulate or discipline her own performance and behaviour. Similarly, observing which groups in the population are most likely to contract a disease (such as lung cancer) can lead to a discovery of its causes (cigarette smoking, or asbestos exposure). Like academic transcripts, this third kind of power – in this case to save lives, by eliminating asbestos or smoke inhalation – does not require a "top of the pyramid" to function. But unlike an academic transcript, this kind of power does not directly address particular individuals, but rather groups of people and populations as a whole. This third example is an illustration of what Foucault calls "biopower".

The second level of Foucault's analyses (the "theoretical" level) transcends historical particularities and is common to the diverse modes of power that Foucault has described. It is at this level that we can grasp the most general and fundamental features of power and its operation, and so we would do well to approach Foucault's work from this theoretical perspective.

Foucault's most explicit thinking about power developed in the 1970s, particularly in two published works, *Discipline and Punish* (1975) and *La Volonté de Savoir* (1976, translated as *The History of Sexuality, Volume I: An Introduction*), as well as his courses at the Collège de France between 1974 and 1979. We will focus upon his most condensed and generalized presentation of power, Part Four of *La Volonté de Savoir*, to accomplish three tasks. First, we will be able to grasp why Foucault's analyses can be called a "theory" of power. Second, we will identify the mistaken theories of power that his analysis is meant to supplant: the theories against which he is arguing. Third, we will be able to articulate the basic characteristics of power according to Foucault's theory: a network of force relations throughout society, relations that are characterized by resistance and which interact by means of local tactics and larger strategies. Since these characteristics serve to describe not only modern forms of power such as disciplinary power, but also earlier forms, they represent the substance of Foucault's *theory* of power.

A "theory" of power

What we can call a "theory" of power emerges from Foucault's mid-1970s analyses of psychiatry, the prison and sexuality. This theory is not restricted to descriptions of one empirical period or "regime", but describes certain general characteristics of power and its operation, across historical epochs and periods.

Foucault disliked the term "theory". He noted in *La Volonté de Savoir* that "The aim of the inquiries that will follow is to move less toward a 'theory' of power than toward an 'analytics' of power ..." (1990a: 82; we will soon see how this sentence ends). Foucault emphasized analysis over theory in part because he was reluctant to make any claim to a permanent or complete understanding of the world in which we live. In his 1976 Collège de France course, Foucault explained at least part of his distrust for theory: "the question 'What is power?' is obviously a theoretical question that would provide an answer to everything, which is just what I don't want to do" (2006a: 13). It is only in so far as theories can be used "untheoretically" in this sense – that is, without claiming to answer everything – that they can be valuable. Nevertheless, he did refer to his own project as a theory: his task "is a question of forming a different grid of historical decipherment by *starting from a different theory of power*" (1990a: 90–91, emphasis added).[2] For Foucault, then, the term "theory" must be used with caution; we should embrace theory only in the sense of "a theoretical production that does not need a visa from some common regime to establish its validity" (*ibid.*: 6).

With this terminological caution in mind, I shall use the term "theory" in an experimental sense: a theory is a hypothesis to organize diverse data, but also to be tested and revised or abandoned in light of that data. That a theory aims to be more general than a description of a single historical period or epoch is an essential part of its value and usefulness for our understanding of the phenomena it encompasses, and it is for these reasons that the term remains a useful term with respect to Foucault's analyses of power. Such a theory does not "answer everything"; its warrant comes from the empirical data that it organizes and that supports it, and it is subject to revision.

Foucault's theory of power suggests that power is omnipresent, that is, power can be found in all social interactions. As he put this in 1977, "it seems to me that power *is* 'always already there', that one is never 'outside' it" (1980e: 141). That power is omnipresent – that is, that power is co-extensive with the field of social relations; that power is interwoven with and revealed in other kinds of social relations – does *not* mean that power functions as a trap or cage, only that it is present in all of our social relations, even our most intimate and egalitarian.[3] Nor is Foucault saying that all relations reduce to, or consist of nothing other than, power relations.[4] Power does not "consolidate everything" or "embrace everything" or "answer everything"; power alone may not be adequate to explain all, or every aspect of, social relations. So

Foucault's theoretical task (and the conclusion of the sentence we left earlier) is to work "toward an 'analytics' of power: that is, toward a definition of the specific domain formed by relations of power, and toward a determination of the instruments that will make possible its analysis" (1990a: 82).

How *not* to understand power

Foucault first distinguishes his own theory from three mistaken, inadequate or misleading conceptions of power (each of which corresponds to a tradition or school of social thought, as I note below in brackets).

> [T]he word *power* is apt to lead to a number of misunderstandings – misunderstandings with respect to its nature, its form, and its unity. By power, I do not mean "Power" as a group of institutions and mechanisms that ensure the subservience of the citizens of a given state [such as characterize many liberal analyses]. By power, I do not mean, either, a mode of subjugation which, in contrast to violence, has the form of the rule [typical of psychoanalytic approaches]. Finally, I do not have in mind a general system of domination exerted by one group over another [i.e. class oppression], a system whose effects, through successive derivations, pervade the entire social body [as in many Marxist views].
> (1990a: 92)

Foucault's worry is not that these analyses are entirely useless, but that they often mischaracterize an accidental feature of power in a particular context as an essential characteristic of power in general.

> The analysis, made in terms of power, must not assume that the sovereignty of the state [liberal], the form of the law [psychoanalytic], or the over-all unity of a domination [Marxist] are given at the outset; rather, these are only the terminal forms power takes.
> (*Ibid.*, my comments in brackets)

So each of these forms of power (sovereignty, law, domination) may in fact be present in certain contexts as terminal forms, but none are fundamental. And Foucault's first task in understanding power is therefore to develop a new method – based on a richer theory – that begins with the basic molecules of power relations and then builds to more complex forms.

16

The most important misconception is what Foucault terms a "juridico-discursive" understanding of power. This misconception, "deeply rooted in the history of the West", is common to many "political analyses of power" (*ibid.*: 83) and approaches to sexuality. His argument is that this misconception, so generally accepted, has functioned as a mask by which much of the actual operation of power is obscured, thereby making many of the actual mechanisms of power tolerable (*ibid.*: 86).

According to this "juridico-discursive" theory, power has five principal characteristics: first, power always operates negatively, that is, by means of interdictions. Second, power always takes the form of a rule or law. This entails a binary system of permitted and forbidden, legal and illegal. These two characteristics together constitute the third: power operates through a cycle of prohibition, a law of interdiction. Hence (and fourth), this power manifests in three forms of prohibition – "affirming that such a thing is not permitted, preventing it from being said, denying that it exists" (*ibid.*: 84) – which reveal a logic of censorship. Fifth and finally, the apparatus of this power is universal and uniform in its mode of operation:

> From top to bottom, in its over-all decisions and its capillary interventions alike, whatever the devices or institutions on which it relies, it acts in a uniform and comprehensive manner; it operates according to the simple and endlessly reproduced mechanism of law, taboo, and censorship. (*Ibid.*)

Notice how Foucault has characterized this uniformity, "in its over-all decisions and its capillary interventions alike". Implicit in this characterization is a distinction between macro-structures (the "over-all decisions") and micro-practices ("capillary interventions"): a distinction that will be very important in the development of Foucault's own understanding of power. Recall our opening illustrations: a transcript would be a "capillary intervention", whereas epidemiological studies of cancer rates reflect macro-patterns. Foucault's analysis begins at the micro-level (in *Discipline and Punish*, for example) and is modified as it encompasses the macro-level (especially in the 1978 and 1979 Collège de France courses).[5] That this distinction is not made in the "juridico-discursive" view is just another indication of how it differs from Foucault's own analysis, and how it is mistaken about, and masks, the actual operation of power.

Why does Foucault term this view a "juridico-discursive" representation of power? First, it is juridical because it is modelled upon law, upon prohibition: "it is a power [more precisely a representation of power] whose model is essentially juridical, centered on nothing more than the statement of the law and the operation of taboos" (*ibid.*: 85). But as Foucault makes clear, the actual operation of power cannot be reduced to one model – the law, the state, or domination – but instead functions in a variety of forms and with varying means or techniques.

Second, according to this view, power is essentially discursive: its prohibitions are tied together with what one can say as much as what one can do; in this way restrictions on language should also function as restrictions upon reality and action – this is the heart of the "logic of censorship" (*ibid.*: 84). While this view emphasizes discourse as the primary arena in which power's effects manifest, Foucault notes that discourses are related to power in much more complicated ways than this view would suggest: "Discourses are not once and for all subservient to power or raised up against it ... discourse can be both an instrument and an effect of power, but also a hindrance, a stumbling-block, a point of resistance and a starting point for an opposing strategy" (*ibid.*: 100–101).

Let us consider another example to illustrate this "juridico-discursive" view of power: is what you are wearing today an effect of power relations? If you picked your clothes to conform to a dress code (skirts must fall below the knee, no profanity on T-shirts, etc.), then your choices can be explained by a "juridico-discursive" account: a prohibitory, discursive law specified what you could or could not wear. Within those rules, on that view, your choices were presumably made without external interference. But when we look more closely, this view is not correct: a number of other, "capillary" (your friends) and "macro" (fashion) as well as extra-legal power relations have almost certainly shaped your choices of what to wear. Foucault's own theory of power is meant to replace these "juridico-discursive" accounts:

> It is this image that we must break free of, that is, of the theoretical privilege of law and sovereignty, if we wish to analyze power within the concrete and historical framework of its operation. We must construct an analytics of power that no longer takes law as a model and a code. (*Ibid.*: 90)

A Foucauldian view of power

It is time now for us to turn to this constructive task, and begin to articulate Foucault's own positive understanding of power. Foucault's self-described task is to use empirical analyses to discover a new theory of power, which will in turn provide a new framework for (and the hypotheses to be tested in) subsequent historical analyses (Foucault 1990a: 90–91). He begins:

> It seems to me that power must be understood in the first instance as [1] the multiplicity of force relations immanent in the sphere in which they operate and which constitute their own organization; as [2] the process which, through ceaseless struggles and confrontations, transforms, strengthens, or reverses them; as [3] the support which these force relations find in one another, thus forming a chain or a system, or on the contrary, the disjunctions and contradictions which isolate them from one another; and lastly, as [4] the strategies in which they take effect, whose general design or institutional crystallization is embodied in the state apparatus, in the formulation of the law, in the various social hegemonies.
>
> (*Ibid.*: 92–3, my numerals)

There is much to unpack in this sentence. The bracketed numbers indicate four principal aspects of Foucault's initial definition. We have a set of "force relations", processes by which these relations are transformed, systems or disjunctions that are constituted by the interplay of these force relations, and larger strategies (or "terminal forms") with general and institutional characteristics that emerge from these relations, processes and systems. He begins at the micro-level, looking at local relations of force rather than at the macro-level of hegemonies and states, which can only be fully understood as functions of the local relations. In other words, Foucault begins with individuals' behaviours and interactions ("local relations" like academic transcripts, or choices of what to wear), to see how larger patterns, and eventually national norms or regulations, grow out of them.

First, then, power must be understood at the micro-level as relations of force. Foucault is unambiguous on this point: "It is in this sphere of force relations that we must try to analyze the mechanisms of power" (*ibid.*: 97). But what are these "force relations" at the basis of power? With this term, Foucault makes an explicit analogy to physics; he refers on numerous occasions, for example, to the "micro-physics of power" (1979: 26; 1990a: 16).[6] Force relations seem to be the basic unit, the undefined or given, in this approach to power. Very broadly, force relations consist of whatever in one's social interactions that pushes, urges or compels one to do something.

We can use the analogy to help us understand this notion of force relations as the basic unit of power. In Newtonian physics, force is defined as mass times acceleration. Force is thus the extent to which a body will be put into motion: larger objects (greater mass) will require a greater force to begin moving; a greater force will also be necessary to make an object move more quickly (greater acceleration). The important point here is that "force" is whatever serves to put an object into motion, *regardless* of the origin or source of that force. Force may be introduced by gravity, magnetism, or some other means. Its action thus can be described independently of any particular agent or object as the "creator" of that force. Analogously, Foucault speaks of power relations in terms of force relations without reference to a source or agent. This suggests that Foucault does *not* mean to imply that individuals cannot act as agents within power relations, but rather to draw our attention, especially for methodological reasons, to the force relations *as such* rather than to agents or actors. Closer examination of the characteristics of these force relations should help to make this clearer.

To recall, Foucault began with the claim that "power must be understood in the first instance as the multiplicity of force relations immanent in the sphere in which they operate and which constitute their own organization" (1990a: 92). Three features of these force relations are thus delineated, as follows.

First, that there is a multiplicity means that we will find many different relations of force, intersecting and overlapping, in our social interactions. What is more, this multiplicity suggests that these force relations will not all be of the same quality or kind: there will be multiple sorts of force relations, which may have different particular characteristics or impacts. To draw on the analogy to physics again, we could say that different forces will be present in the same field, as are gravity and magnetism, and that some of these forces will be stronger than others, and some stronger in certain contexts but not in others. To make this more concrete, recall (or imagine) yourself as a high school student, and consider what you chose to wear to school each day. You probably considered a number of different perspectives – or relations of force: what will my best friends say? Will a certain special someone think I look "cool" or "geeky" if she or he sees me in this? (Indeed, what constitutes "cool" or "geeky" is defined through multiple overlapping relations.) What "group" (the "popular" set, jocks, brains, punks, skaters, etc.) does dressing like this put me in? Is it fashionable? What will my parents and teachers think? Is it in accord with the school's official dress code? Most or all of these questions probably influenced your choice – whether you aimed to please or annoy any particular one of these groups – and they represent the very different, but intersecting relations within which you decide what to wear.

What sort of presence do these relations have then? The second feature delineated in this description is that force relations are "immanent in the sphere in which they operate". That these relations are "immanent" means that they exist only within a certain domain or discourse. In other words, they are not concrete, like bodies, but incorporeal, like the laws of physics. They are nevertheless genuinely present – and, like laws, their presence can be felt in very concrete ways. The analogy to physics is again useful here. As physical bodies interact, they exert relations of gravity, magnetism and so on upon each other. Similarly, social interactions are constantly permeated by these relations of force, power relations. Foucault thus describes force relations as a "substrate": "it is the moving substrate of force relations which, by virtue of their inequality, constantly engender states of power, but the latter are always local and unstable" (*ibid.*: 93). He notes in the 1976 Collège de France course that "power is never anything more than a relationship that can, and must, be studied only by looking at the interplay of the terms of the relationship" (2006a: 168).[7] This means that power relations are not outside but rather "immanent in" other kinds (economic, knowledge, sexual) of relationships (1990a: 94). So "power is not an institution [or] a structure", nor an individual capacity, but rather a complex arrangement of forces in society (*ibid.*: 93). Excepting an explicit dress code, none of the questions we asked above about what to wear could be answered institutionally, but they all have a significant impact on your status in school. And we are all quite aware of them, at least implicitly. Your choices of what to wear thus reveal "a complex strategical situation [how you want to be perceived by various groups] in a particular society [your school]". And so your self-presentation has been shaped by power relations. This has an important corollary: power is omnipresent (as discussed above) "because it is produced from one moment to the next, at every point, or rather in every relation from one point to another. Power is everywhere; not because it embraces everything, but because it comes from everywhere" (*ibid.*: 93). It even shapes our choices of how to dress on a daily basis.

So there is a multiplicity of force relations, which are immanent in social interactions. The third feature in this initial characterization is that these force relations "constitute their own organization". On the one hand, these force relations "are the immediate effects of the divisions, inequalities, and disequilibriums which occur in [other types of relationships]" (*ibid.*: 94). But on the other hand,

If in fact [force relations] are intelligible, this is not because they are the effect of another instance that "explains" them, but rather because they are imbued, through and through, with calculation:

there is no power that is exercised without a series of aims and objectives. (*Ibid.*: 94–5)

Each school has its own distribution of social groups or cliques, with inequalities and occasionally shifting alliances. These calculations, these aims and objectives, which Foucault will refer to as tactics and strategy, constitute the internal organization of power relations.

Several other propositions also emerge from this core understanding of power. Foucault delineates five. First, since power emerges in relationships and interactions, power is not possessed, but exercised. "It is not the 'privilege,' acquired or preserved, of the dominant class, but the overall effect of its strategic positions" (*ibid.*: 26). At stake here are two competing models of power: one based on a contract (possession), the other based on perpetual battle (strategies or war). As he notes in *Discipline and Punish*, his analysis of power "presupposes that the power exercised on the body is conceived not as a property, but as a strategy … that one should take as its model a perpetual battle rather than a contract regulating a transaction or the conquest of a territory" (1979: 26). Second, reiterating the point about immanence, power relations are not exterior to other relations.

Third, "power comes from below; that is, there is no binary and all-encompassing opposition between rulers and ruled at the root of power relations and serving as a general matrix" (1990a: 94). So power is not reducible to a binary relationship (we cannot reduce all sorts of power to one model); furthermore, power comes from below (as discussed above, a multiplicity of power relations exist; power emerges from a variety of overlapping and intertwined relationships rather than from a sovereign individual).

That power comes from below means we cannot best understand power by looking at monarchies or states, at the top of any chain of command. Rather, we must look at the complex webs of interwoven relationships: what Foucault calls the "microphysics" of power (1979: 26). Power develops in the first instance in specific, local, individual choices, behaviours and interactions. These combine in myriad ways to constitute larger social patterns, and eventually yield macroforms, which one typically thinks of when one thinks about "power" (societies, states, kings) – just as everyday objects are constituted by atoms and molecules. We thus have a micro-level of individuals (disciplinary techniques of the body) and a macro-level of populations (biopolitics).

Fourth of the five propositions that emerge from Foucault's conception of power is that "power relations are both intentional and nonsubjective" (1990a: 94). This juxtaposition is, frankly, puzzling, and this claim has led to a fair amount of misunderstanding about Foucault's analysis. First, power is intentional: power relations are "imbued, through and through, with calculation: there is no power that is exercised without a series of aims and objectives" (*ibid.*: 95). What you wear says much about you, and your status at school – not to mention your broader socioeconomic status (not everyone can afford designer labels) – and you have intentionally chosen to communicate a number of messages with your clothing. Foucault refers to these aims and objectives as "tactics" and "strategies", and notes that these are what constitute its "rationality". But power, he insists here, is also nonsubjective: "But this does not mean that it results from the choice or decision of an individual subject" (*ibid.*: 95). Nor, he continues, can it be located in groups such as economic decision makers, governing castes or the state apparatus. No one student, or social caste, or administrator can control what will be "cool" or "loser". Indeed, what is "cool" today could be "out" tomorrow, and an out-group can rise in prestige (or vice versa).

The problem here, the apparent paradox, is that according to Foucault's description, power has to be exercised by someone or something, but if it is nonsubjective, there cannot be a "someone" exercising that power. Foucault seems to be erasing agency – individuals' capacity to choose and act for themselves – or rather, locating this capacity to act in a noncorporeal "power" rather than in individuals and institutions. It is as if "power", not you, decides what you are wearing today. I think this problem can be resolved with two observations. First, part of his point here is that the effects of the exercise of power reach beyond any individual's (or group's) intentions or control. As we have already seen, Foucault is arguing against the view that "the state" acts as a monolith, and he is arguing for the importance of micro-events, with their ripples and interactions, in order to understand macro-phenomena. This means that local actions often have unintended macro-consequences, and that one's control of macro-processes will always be limited and incomplete. Macro-phenomena result from the concatenation of many micro-events, but they are not the direct result of any *particular* individual action or choice. This is, then, an argument for a system-level, rather than individual-level, understanding of power relations. Foucault's distinction between tactics and strategy parallels this micro/macro distinction. Tactics are local, micro (individual choices about what to wear today); and strategies are macro, systemic (school- or culture-wide understandings of "cool" and "uncool").

The second observation to be made here is a logical one. To understand subjectivity as constituted (in part) through power relations is not to deny that subjects can act intentionally. You still choose what you'll wear each day, even if those choices are conditioned and limited by the "strategical situation" in which you find yourself. Given this problem, the status of subjectivity will become a focal point of Foucault's investigations in later years. It is an important point, because one of the fundamental questions for ethical action has to do with the individual's ability to make decisions that are not "merely" determined by the relations of power in which they emerge – in other words, a question of freedom.

This question may in fact lie at the heart of readers' varied reactions to Foucault's analyses. Those who understand the claim that individuals are constituted by power relations to constitute a denial of freedom find his vision to be bleak. Those of us, on the other hand, who find in his analyses the tools with which to increase our self-awareness, and hence our own freedom, hear wellsprings of hope in his discussion of the continuous transformations of power through history. (Understanding how "cool" comes to be defined and how certain groups are "cooler" than others, one can – perhaps even through one's choice of clothes – begin to break free of or even redefine these categories and groups.) At a minimum, on the latter view, if power relations are in fact best understood as a necessarily ongoing battle, then the battle is never utterly lost.

Indeed, Foucault seems to anticipate this objection, this worry about freedom, in the fifth of five propositions that he discusses here. Power is always accompanied by resistance; resistance is in fact a fundamental structural feature of power: "Where there is power, there is resistance, and yet, or rather consequently, this resistance is never in a position of exteriority in relation to power" (1990a: 95). Without resistance, without two bodies (or minds) pushing or pulling against each other, there is no power relation. And through resistance, power relations can always be altered.

This fifth point encapsulates each of the preceding four. Power is exercised (first proposition) in the very interplay of force and resistance; this interplay is present in all social interactions (second proposition); force and resistance are manifest even in micro-interactions between individuals as well as states (third proposition); and while each person may choose to apply force or resist, the ultimate outcome of the relation cannot be controlled by one party (power is intentional and nonsubjective – fourth proposition).

On the role of resistance in constituting power, Foucault's position will not change. In a 1984 interview, for example, Foucault reiterates that "in the relations of power, there is necessarily the possibility of resistance, for if there were no possibility of resistance – of violent resistance, of escape, of ruse, of strategies that reverse the situation – there would be no relations of power" (1994: 12). He adds that "there cannot be relations of power unless the subjects are free ... [I]f there are relations of power throughout every social field it is because there is freedom everywhere" (*ibid.*: 12).

Let us stop for a moment and recall where we are in the discussion. We began this section with a long quotation, in which Foucault identified four principal aspects of power.[8] Our discussion so far has focused on explicating only the first of these, that power consists of multiple force relations. (We have covered a good deal of ground along the way. Indeed, we have implicitly addressed the other three aspects of power.)

The second aspect that Foucault identifies here is that these force relations are processes, not static, and are constantly being transformed. These transformations take the form of ceaseless struggles and confrontations – between the original force and its accompanying resistance – and sometimes strengthen the power relations, but sometimes weaken or reverse it. These processes also produce a number of interrelationships and systems, as various power relations reinforce or undermine each other (third aspect). Here Foucault introduces a distinction between tactics and strategy: tactics are the local rationalities of power in particular cases; strategies, on the other hand, are the larger systemic or global patterns of power. And (fourth aspect) these strategies are built out of combinations and concatenations of those local tactics.

> [T]he rationality of power is characterized by tactics that are often quite explicit at the restricted level where they are inscribed ... tactics which, becoming connected to one another, attracting and propagating one another, but finding their base of support and their condition elsewhere, end by forming comprehensive systems. (1990a: 95)

These comprehensive systems, or strategies, constitute "institutional crystallizations" out of the interaction and combination of locally fluid power relations, and become recognizable terminal forms like the state and the other types he enumerated.

The movement of Foucault's analysis here is from the micro-level to the macro, from the molecular to the everyday – from (1) specific, individual force relations through (2) their processes of transformation and (3) the networks or systems that their interplay produces, to (4) their larger, strategic manifestations in the state, the law and other hegemonies, such as ownership of the means of production. In the end-forms that Foucault identifies here, we should recognize the three traditions of analysis that Foucault earlier criticized as partial and inadequate (liberalism, psychoanalysis, Marxism). Even though each of these strategies may be one-dimensional, the networks of power taken in sum are multi-dimensional and cannot be reduced to only one strategic mode, "juridico-discursive" or otherwise. Foucault's point is that while they may have adequately described some particular strategy (or terminal form) of power, each approach fails to grasp the fundamental form or operation of power at the molecular level. But as Foucault reminds us again, analysis of power must begin not with these end-forms, but with "the moving substrate of force relations which, by virtue of their inequality, constantly engender states of power" (*ibid.*: 93). Observing power in its local and peripheral effects provides a new viewpoint from which to begin a study of power, and will thus entail a new methodological approach: the theory of power that we have just outlined.

An ongoing project

To review, we have unpacked a dozen or so dense pages at the heart of *La Valonté de Savoir*. What we have discussed provides only a *basic framework*: a set of theoretical presuppositions that constitutes the heart of Foucault's theory of power. There are important elements of this theory that we have not discussed, and many aspects of Foucault's analysis of power would continue to evolve over the next decade, as Foucault's ongoing self-critique continued. This basic framework, however, is consistent throughout the theory's subsequent development and elaboration.

Notes

1. Special thanks to David Cylkowski, Stacy Klingler and Dianna Taylor for their very thoughtful responses to earlier versions of this essay.
2. The French original is at Foucault (1976: 120): "en se donnant une autre théorie du pouvoir".
3. These are not necessarily the same relationships.
4. Lynch (1998) gives a fuller discussion of Foucault's view of the omnipresence of power.
5. For more on this shift, see Lynch (2009).
6. We must be careful not to make too much of the analogy to physics; I do not think, for example, that Foucault means that analysis of social relations should be reduced to equations of force relations. Given this caution, however, we can note certain implications of the analogy.
7. In this passage, Foucault is making an observation about Henri de Boulainvilliers' eighteenth-century history of France. But his point here, in fact, speaks to Foucault's own methodology.
8. On page 19, above.

TWO

Disciplinary power

Marcelo Hoffman

Michel Foucault's *Discipline and Punish: The Birth of the Prison*, published in 1975, contains his most famous and elaborate exposition of disciplinary power. A bird's-eye view of his preceding and succeeding analyses reveals, however, that this concept arose in overlapping stages and served a variety of purposes. From roughly 1973 to 1976, in analyses of punishment, proto-psychiatry, criminology and race war, Foucault attempted to articulate disciplinary power in contradistinction to sovereign power. From about 1976 to 1979, he used disciplinary power as a springboard for delineating modalities of power concerned with population, namely, biopolitics, security and governmentality. Finally, in the early 1980s disciplinary power figured more as an implicit background to his analyses of subjectivity in Greco-Roman antiquity and early Christianity. The long shadow cast by this concept renders it absolutely crucial to understanding the trajectory of Foucault's thought.

Using a composite account of disciplinary power drawn from Foucault's seminal presentation in *Discipline and Punish* as well as his Collège de France course for the academic year 1973–74, *Psychiatric Power*, I will provide an overview of disciplinary power and then exemplify the exercise of this power through Frederick Winslow Taylor's *The Principles of Scientific Management*, published in 1911. Taylor's *Principles*, which influenced American and European industrialists as well as Lenin and Antonio Gramsci, enriches our understanding of disciplinary power in two ways. First, the presentation of scientific management at the core of *Principles* reflects nothing short of a full-fledged disciplinary programme. Indeed, it is hard to read a page of *Principles* without noticing that Taylor suffuses his presentation with

27

a thoroughly disciplinary aspiration. Second, Taylor's *Principles* high-lights the limitations to the exercise of disciplinary power by attesting that disciplinary practices bound up with the application of scientific management are deeply contested. Taylor thus de-naturalizes this form of power even as he seeks to extend its reach not only within factories, but also within "all social activities", including the management of homes, farms, businesses, churches, charities, universities and govern-mental agencies (F. W. Taylor 1967: 8).

Subjected individuals

The concept of disciplinary power concerns individuals. As Foucault notes with reference to what he takes to be the ideal exercise of this power, "We are never dealing with a mass, with a group, or even, to tell the truth, with a multiplicity: *we are only ever dealing with individuals*" (2006a: 75, emphasis added). However, in opposition to political theories which take the individual as a given for the purpose of constructing sovereignty, as in the notable case of Thomas Hobbes's version of the social contract, Foucault sets about showing that the individual first and foremost amounts to a construction of disciplinary power. The individual is an effect of this form of power rather than the raw material upon which it impinges. Foucault writes, "Discipline 'makes' individuals; it is the specific techniques of a power that regards individuals as objects and as instruments of its exercise" (1979: 170). As a first approximation, we can therefore say that disciplinary power produces individuals as its objects, objectives and instruments.

Disciplinary power yields such effects by targeting bodies. The tar-geting of bodies may not seem terribly unique, especially in light of Foucault's sweeping assertion that "what is *essential* in *all* power is that *ultimately* its point of application is *always* the body" (2006a: 14, emphasis added). It seems even less singular in light of his sugges-tion that pastoral power treats the body as an object of care (2007: 126–8) and that even sovereign power sets its sights on the body as an object of violence or honour (2006a: 44–5). However, what dis-tinguishes disciplinary power from these other modalities of power is its endeavour to meticulously, exhaustively and continuously control the activities of bodies so as to constitute them as bearers of a highly particular relationship between utility and docility, whereby increases in utility correspond to increases in docility and vice versa. In Foucault's words, disciplinary power strives to make the body "more obedient as it becomes more useful, and conversely" (1979: 138). This increase entails the augmentation of the skills and aptitudes of bodies without at the same time allowing these skills and aptitudes to serve as a source of resistance to disciplinary power. This form of power thereby attempts to resolve the problem of the resistances aroused from its own incessant investments in the body. Disciplinary power controls the body to effectuate this result through the production not only of an individual but also of individuality, the amalgam of qualities that render an individual distinct from others (Arendt 1985: 454). This individuality consists of cellular, organic, genetic and combinatory traits. Let us now outline the production of these traits.

Foucault insists that disciplinary power creates a cellular form of individuality by ordering individuals in space. He calls this ordering "the art of distributions". Cellular individuality rests on the division of individuals from others. The art of distributions produces this individuality by first of all enclosing a space different from all others through the use of walls or gates, as in the case of barracks and factories (Foucault 1979: 141–3). It partitions this space into individual cells in order to break up collective activities that deter from the goal of utility, such as desertion or vagabondage. The art of distributions also codes a space with specific functions to make it as useful as possible (*ibid.*: 143–5). As an example of this coding, Foucault refers to the production of printed fabrics at the Oberkampf manufactory at Jouy. The workshops at the manufactory were divided into operations "for the printers, the handlers, the colourists, the women who touched up the design, the engravers, the dyers" (*ibid.*: 145). Each worker occupied a space defined by his or her specific function within the overall production process. Lastly, the art of distributions creates a cellular individuality by ascribing the unit of rank to individuals. As an example of rank, Foucault discusses the seating of pupils in a classroom according to their age, grade and behaviour (*ibid.*: 146–7).

Within this enclosed space, disciplinary power produces an organic individuality by exerting a control over bodily activities. This individuality is "organic" in so far as it lends itself to disciplinary practices all on its own, as if spontaneously and naturally (*ibid.*: 155–6). The control of bodily activities realizes this organic individuality first of all through a temporal enclosure afforded by the use of timetables, which prevent idleness by partitioning activities into minutes and seconds (*ibid.*: 150–51). The control of activities also breaks down movements of the body into an ever-greater number of acts and indexes these acts to temporal imperatives. Foucault identifies the prescription of the duration and length of the steps of marching soldiers as an example of this temporal elaboration of the act (*ibid.*: 151–2). The control of activities further implies a relationship between the general position of the body and its gestures. In this regard, Foucault mentions the example of the upright posture of pupils and the correct positioning of their elbows, chins, hands, legs, fingers and stomachs as the conditions for good handwriting (*ibid.*). The control of activities goes even further, correlating the gestures of the body to the parts of the object used by it, as in the case of manifold gestures employed by a soldier to manipulate the barrel, butt, trigger-guard, notch, moulding, lock, screw and hammer of a rifle (*ibid.*: 153). Finally, rather than merely preventing idleness, the control of activities forges an organic individuality by exhaustively using time.

With the activities of the body controlled, disciplinary power proceeds to constitute a genetic form of individuality by subjecting the body to the demand for a perpetual progress towards an optimal end. Foucault dubs this demand the "organization of geneses". Drawing from the example of the military, he submits that perpetual progress towards an end yields a genetic individuality in the following ways: first, through the division of time into distinct segments, such as periods of practice and training; second, through the organization of these segments into a plan proceeding from the simplest elements, such as the positioning of the fingers in military exercise; third, through the ascription of an end to these segments in the form of an exam; and, finally, through the production of a series that assigns exercises to each individual according to rank (*ibid.*: 157–9).

Finally, disciplinary power establishes a combinatory form of individuality characterized by articulations with other bodies to obtain a level of efficiency greater than that realized by the mere sum of the activities of these bodies (*ibid.*: 167). Foucault calls this process the composition of forces. This composition gives rise to a combinatory individuality by first treating individual bodies as mobile elements to be connected to other individual bodies as well as the totality of bodies; second, by coordinating the time of each of these bodies to maximize the extraction of their forces and to combine them with others for the optimal results; and, lastly, by commands that may be transmitted through signs and that therefore need not be verbalized, much less explained (*ibid.*: 164–7).

We now know *how* disciplinary power works and *what* it produces. It works by distributing individuals, controlling activities, organizing geneses and composing forces, and these functions correspond to the production of cellular, organic, genetic and combinatory individualities, respectively. Yet, at the risk of drawing too fine a distinction, Foucault goes further in his analysis to impart a sharp sense of how disciplinary power *gets going* and *keeps going*. He attributes the success of this power

to several basic techniques: hierarchical observation, normalizing judgement and the examination.

If architecture figures within the art of distributions as a means of
ordering multiplicities into cellular individuals, it plays the role within
hierarchical observation of rendering individuals visible with the overall
effect of structuring their behaviour. In making individuals seeable,
architecture serves, as Foucault writes, "to act on those it shelters, to
provide a hold on their conduct, to carry the effects of power right to
them, to make it possible to know them, to alter them" (*ibid.*: 172). Still,
he suggests that outside of any ideal schema, architecture alone falls
short of making visibility constant. What makes this visibility perpetual
is the implementation of a hierarchical network within the group of
individuals who occupy a particular architectural space. Foucault offers
many examples of these networks. While we will not dwell on them
here (we have an opportunity to gauge their presence in Taylor's *Principles*), it is instructive to mention briefly one particularly rich example.
Foucault suggests that surveillance operated in the asylum in the early
nineteenth century not only through a doctor but also through supervisors who reported on patients, and servants who feigned servitude
to patients while gathering and transmitting information about them
to the doctor (2006a: 4–6). This example clearly demonstrates the
communication of the gaze from the top to the bottom, its manifestly
"hierarchical" character. Yet, Foucault is keen to remind us that the
gaze may operate in a more multi-directional manner to the point of
bearing on the supervisors themselves.

> Although surveillance rests on individuals, its functioning is that
> of a network of relations from top to bottom, but also to a certain
> extent from bottom to top and laterally; this network "holds"
> the whole together and traverses it in its entirety with effects of
> power that derive from one another: supervisors, perpetually
> supervised.   (1979: 176–7)

Such a dense network of vigilant and multi-directional gazes no doubt
causes disciplinary power to appear ubiquitous, but the sheer simplicity
of its mechanism also makes it seem rather inconspicuous (*ibid.*: 177).

In a disciplinary world, however, it is not enough to see bodies so
as to yield from them specific effects. One must be able to *judge* them
as well. This modality of power therefore depends on normalizing
judgement for its continued exercise. Foucault indicates that this form
of judgement consists of features that make it look quite different from
judgement in, for example, criminal courts. These features are summed

up in terms of the following forms of punishment: first, even minute departures from correct behaviour are punished; second, failure to adhere to rules established on the basis of regularities observed over time is punished; third, exercise is used specifically as a corrective punishment; fourth, gratification is used in addition to punishment for the purposes of establishing a hierarchy of good and bad subjects; and, finally, rank understood as the place occupied in this hierarchy is used as a form punishment or reward (*ibid.*: 177–83). What ultimately stands out here for Foucault is the concept of the norm. Disciplinary power judges according to the norm. By "norm", however, it should be obvious that Foucault has in mind something other than a strictly legal concept. He depicts the norm as a standard of behaviour that allows for the measurement of forms of behaviour as "normal" or "abnormal". In his words, "the norm introduces, as a useful imperative and as a result of measurement, all the shading of individual differences". The norm thus establishes the figure of the "normal" as a "principle of coercion" for the figure of the "abnormal" (*ibid.*: 184).

The examination combines the techniques of hierarchical observation and normalizing judgement in "a normalizing gaze" to lend further sustenance to the exercise of disciplinary power (*ibid.*). This gaze, as Foucault points out in a splendidly economical formula, "manifests the subjection of those who are perceived as objects and the objectification of those who are subjected" (*ibid.*: 184–5). Put differently, the examination binds the exercise of disciplinary power to the formation of a disciplinary knowledge. It does so in several ways. First of all, the examination facilitates the exercise of disciplinary power by objectifying subjects through observation. As Foucault posits, "Disciplinary power manifests its potency, essentially, by arranging objects. The examination is, as it were, the ceremony of this objectification" (*ibid.*: 187). In this regard, he mentions the first military review of Louis XIV as a form of examination yielding the objectification of subjects. This review subjected 18,000 soldiers to the gaze of a barely visible sovereign who commanded their exercises (*ibid.*: 188). Second, the examination constitutes individuality through an administrative form of writing that leaves behind a dense layer of documents, as in the examples of medical records and student records. This writing makes it possible to describe individuals as objects and track their development, or lack thereof, as well as to monitor through comparison phenomena within the larger aggregate of population (*ibid.*: 189–91). Finally, the accumulation of documents through the examination forges the individual as a case defined in terms of a status bound up with all of the "measurements", "gaps" and "'marks'" characteristic of disciplinary power (*ibid.*: 192).

In historical terms, Foucault sketches the shift from a society (prior to the sixteenth century) in which disciplinary power played a marginal but critical and innovative role from within the confines of religious communities to a society (beginning in the eighteenth century) in which it played a preponderant role from a myriad of institutions. In this sketch, disciplinary power spread initially through several "points of support" (2006a: 66) with religious underpinnings, such as the education of youth inspired by the ascetic ideal embraced by the Brethren of the Common Life with its focus on progressive stages of education, rules of seclusion, submission to a guide and military organization; colonization as practised by the Jesuits in the Guarani republic of Paraguay with its emphasis on the full employment of time, permanent supervision and the cellular constitution of families; and, lastly, the confinement of marginal elements of the population under the management of religious orders. From these peripheral positions, disciplinary power began to cover more spheres of society without any religious backing, appearing in the army by the end of the seventeenth century and working class by the eighteenth century (*ibid.*: 66–71).

Foucault maintains that this formidable extension of disciplinary power across the surface of society reflected a deeper ensemble of transformations. First, disciplinary power began to function as a technique more for the constitution of useful individuals than for the prevention of desertion, idleness, theft and other problems. Second, disciplinary mechanisms began to extend beyond their institutional parameters to yield lateral effects. In this regard, Foucault mentions the quite fascinating example of schools using information gathered from students to monitor parental behaviour. Lastly, disciplinary power began to bear on society as a whole through the organization of a police apparatus concerned with intricacies of individual behaviour (1979: 210–16).

These transformations were bound up in their turn with broad historical processes in economic, juridical and scientific domains. The generalization of disciplinary power took place against the background of the eighteenth-century problem of indexing the rapid growth in population to the rapid growth in production apparatuses (*ibid.*: 218–20). It attempted to resolve this problem by offering a means of administering the growth in the number of human beings and making them useful. The generalization of disciplinary power also entailed consequences for the juridical system, introducing asymmetries that vitiated the egalitarian juridical framework forged in the eighteenth century. As Foucault explains, disciplinary power established relationships of constraint between individuals rather than relationships of contractual obligation, and it defined individuals hierarchically rather than universally. The play of such asymmetries within the time and space proper to the exercise of disciplinary power effectively suspended the law (*ibid.*: 222–3). Lastly, the generalization of disciplinary power implied a tightening of relations between power and knowledge to the point of their mutual constitution by the eighteenth century. The objectification of individuals became the means for their subjection and the subjection of individuals became the means for their objectification (*ibid.*: 224). Through the diffusion of psychology and psychiatry, the examination became incarnated in "tests, interviews, interrogations and consultations" that reproduced mutually constitutive power–knowledge relations within disciplinary institutions (*ibid.*: 226–7).

Foucault finds the "formula" for the generalization of the exercise of disciplinary power in Jeremy Bentham's architectural plan for the model prison, *Panopticon*, published in 1791 (Foucault 2006a: 41). Foucault relates that Bentham depicts the Panopticon as an annular building with an internal periphery consisting of cells containing iron grate doors opening to the interior and windows opening to the exterior as well as a multi-floored central tower containing wide windows with blinds and partitions. Foucault considers this building *the* perfect expression of disciplinary power for a host of reasons. First, with each of the cells designed to be occupied by only one inmate at a time the building produces individualizing effects at its periphery. Second, venetian blinds and partitions on the tower conceal whether anyone actually occupies it, guaranteeing anonymity at the centre. Third, the artificial light from the central tower as well as the natural light entering through the cell windows assure the visibility of inmates in the cells. Finally, this visibility allows for the perpetual writing about inmates and, consequently, the constitution of an administrative knowledge about them (*ibid.*: 75–8).

These features render the Panopticon a magnificent machine not only for subjection but also for *self*-subjection. By inducing *in* inmates an awareness of their own constant visibility, the Panopticon compels them to structure their own behaviour in accordance with its power mechanism (Foucault 1979: 201). Notably missing from this ideal process is any reliance on violence or ostentatious displays of force. Remarkably, the play of visibility facilitated by spatial arrangements and lighting suffices to make inmates the very *conduits* of the power mechanism embodied in the Panopticon.

Though Bentham conceived of the Panopticon as an ideal prison for the resolution of the vexing problem of pauperism (Polanyi 2001: 111–13), Foucault does not tire of reminding us that Bentham considered it applicable to a broad array of settings *besides* the prison. As

Foucault explains on Bentham's behalf, "Whenever one is dealing with a multiplicity of individuals on whom a task or a particular form of behavior must be imposed, the panoptic schema may be used" (1979: 205). Moreover, lest we think that the Panopticon simply remained a product of Bentham's imagination, Foucault points out that, "In the 1830s, the Panopticon became the architectural program of most prison projects" (*ibid.*: 249) and that institutions apart from the prison adopted its architectural dispositions for a wide variety of purposes. As an example of this adoption, Foucault details all of the Panoptic features of the architecture of the asylum in the early nineteenth century, demonstrating that the panoptic architecture of the asylum building was construed as the very cure to madness (2006a: 102–7). This cross-institutional takeover of Panoptic architectural dispositions intensified the spread of disciplinary power.

For all of the reasons elaborated above, namely, the diffusion of disciplinary power from one institution to another as well as its various transformations into an ever more productive and pervasive modality of power culminating in the extension of Panoptic architectural features, Foucault finds warrant in speaking somewhat grandiosely about the advent of a "disciplinary society". Yet his employment of this expression is not without qualification. Foucault clearly wants us to take away from the phrase "disciplinary society" an understanding of a society in which disciplinary power is pervasive enough to interact with and alter other modalities of power rather than one in which it simply effaces these other modalities (1979: 216). Such complex articulations derive precisely from the *incompleteness* of the exercise of disciplinary power *even* in the context of a "disciplinary society". This incompleteness will become abundantly evident as we turn to Taylor's *Principles*.

Taylor's *Principles* as a disciplinary programme

At its core, scientific management as propounded by Taylor in his *Principles* attempts to increase the efficiency of workers by divesting them of any roles in planning and controlling their own work, and by placing these roles squarely in the hands of the management. Scientific management is manifestly disciplinary in this overall goal of increasing efficiency. However, Taylor devotes the bulk of his *Principles* to illustrating the efficacy and superiority of scientific management with reference to concrete examples drawn from a range of industrial activities, and it is within the inglorious intricacies of these examples that his espousal of a disciplinary perspective becomes altogether striking. Let us turn to a couple of his most pertinent illustrations.

Taylor's first illustration comes from his experience of attempting to increase the amount of pig iron loaded at the Bethlehem Steel Company from 12.5 tons to 47 tons per worker per day. Taylor recounts that he sought this nearly fourfold increase from workers without at the same time provoking their resistance. In his words, "It was further our duty to see that this work was done without bringing on a strike among men" (F. W. Taylor 1967: 43). Taylor addresses here the disciplinary problem of maximizing the utility as well as docility of individual bodies. He goes on to explain that he set about resolving this problem by, first of all, selecting out of the 75 workers at Bethlehem Steel four workers capable of loading 47 tons of pig iron per day. This selection took place on the basis of the deployment of a veritable myriad of disciplinary practices, which Taylor describes in the following passage:

> In dealing with workmen under this type of management, it is an inflexible rule to talk to and deal with only one man at a time, since each workman has his own special abilities and limitations, and since we are not dealing with men in masses, but are trying to develop each individual man to his highest state of efficiency and prosperity. Our first step was therefore to find a proper work-man to begin with. We therefore carefully watched and studied these 75 men for three or four days, at the end of which time we had picked out four men who appeared to be physically able to handle pig iron at the rate of 47 tons per day. A careful study was then made of each of these men. We looked up their history as far back as practicable and thorough inquiries were made as to the character, habits and the ambition of each of them. Finally we selected one from among the four as the most likely man to start with.   (*Ibid.*)

One of the most obvious disciplinary effects in this passage is individualization. Taylor informs us of the importance of having treated workers individually rather than collectively, thereby reminding us of Foucault's discussion of the constitution of a "cellular" individuality. However, he proceeds to indicate that the individualizing effects sought in the selection process rested on the observation of the mass of workers, and that this observation and the knowledge obtained from it facilitated a judgement about the most able-bodied workers. Lastly, Taylor tells us that he made the selection of the most able-bodied worker at Bethlehem Steel on the basis of an enquiry into the identities of the four most able-bodied workers. Individualization, observation and the constitution of an administrative identity on the basis of knowledge obtained through observation all figure centrally in Taylor's account of the selection of the appropriate worker to load 47 tons of pig iron per day.

This worker turned out to be "a little Pennsylvania Dutchman" dubbed Schmidt (*ibid.*). Taylor explains that his team selected Schmidt as the first worker to try out the increase in pig iron loading because it had learned through its enquiries that Schmidt placed an unusually high premium on his earnings. It was on the basis on this knowledge about Schmidt that Taylor's team approached him, first to entice him with the monetary incentive of a pay of $1.85 rather than standard $1.15 a day and then to inform him that the increase in pay would presuppose a strict obedience (*ibid.*: 44–5). Taylor relates that Schmidt was told the following in particular:

> Well, if you are a high-priced man, you will do exactly as this man tells you to-morrow, from morning 'til night. When he tells you to pick up a pig and walk, you pick it up and you walk, and when he tells you to sit down and rest, you sit down. You do that right straight through the day. And what's more, no back talk. Now a high-priced man does just what he's told to do, and no back talk. Do you understand that? When this man tells you to walk, you walk; when he tells you to sit down, you sit down, and you don't talk back at him. (*Ibid.*: 45–6)

As in the case of the previous passage, several disciplinary practices leap out at us from this excerpt of "rough talk" to Schmidt (*ibid.*: 46). The first of these practices is the exhaustive regularity of the movements of the body. The person in charge of Schmidt would command him not only how to work but also when and how to rest so as to work all the more efficiently. Moreover, this person would insist that Schmidt follow his orders without any "back talk", once again illustrating the disciplinary relationship between increased utility and increased obedience. In this instance, we are further reminded of Foucault's contention that commands in the exercise of disciplinary power need not be premised on *any* explanation. They need only "trigger off the required behavior and that is enough" (1979: 166).

We learn from Taylor's narrative that Schmidt accepted the conditions spelled out in the passage above and succeeded in loading 47 tons of pig iron per day under the meticulous control of the aforementioned person from Bethlehem Steel. Presumably, Schmidt could have used

his demonstrated skill in loading so much pig iron to extract conces-
sions from management at Bethlehem Steel. However, Taylor adds
that under the continued presence of an overseer Schmidt "practically
never failed to work at this pace and do the task that was set him during
the three years that the writer was at Bethlehem" (1967: 47). He thus
leaves us with the distinct impression that the application of scientific
management succeeded in yielding Schmidt as a docile as well as useful
individual.

Another illustration that reveals the disciplinary character of scientific management derives from Taylor's account of efforts to increase
the output of shovellers at Bethlehem Steel. Unlike the example above,
Taylor in this instance discloses the process used to determine the appropriate load for the maximum daily output of shovellers, explaining
that experimentation with and the observation of several of the best
shovellers led to the discovery of 21 pounds as the appropriate load
(*ibid.*: 65). On the basis of this knowledge, Bethlehem Steel set up
an intricate instructions and record-keeping procedure. Taylor recalls
the emphasis on individualization in this procedure, stressing that this
emphasis was reflected in a system of writing detailing not only what
each worker should do on a given day and how he should do it but
also whether he had worked enough to earn his $1.85 on the *previous*
day, presumably by loading his 21 pounds per shovel. This system of
writing used a norm – work equivalent to $1.85 a day or 21 pounds
per shovel – to distinguish normal from abnormal workers, with the
former denoted by the receipt of white slips and the latter denoted by
the receipt of yellow slips. According to Taylor, the consequences of
this distinction were perfectly clear. Workers in receipt of yellow slips
were faced with the choice of working in adherence to the norm and,
consequently, normalizing themselves, or being demoted to a type of
work corresponding to their comparatively low levels of productivity.
We have in his discussion of the consequences of the distribution of
these slips a fairly clear and vivid illustration of normalizing judgement.

Taylor draws the following lesson from the experience of individual-
ized instructions and record keeping at Bethlehem Steel:

> If the workman fails to do his task, some competent teacher
> should be sent to show him exactly how his work can best be
> done, to guide, help, and encourage him, and, at the same time, to
> study his possibilities as a workman. So that, under the plan which
> individualizes each workman, instead of brutally discharging the
> man or lowering his wages for failing to make good at once, he
> is given the time and the help required to make him proficient at

his present job, or he is shifted to another class of work for which he is either mentally or physically better suited. (*Ibid.*: 69–70)

This prescription is most obviously disciplinary in its preference for first training abnormal workers on an individual basis rather than simply discharging them. Training in this instance also facilitates an intimate examination of the aptitudes of these workers with the effect of allowing for the production of additional knowledge about them.

Taylor identifies the point of support for such prescriptions as a ramified structure consisting as it did at Bethlehem Steel of superintendants and clerks planning the fine details of work, preparing instruction slips and managing records, subtended by teachers working intimately with workers to make sure that they carry out the tasks spelled out in the instruction slips as well as tool-room men preparing standardized implements for the execution of these tasks (*ibid.*). This structure nicely illustrates the network of gazes facilitating the play of hierarchical observation.

Taylor's exposition of scientific management abounds with such examples of disciplinary power but it also de-naturalizes this modality of power by demonstrating that disciplinary practices bound up with the application of scientific management have yet to take root, and that they are subject to great contestation (at the risk of belabouring the obvious, it is worth keeping in mind that if these disciplinary practices *had* taken root, Taylor would not have needed to compose *Principles*). Indeed, Taylor paints his vision of scientifically managed labour-processes on a canvas of sceptical employers as well as a mass of recalcitrant, if not openly hostile, workers. Against the disciplinary demand for maximized utility, we find in Taylor's narrative workers who threaten to strike, workers who intimidate managers and workers who damage machinery (*ibid.*: 49–52). Taylor is acutely aware of the prospect of inciting warfare within the interstices of the labour process. For this reason, he warns prospective practitioners against the hasty application of his principles of scientific management and insists that only a prolonged period of habituation will result in the successful application of these principles (*ibid.*: 128–35). To paraphrase Foucault, we could therefore say that the not so distant "roar of battle" (Foucault 1979: 308) resounds throughout Taylor's theory, suggesting that *only* an ensemble of deeply contested practices sustain the exercise of a disciplinary power that strives to appear natural and spontaneous in the very bodies of individuals.

THREE

Biopower

Chloë Taylor

French philosopher Michel Foucault is perhaps best known as a theorist of power. Foucault analysed several different types of power, including sovereign power, disciplinary power and the subject of the current chapter: biopower. In what follows, I will first provide an overview of biopower as Foucault conceives of it. This overview will distinguish biopower from sovereign and disciplinary power, identify and discuss distinctive characteristics of biopower and provide examples which illustrate these characteristics. The final section of the chapter undertakes an extended example of a particular occurrence of biopower within modern and contemporary Western societies.

Powers of life and death: from sovereign power to biopower

In *The History of Sexuality: An Introduction* (1990a) and in his 1975–76 Collège de France course, *Society Must Be Defended* (2003) Foucault describes biopower as a power which takes hold of human life. In both these works Foucault traces the shift from classical, juridico-legal or sovereign power to two typically modern forms of power, discipline and biopower, as a shift from a right of death to a power over life: "in the classical theory of sovereignty, the right of life and death was one of sovereignty's basic attributes ... The right of sovereignty was the right to take life or let live. And then this new right is established: the right to make live and to let die" (2003: 240–41). Sovereign power is a power which deduces. It is the right to take away not only life but wealth, services, labour and products. Its only power over life is to seize that life, to end, impoverish or enslave it; what it does not seize it leaves alone. Sovereign power's right over life is merely the right of subtraction, not of regulation or control. As Foucault writes:

> The sovereign exercised his right of life only by exercising his right to kill, or by refraining from killing; he evidenced his power over life only through the death he was capable of requiring. The right which was formulated as the "power of life and death" was in reality the right to *take* life or *let* live. Its symbol, after all, was the sword. (1990a: 136, emphasis added)

The seventeenth-century theorist of sovereign power Thomas Hobbes illustrates Foucault's points, writing:

> For seeing there is no Common-wealth in the world, wherein there be Rules enough set down, for the regulating of all the actions, and words of men, (as being a thing impossible:) it followeth necessarily, that in all kinds of actions, by the laws praetermitted, men have the Liberty, of doing what their own reasons shall suggest, for the most profitable to themselves. (1986: 264)

Hobbes notes in particular that it would be ludicrous for a sovereign to attempt to regulate the corporeal dimensions of a subject's existence, and hence no covenant with the sovereign could be concerned with these aspects of a subject's life. Hobbes argues that so far as "corporall Liberty" is concerned, subjects of any commonwealth are free: "For if wee take Liberty in the proper sense, for corporall Liberty; that is to say, freedome from chains, and prison, it were very absurd for men to clamor as they doe, for the Liberty they so manifestly enjoy" (*ibid.*). The freedom of subjects, for Hobbes, consists of those aspects of life with respect to which there are no covenants with the sovereign. For Hobbes, it would be *absurd* to imagine certain mundane aspects of life, such as liberty over one's body and private life, being the subject of such covenants. Hobbes simply cannot imagine these being of interest to the king or to the commonwealth, or mechanisms of power which might function at this level. He elaborates:

> The Liberty of a Subject, lyeth therefore only in those things, which in regulating their actions, the Soveraign hath praetermitted: such as is the Liberty to buy, and sell, and otherwise contract with one another; to choose their own aboad, their own diet, their own trade of life, and institute their children as they themselves

think fit: & the like." Hobbes adds that "Lawes are of no power
... Without a Sword in the hands of a man, or men, to cause those
laws to be put in execution.   (*Ibid.*)

And he assumes that concerns such as dwelling, diet and childcare
could never warrant the wielding of a sword or the exercise of law.
Sovereign power is, then, for Hobbes as for Foucault, a juridico-legal
power to kill which leaves the daily life of the body alone, and its
symbol is the sword or the threat of death. In those realms where one
would not wield a sword or the force of law, one is free or escapes
from power. In particular, Hobbes thinks that our bodies are free, or
that we have "corporall Liberty" unless the sovereign has us literally
in chains.

In contrast to sovereign power which could "*take life* or *let live*",
biopower is the power "to *foster life* or *disallow* it to the point of death"
(Foucault 1990a: 138, emphasis added). Foucault writes,

> Power would no longer be dealing simply with legal subjects over
> whom the ultimate dominion was death, but with living beings,
> and the mastery it would be able to exercise over them would have
> to be applied at the level of life itself: it was the taking charge of
> life, more than the threat of death, that gave power its access even
> to the body.   (*Ibid.*: 142–3)

Hobbes deems corporeal aspects of life such as dwelling (abode),
desires (what we want to purchase and consume), the care of the body
(diet), and childcare and education to be outside of the interests of
the sovereign and hence free. Yet for Foucault these aspects become
some of the privileged loci of the mechanisms of biopower, indicating
a transformation of power which Hobbes would have deemed "a thing
impossible".[1] Biopower is able to access the body because it functions
through norms rather than laws, because it is internalized by subjects
rather than exercised from above through acts or threats of violence,
and because it is dispersed throughout society rather than located in
a single individual or government body. While the sovereign power
which Hobbes describes could only seize life or kill, Foucault writes of
"a very profound transformation of these mechanisms of power", in
which "deduction" would be replaced by a power "working to incite,
reinforce, control, monitor, optimize, and organize the forces under
it: a power bent on generating forces, making them grow, and ordering them, rather than one dedicated to impeding them, making them
submit, or destroying them" (*ibid.*: 136).

Two levels of biopower: discipline and regulation

In his 1977–78 Collège de France course, *Security, Territory, Population*, Foucault takes the example of a prohibition such as "do not steal" or "do not murder" in order to illustrate the differences between sovereign power, discipline and biopower in a simple way (Foucault 2007). Under sovereign power, which predominated up until the end of the seventeenth century when Hobbes was writing, an individual who transgressed these prohibitions against theft and murder would be subjected to the law and punished solely on the basis of his crime; he might, for instance, be executed, exiled or fined. Under disciplinary power, which emerged in the eighteenth century, the criminal will still be subjected to the law or punished, however it will no longer be a mere matter of his crime. Rather, power will now be at least as interested in the thief's or murderer's character. It will want to know the conditions, both material and psychological, under which the individual committed his crime. This information will be deemed important in order to anticipate and intervene in the likelihood that the criminal will reoffend. In order to predict and control the individual's chance of recidivating, the criminal needs to be subjected to psychological examinations, surveillance and rehabilitative practices unknown under sovereign power. For this reason, the punishment is less likely to put an end to the criminal's life, and more likely to control his life through tactics such as prison, psychiatric treatment, parole and probation. Finally, under biopower, which emerged later in the eighteenth century, the focus and target of power becomes the numbers of thefts and murders occurring in the population. Power now takes an interest in whether crime rates are rising or falling, in which demographic groups particular crimes are predominant, and how crime rates can be optimally controlled or regulated. While many of the same tactics will be employed under biopower as under disciplinary power, the focus will now be on the population rather than the individual.

If at times Foucault describes discipline and biopower as two distinct (although intersecting and overlapping) forms of power,[2] at other times he includes discipline within biopower, or describes discipline as one of the two levels at which biopower works. Biopower is a power over *bios* or life, and lives may be managed on both an individual and a group basis. While at one level disciplinary institutions such as schools, workshops, prisons and psychiatric hospitals target individual bodies as they deviate from norms, at another level the state is concerned with knowing and administrating the norms of the population as a whole and thus with understanding and regulating "the problems of birthrate, longevity, public health, housing, and migration" (Foucault 1990a: 140). Disciplinary power works primarily through institutions, while biopower works primarily through the state, however the state is also involved in many institutions, such as the prison. In *The History of Sexuality: An Introduction*, Foucault writes of biopower:

> this power over life evolved in two basic forms; these two forms were not antithetical, however; they constituted rather two poles of development linked together by a whole intermediary cluster of relations. One of these poles – the first to be formed, it seems – centered on the body as a machine: its disciplining, the opti-mization of its capabilities, the extortion of its forces, the paral-lel increase of its usefulness and its docility, its integration into systems of efficient and economic controls, all this was ensured by the procedures of power that characterized the *disciplines: an anatomo-politics of the human body*. The second, formed some-what later, focused on the species body, the body imbued with the mechanics of life and serving as the basis of the biological proc-esses: propagation, births and mortality, the level of health, life expectancy and longevity, with all the conditions that can cause these to vary. Their supervision was effected through an entire series of interventions and *regulatory controls: a bio-politics of the population*. (*Ibid.*: 139, emphasis added)

Discipline may be seen as biopower as it targets the individual body, therefore, while another level of biopower targets the species-body. Foucault will describe these two levels as "the two poles around which the organization of power over life was deployed" (*ibid.*). These two levels of power are necessarily intertwined, since bodies make up popu-lations and populations are made up of individual bodies. In *Society Must Be Defended*, Foucault insists that a biopolitics of the population:

> does not exclude disciplinary technology, but it does dovetail into it, integrate it, modify it to some extent, and above all, use it by sort of infiltrating it, embedding itself in existing disciplinary techniques. This new technique does not simply do away with the disciplinary technique, because it exists at a different level, on a different scale, and because it has a different bearing area, and makes use of very different instruments. (2003: 242)

One way of conceptualizing the point of this passage is to say that dis-cipline is the micro-technology and biopolitics is the macro-technology

Table 3.1 Two levels of biopower

Type	Target	Aim	Institutions	Tactics
Regulatory power (biopolitics)	Populations, species, race	Knowledge/ power and control of the population	The state	Studies and practices of demographers, sociologists, economists; interventions in the birthrate, longevity, public health, housing, migration
Disciplinary power (anatomo-politics)	Individuals, bodies	Knowledge/ power and subjugation of bodies	Schools, armies, prisons, asylums, hospitals, workshops	Studies and practices of criminologists, psychologists, psychiatrists, educators; apprenticeship, tests, education, training

of the same power over life. Table 3.1 schematizes the distinctions between these two levels of biopower.

Administering life: from the census to sexuality

Biopower administers life rather than threatening to take it away. In order to administer life, it is important for the state to obtain forecasts and statistical estimates concerning such demographic factors as fertility, natality, immigration, dwelling and mortality rates (Foucault 1990a: 25). For this reason, an important moment in the history of biopower is the development of the modern census. While inventories of heads of households, property and men who could serve in the military were taken in ancient Rome, China, Palestine, Babylonia, Persia and Egypt, they were almost unknown throughout the Middle Ages (an exception being the Domesday Book of William the Conqueror), and differed from the modern census in that they did not attempt to gather information about the entirety of the population, but only about specific types of individuals: those who could be taxed, drafted or forced to work. The idea of enumerating the entirety of a population was only introduced in Western countries at the end of the seventeenth century and became increasingly detailed in the centuries that followed. Soon, the census secured data on dates and places of birth, marital status and occupations. Modern states recognized the necessity of understanding the characteristics, structures and trends of their populations in order to manage them or to compensate for what they could not control.

One subject of biopolitical concern is the age of a population, "together with a whole series of related economic and political problems" (Foucault 2003: 243). The state is concerned with demographic forecasts which foresee a "sapp[ing of] the population's strength, [a] shorten[ing of] the working week, wasted energy, and cost money [...]" (*ibid.*: 244). We often hear of the ageing of the "baby boomer" generation, for example, when unprecedented segments of the population will retire from the work force and require expensive geriatric care. Both a "sapping" of the labour force and of medical resources are predicted as a result and need to be compensated for, while retirement and geriatric care facilities need to be established and staffed in anticipation of this event.

Another area of biopolitical study and intervention is the health and survival of neo-nates, managed, for instance, through government-sponsored breastfeeding advocacy campaigns (see Kukla 2005: chs 2, 5). States may also be concerned with what sorts of babies are born, or which demographic groups they are born into. The French Canadian province of Québec has a profound interest in keeping the French language alive in its territory, for instance, and is thus concerned with increasing its francophone population in particular. Since the census reveals that French Canadians have fewer children than English Canadians, "allophones" and immigrants, the province compensates with pro-natal policies, by promoting immigration from francophone countries (through financial incentives), and by promoting immigration in general (through attractions such as inexpensive day-care) while obliging children of non-francophone families to attend French-language schools.

As Foucault writes in *The History of Sexuality*:

> At the heart of this economic and political problem of population was sex ... It was essential that the state know what was happening with its citizens' sex, and the use they made of it ... Between the state and the individual, sex became an issue, and a public issue no less. (1990a: 26)

While non-reproductive sexual acts had long been considered sinful, since the eighteenth century they have come to be seen as a threat to society. At the disciplinary level, individuals engaging in non-reproductive sexual acts and women uninterested in procreative sex have been medically treated for perversion, frigidity and sexual dysfunction. At the biopolitical level, non-reproductive sexual acts and the rejection of reproductive sexuality are issues which need to be managed. It is necessary to know what proportion of the population is engaging in specific sexual acts, or is using contraceptives, in order to intervene in this behaviour or to compensate for it. While in some segments of society the state is concerned with promoting procreation and thus with providing incentives to parenthood, in other segments of the population the state is concerned with containing and preventing procreation. In particular, certain groups, such as unwed women, the poor, criminals and the mentally or physically ill or disabled have been deemed (and in some instances continue to be deemed) unfit to procreate or to raise children.[3]

As these cases show, sex is important at both levels of biopower, concerning as it does both the individual's use of his or her body and the growth and health of the population. As Foucault notes, "Sexuality exists at the point where body and population meet. And so it is a matter for discipline, but also a matter for regularization" (2003: 251–2).

> Sex was a means of access both to the life of the body and the life of the species. It was employed as a standard for the disciplines and as a basis for regulations. This is why in the nineteenth century sexuality was sought out in the smallest details of individual existences .... But one also sees it becoming the theme of political operations, economic interventions (through incitements to or curbs on procreation), and ideological campaigns for raising standards of morality and responsibility: it was put forward as an index of a society's strength, revealing of both its political energy and its biological vigor. Spread out from one pole to the other of this technology of sex was a whole series of different tactics that combined in varying proportions the object of disciplining the body and that of regulating populations.   (1990a: 146)

Far from being something which we have recently liberated (or still struggle to liberate) from an archaic and repressive power, Foucault therefore argues that sex is in fact a privileged site and indeed *a product* of the workings of modern forms of power.

Death in the age of biopolitics

In contrast to sex, Foucault argues that death has now receded from view, becoming private and hidden. While sovereign power entailed the right to impose death, the aims of biopower are to foster and manage life, and so death becomes a "scandal". Under sovereign power death was ritualized as the moment of passing from one sovereign authority to the next. Death was the ultimate expression of the sovereign's power

48

and was made into a public spectacle whenever this power needed to be affirmed. In contrast, under biopower, death is the moment in which we escape power (Foucault 2003: 248). Foucault writes of the "disqualification of death" in the biopolitical age, and observes that the "great public ritualization of death gradually began to disappear" (*ibid.*: 247). For this reason suicide was illegal under sovereign power, perceived as a seizure of the king's power to take life, whereas today it is a medical problem, a shameful secret and a bewildering threat. As an escape from bio-disciplinary power, suicide is described by Foucault as a subversive act of resistance in works such as *"I, Pierre Rivière ..."* (1982b) and *Herculine Barbin* (1980a).

One manifestation of the shift from the sovereign power to kill to the biopolitical interest in fostering life is that capital punishment came to be contested in the modern period and new forms of punishment were invented to replace it, most notably the prison. While the death penalty was abolished in most Western democracies by the 1970s, its practice had long since become rare. In those places where it is still legal and regularly practised today, such as the United States, it is widely criticized as backward and anachronistic.[4] In earlier eras, execution for murder or theft was understood as punishment for having broken the sovereign's law and for undermining his power. Crime was conceived as a personal attack on the sovereign rather than on the individual victims of the crime or on the security of the population as a whole. Punishment was the sovereign's counter-attack, his reaffirmation of power. In contrast, the current view of punishment is a "paying of one's debt to society", while executions, where they are permitted at all, are justified in the name of security. A criminal condemned to death must be perceived as a threat to the population rather than to the ruler's power. For this reason serial killers are executed in the United States today but the president's political opponents are not.

Capital punishment aside, there is little direct control over death under biopower. As Foucault notes, we now have the power to keep people alive when they should be dead and to decide when to "let them die", or to regulate their lives even after, biologically speaking, they should be dead (2003: 248–9). We may thus choose to cease managing an individual's life by letting her die, or to not foster certain lives to begin with, but this is not the same thing as the sovereign right to kill. While a person might be allowed to die or her life may be disallowed to the point of death, and while the state monitors the morbidity rate, you can be fairly sure that your death will not be claimed by the state, and that your life will be managed but not seized. This is why death is now privatized – it is, according to Foucault, "outside the power relationship" (*ibid.*: 248). While we claim that sex is silenced and repressed, Foucault compellingly argues throughout *The History of Sexuality* that this is not the case and that we in fact talk about sex more than anything else; on the other hand, death today truly is taboo.

Foucault thinks that the irony of this "disqualification of death" is that wars are bloodier than ever but are justified in the name of life. He writes:

> Yet wars were never as bloody as they have been since the nine-teenth century, and all things being equal, never before did regimes visit such holocausts on their own populations. But this formida-ble power of death … now presents itself as the counterpart of a power that exerts a positive influence on life, that endeavors to administer, optimize, and multiply it … Wars are no longer waged in the name of a sovereign who must be defended; they are waged on behalf of the existence of everyone; entire populations are mobilized for the purpose of wholesale slaughter in the name of life necessity: massacres have become vital. (1990a: 137)

The Holocaust of the Jews, along with the extermination of gypsies and the "euthanasia" of the mentally ill and persons with developmental disabilites, were justified under the Nazi regime as "racial hygiene", nec-essary or beneficial to German flourishing. Nazi propaganda depicted Jews as a plague of rats that posed a threat to German well-being, and presented medical care for the mentally ill and disabled as a drain on German resources better used for those fit to survive. Indeed, despite the "disqualification of death" in the modern era, Foucault argues that there will be more genocides under biopower than under sovereign power, because biopower wants to manage the health of populations. When combined with racism, this management becomes cast as a con-cern for the racial purity of a people. In *Society Must Be Defended*, Foucault argues that biopower is almost *necessarily* racist, since racism, broadly construed, is an "indispensable precondition" that grants the state the power to kill (2003: 256).[5] Under such conditions, eradicating sub-groups of that population is perceived as a justifiable form of man-aging and protecting a people. Foucault writes: "If genocide is indeed the dream of modern powers, this is not because of a recent return of the ancient right to kill, it is because power is situated and exercised at the level of life, the species, the race, and the large-scale phenomena of population" (1990a: 137).

We can take the example of the recent US-led invasion of Iraq to illustrate the manner in which the modern biopolitical state justifies mass killings in the name of life, and both produces and exploits racism in order to do so. The original justifications for the invasion of Iraq involved claims that Iraq had weapons of mass destruction and was affiliated with Al-Qaeda. The Bush and Blair administrations suggested that Iraq would use its weapons of mass destruction to attack the United States and its allies, affiliated as it was with the attacks of 9/11. Anti-Muslim and anti-Arab racism abounded in this period in the US and was exploited in the arguments for invading Iraq. In this way Iraq was presented as a racialized threat to American existence or to the Western way of life, and invasion of this country was deemed necessary to protect life in Western democracies. When no weapons of mass destruction and no link to Al-Qaeda were found, the Bush and Blair administrations shifted tactics, emphasizing the slaughters and massacres that Saddam Hussein had committed against his own people, much like the oppression of women and girls in Afghanistan is exploited to justify the military incursions into this country. Over time these wars are recast as charity missions, undertaken not so much to protect lives in the West as to save innocent lives in the East. While critics point out that the alleged desires to save Iraqi lives and to liberate oppressed women are pretences, the important point is that we now *need* pretences such as these in order to justify war. We no longer pursue military invasions for the overt sake of glory, gain or conquest, or to defend the honour of the sovereign. While the ancient Romans could invade a foreign country for the undisguised purposes of occupying a land, enslaving a people and gaining access to resources, today we must mask our massacres as humanitarian efforts even while bringing about the deaths of thousands of civilians, turning millions more into refugees, and immediately securing the oil fields.

Social Darwinism and eugenics

In the nineteenth century, Europeans and North Americans grappled with the effects of increased urbanization, including the steady growth of slums inhabited by an underclass of paupers, prostitutes and thieves, many of whom were sickly and, the middle class thought, lazy and immoral. Rates of crime, disease, mental illness, alcoholism, promiscuity and prostitution were rampant in this segment of the population, which was, moreover, reproducing itself more quickly than the middle classes. The result was a growing fear among the bourgeoisie that the "dregs" of society would eventually overtake them. The middle classes in Western countries began to suspect that their race was degenerating, both because they were not reproducing quickly enough and because the lower class was reproducing too quickly. These fears were exacerbated in Britain when studies of the records of the height, weight and health of soldiers throughout the nineteenth century suggested "a progressive physical degeneracy of race" (Childs 2001: 1). European exploration of non-Western countries also confronted Europeans with races they deemed inferior, but which, because they must have a common ancestry with Europeans in Adam and Eve, were believed to have degenerated over time, falling from their original nobility (*ibid.*). The possibility of nationwide racial degeneration was thus posed, and anxiety mounted that Europeans could descend to the level of these "inferior races" if procreation patterns were not controlled.

In response to these fears, the science of eugenics was born in the late nineteenth century in Britain with the works of the statistician Francis Galton, and reached its height in the first half of the twentieth century throughout the Western world. Galton drew on his cousin Charles Darwin's theory of natural selection and argued that human societies were preventing natural selection or the "survival of the fittest" by protecting the sick, the poor and the weak through welfare programmes, charity and medicine. He coined the term "eugenics" from the Greek roots *eu* (good or well) and *genēs* (born), and described the science as "the study of all agencies under human control which can improve or impair the racial quality of future generations" (Black 2004: 18). Social Darwinists argued that the "survival of the fittest" human beings would come about naturally if welfare systems were simply withdrawn: although the poor would continue to have more children than the middle classes, this would be compensated for by higher mortality rates resulting from poverty and lack of medical care. As one Social Darwinist, Herbert Spencer, explains:

> It seems hard that an unskilfulness ... should entail hunger upon the artisan. It seems hard that a laborer incapacitated by sickness ... should have to bear the resulting privations. It seems hard that widows and orphans should be left to struggle for life or death. Nevertheless, when regarded not separately but in connexion with the interests of universal humanity, these harsh fatalities are seen to be full of beneficence.   (Childs 2001: 2–3)

Spencer thus suggests that nature be allowed to run its course, eliminating the weak from society. Individuals such as Spencer rejected the argument that improving the environment of the poor might reduce their rates of mental illness, infection, alcoholism, promiscuity and crime. While those advocating environmental reform suggested improvements in education and health care for the urban poor, and thus argued for biopolitical interventions of a different order (carried out at the level of *disciplinary* incursions into the lives of disorderly and abnormal members of society), Social Darwinists opposed such methods, arguing that they would only exacerbate the problem by helping to sustain those segments of society better left to die.

While Spencer's approach is to let the poor and the weak die out through non-intervention, other eugenicists advocated more active tactics. These tactics were divided into what were called "negative" and "positive" eugenics. "Negative eugenics", as the philosopher and eugenist F. C. S. Schiller puts it, "aims at checking the deterioration to which the human stock is exposed, owing to the rapid proliferation of what may be called human weeds" (*ibid.*: 3). This strategy entails preventing individuals and groups deemed "degenerate" from procreating through abortions, forced sterilization, incapacitation (such as locking up the mentally ill), "euthanasia" or, as in the case of Nazi Germany, genocide. Such "negative" tactics, however, can only prevent further deterioration; they cannot improve the species and so strategies of "positive eugenics" were simultaneously promoted. "Positive eugenics" involved encouraging or compelling "human flowers" to produce large families, for instance through economic stimuli. Abortion by "fit" women was illegal in Nazi Germany, and middle-class women who attempted to enter the work force were discouraged on the grounds that jobs outside the home were "race-destroying occupations" (*ibid.*: 7).

Eugenics thus attempts to improve the gene pool; however, what is meant by "improve" is inevitably socioculturally defined and has always been tainted by classism, racism and abilism. Early eugenicists were concerned with increasing the intelligence of the population, for instance, but this concern tended to promote births in the middle class while preventing them among the working classes. Racist eugenicists are opposed to miscegenation. With the Immigration Act of 1924, eugenicists successfully argued against allowing "inferior stock" from southern and eastern Europe into the United States. Laws were written in the late 1800s and early 1900s to prohibit the mentally ill from marrying and to allow them to be sterilized in psychiatric institutions. These laws were upheld by the Supreme Court in 1927 and were only abolished in the mid-twentieth century. As a result, 60,000 mentally ill Americans were sterilized in order to prevent them from passing on their genes. This is particularly problematic since what qualifies as "mental illness" is notoriously unstable and, as Foucault argues in works such as *The History of Madness* (2006b) and *Psychiatric Power* (2006a), has tended to describe social mores and norms rather than genuine medical conditions.[6]

Social Darwinism and eugenics may be described as biopolitical movements since they involve strategies for managing the health and productivity of populations through interventions in natality and mortality rates, mental and physical health, and immigration, even if what is taken to be "healthy" is highly problematic, entailing as it does prejudices ranging from abilism and classism to sexism, nationalism and racism. Following the Second World War, there has been a tendency to repress the fact that other countries besides Germany have histories of eugenics, histories which quietly continued long after the defeat of the Nazis (Childs 2001: 15). Ladelle McWhorter not only traces the extensive history of eugenics in the United States, however, but argues that the contemporary and mostly unquestioned pro-family movement in this country is a mere recasting and extension of the eugenics movement (McWhorter 2009). Eugenic uses of science also arguably continue in the cases of pro-family financial, social and political incentives, designer babies, genetic counselling, preemptive abortions, and the creation of "genius sperm banks". Many of these examples entail the use of new scientific technology to improve the genes of individual babies and of the population as a whole while preventing babies deemed "unfit" from ever being born. These biopolitical practices thus further entrench the prejudices of an abilist society while continuing the goals of eugenics in manners which have become increasingly unbounded by the state.

Notes

1. For a Foucauldian study of how biopower and discipline control the care of one's body, see Bartky 1988; for how disciplinary power controls diet, see Bordo (2003) and Heyes (2006); for a Foucauldian study of how biopower controls housing choices and opportunities and the raising and education of children, see Feder (1996, 2007).
2. In the second and third lectures of *Security, Territory, Population*, Foucault contrasts disciplinary mechanisms and security measures aimed at the level of population which, at the beginning of the first lecture, he calls "somewhat vaguely, bio-power" (2007: 1).
3. See Kukla (2005: chs 2, 5).
3. For an extended discussion of biopolitical interventions in the birthrate among these demographic groups in the United States, see McWhorter (2009).
4. Bedau, "The Case Against the Death Penalty": www.skepticfiles.org/aclu/case_aga.htm (accessed August 2010).
5. Foucault writes of "racism against the abnormal" in this lecture, and hence is not limiting himself to racism based on skin colour in making these claims.
6. To take but one example, homosexuality was included in the *Diagnostic and Statistical Manual of Mental Disorders* until 1973.

FOUR

Power/knowledge
Ellen K. Feder

Foucault explicitly introduces the composite term, "power/knowledge" (*pouvoir/savoir*) in the middle, "genealogical" period of his work. At the same time, however, the concept of power/knowledge in many ways encompasses the entire corpus, characterizing the implicit project of his "archaeological" works, the explicit focus of the "genealogical", and the working out of the implications for living a good life in the later "ethical" work.

To understand what Foucault means by power/knowledge we first have to engage in a little translation. Notice that when the term is used in philosophy written in English, the original French in which Foucault spoke and wrote often follows it. In French, there are different ways of expressing distinctive categories of knowledge which English speakers mark by qualifications such as "folk knowledge" or "book knowledge". In many of his earlier, archaeological works, Foucault is interested in investigating how a particular kind of implicit knowledge – the *savoir* – permeating a historical period, that is, the understanding that counts as the "common sense" of that time/place/people, shapes the explicit knowledge – the *connaissance* – that is institutionalized in the disciplines that make up the human sciences, including natural (e.g. biology) or social (e.g. psychology) science (Foucault 1972: 182–3).

As a noun, *pouvoir* is most typically translated as "power", but it is also the infinitive form of the verb meaning "to be able to", and is the most common way of saying "can" in Romance languages. In Foucault's work, *pouvoir* must be understood in this dual sense, as both "power" as English speakers generally take it (which could also be rendered as *puissance* or *force* in French), but also as a kind of potentiality, capability or capacity. Power, Foucault tells us, must be understood to be more complex than a term like *puissance* conveys; it has multiple forms and can issue from "anywhere". Foucault urges us not to think of power only in terms of its "old" monarchical form, as something an individual possesses or wields over another or others. For him power works *through* culture and customs, institutions and individuals. Likewise, its effects are also multiple, not simply negative or positive, but, as he puts it, "productive": they are both positive and negative, unstable valuations that can be reversed through history.

The composite "power/knowledge" is also not quite translatable. Literary theorist and translator Gayatri Spivak helpfully calls our attention to what she describes as the "homely verbiness of *savoir* in *savoir-faire* [a ready and polished kind of 'know-how', in English], *savoir-vivre* [an understanding of social life and customs] into *pouvoir*", and suggests that regarded in this way:

> you might come up with something like this: if the lines of making sense of something are laid down in a certain way, then you are able to do only those things with that something that are possible within and by the arrangement of those lines. *Pouvoir-savoir* – being able to do something – only as you are able to make sense of it. (1993: 34)

The kind of knowledge to which Foucault directs us with this term, then, is one that has no clear source, but that a genealogical analysis – an examination of the historical conditions of possibility – illuminates, describing the accidents of history that result in particular consolidations of what counts as truth or knowledge. It is not the knowledge that is decreed by some authoritative body "from on high", but is more precisely described in the passive voice: it is the kind of knowledge that is "recognized as true", "known to be the case". For Foucault, this knowledge can only exist with the support of arrangements of power, arrangements that likewise have no clear origin, no person or body who can be said to "have" it.

An example illustrates many of the dimensions of power/knowledge as they are taken up in Foucault's work. It will also help to clarify how the concept of power/knowledge is salient throughout the different periods into which scholars generally divide Foucault's corpus: the early (archaeological) texts where, Foucault later says, power/knowledge was present even if unnamed;[1] the middle (genealogical) texts where the concept power/knowledge is explicitly introduced; and finally the late (ethical) reflections, where power understood as capacity becomes more central. In what follows, I examine the concept of sexual difference and its enforcement. Despite his famous interest in questions concerning "sexuality", Foucault does not take up the matter of sexual difference directly; nevertheless, Foucault's work has been highly influential among scholars and activists over the past several decades who have done so, and have compellingly demonstrated how the tools offered by Foucault's analysis can help us to clarify and deepen our understanding of a critical, yet surprisingly under-studied, concept.

Example: dividing the sexes, or boys *will* be boys

We take for granted sexual difference. It seems obvious that men and women, boys and girls, make up the world's populace. We may recognize that sexual difference can be understood somewhat differently across the globe; some cultures have standards for masculine and feminine behaviour that differ from others. But there remains under the blanket of social distinctions what we take to be a brute biological or genetic "fact" of sexual difference. Common sense – a kind of unquestioned knowledge – tells us that this sexual division into male and female is true, how things are. But if this difference is so obvious we might ask why the distinction between the sexes requires enforcement.

Take the example of four-year-old Nathan who is teased by his classmates because he enjoys playing "like a girl", dressing up in high heels and dresses instead of like a cowboy, enjoying play with baby dolls instead of trucks. Perhaps we could say that the boy suffers the teasing of his preschool classmates because his play violates the other children's common sense. "You can't be a little girl" (Rekers & Varni 1977: 428), the other children tell Nathan.

What happens to Nathan is not unusual among preschoolers. But Nathan's story is distinctive because his is a published case, among the first of a number of cases, of a condition that was first discussed in US psychiatry in the early 1970s. "Gender Identity Disorder", or GID, continues to be actively treated today. In the paper in which Nathan's story is featured, the authors recount how Nathan's diagnosis led to a long period of therapy designed to help him accept that as a boy he was expected to play with "boys' toys". His parents were instructed to observe him and offer positive reinforcement for playing with gender-appropriate toys, and to ignore him when he played with inappropriate toys. Eventually, the case study reports, Nathan was given a wrist counter and told to press the counter when he played with boys' toys but not when playing with girls' toys. When he accumulated enough points he received a prize.

Reading the story of Nathan through the theoretical lens of Foucault, it is striking how closely Nathan's treatment regimen corresponds to the levels and character of surveillance Foucault describes in *Discipline and Punish*, and to the levels of surveillance the Panoptic structure organizes. Most accounts of the Panopticon focus on the prisoners (or madmen, paupers, schoolchildren) in the machine, those who are isolated and are the clear objects of the anonymous gaze signified by the invisible inhabitant(s) of the central tower. The objective of panopticism is the "internalization" of the authoritative gaze, where one:

> subjected to a field of visibility ... assumes responsibility for the constraints of power; he makes them play spontaneously upon himself; he inscribes in himself the power relation in which he simultaneously plays both roles; he becomes the principle of his own subjection.   (Foucault 1979: 202–3)

But among the many lessons of panopticism is that the power that seems focused on one individual is in fact "distributed" throughout the structure, so that every individual is at the same time both "object" and "subject" of this power: the prisoner is "watched", but is being trained to watch himself, to be his own inspector. The inspector is by definition the "watcher", and yet he, too, is the object of a gaze: his performance as watcher is ever under scrutiny. The Panopticon is Foucault's best lesson in unsettling the way we typically conceive power and its operation.

Foucault's analysis points us to ways that power can be exercised from unexpected places. As the study reports the succession of events, it is not *Nathan's* distress – over his desire to play with girls' toys, or the teasing he faces – or worry by his parents or teacher about his behaviour that brings him to the team of psychologists and researchers who subject him to treatment; it is, rather, the *other children's teasing* that distresses the teacher, who alerts the parents, who finally bring Nathan to treatment. It may seem obvious that children's interaction with one another is an important dimension of their psychosocial development, but the authority the children's voices command is arresting. We could speculate that the parents, teacher and treatment team see something important, even "natural", about the other children's intolerance of Nathan's behaviour. Viewing children as natural arbiters of gender norms might capture something of the intuitive sense of the adults involved in the case of Nathan, but this perspective calls for analysis of how such authority is vested in Nathan's four-year-old peers.

In *Discipline and Punish*, Foucault contrasts disciplinary power with the ordinary understanding of power as something that can be "possessed as a thing" and brandished against another (1979: 177; see also 1990a: 94). Disciplinary power, according to Foucault, is instead an expression of power that is associated with what he calls, in *The Archaeology of Knowledge*, the "assignment" of subjective positions (1972: 95), whereby individuals are allotted roles in the social world, positions that provide different possibilities for the exercise of power. The power that one can exercise as parent, simply by virtue of being a parent – power that is supported by society and by law – is one good example, but so is the power that is exercised by a bureaucrat in the Department of Motor Vehicles (DMV). It is not that the individual in one or the other of these positions "is" powerful in Foucaultian terms, but that different positions individuals take up or are assigned afford specific arenas for the exercise of power. Once an individual no longer occupies a given position – the parent goes to school to finish his college degree and at least for some part of the day occupies the position of student, or the clerk at the DMV goes home after a day of work – the power associated with that position can no longer be exercised. In the first volume of *The History of Sexuality*, Foucault clarifies that "power is not an institution, and not a structure; neither is it a certain strength we are endowed with; it is the name that one attributes to a complex strategical situation in a particular society" (1990a: 93). The story of a little boy who is teased in the playground and becomes a psychological case-study illustrates how power relations are distributed widely among young children, teachers and mental health professionals, forming what Foucault described as a "dense web that passes through apparatuses and institutions, without being localized in them" (*ibid*.: 96). Power is for Foucault inaccurately described as issuing "from above" or "outside"; instead, it is more instructive to understand first the way it "comes from below" (*ibid*.: 94).

In Bentham's design of the Panopticon, the occupants of the central tower take up positions of surveillance *vis-à-vis* each of the inmates (and indeed, of one another). Nathan's classmates are similarly enjoined, enlisted in a panoptic apparatus that operates to ensure properly gendered subjects. If the exercise of the classmates' gaze is evidenced by their teasing, it should be counted among the "essential techniques" of disciplinary power. Foucault describes such techniques as:

> always meticulous, often minute techniques, but they defined a certain mode of detailed political investment of the body, a "new micro-physics of power" [that] had constantly reached out to

> ever broader domains, as if ... intended to cover the entire social
> body.   (1979: 139)

Loosed from its discursive field, the children's forthright announce-
ment to Nathan that "You can't be a little girl" resists characterization
as a subtle expression of power. Conceived within the terms of its
field, however, their blunt repudiation is precisely the sort of "capillary
intervention" (1990a: 84) that epitomizes a microphysics of power. It
is consequential not for its sheer force but for the disciplinary effects
it can provoke, that is, for its ability to "reach out to ever broader
domains". The children's intervention in the case of Nathan activates
a complex machinery of interlocking institutional interests – embodied
by his teacher, his parents and an entire team of psychologists, assistants
and technicians – functioning to subject Nathan to a "field of visibility"
whereby he will learn, as his peers have already learned, to assume
"responsibility for the constraints of power ... [to] become the principle of his own subjection" (1979: 202–3). Located at the extremities
of this "productive network of power which runs through the whole
social body" (1980d: 119), the children's exposure of Nathan's viola-
tion is instrumental in two linked ways: it rouses the apparatus that will
therapeutically draft Nathan into his prescribed role and correct the
parental missteps that resulted in Nathan's deviation; it also provides
an opportunity to produce new knowledge, that is, new "understandings", new "truths", not only about Nathan, but about the increasing
numbers of children – and their parents[2] – who would be identified
under this new disorder.[3]

Bentham himself understood that "panopticism" functions not only
to circulate power, as it clearly does in the example of the prison, but
also to produce knowledge. Foucault's formulation of the term "power/
knowledge" is developed from Bentham's own expectation that the
Panopticon would serve as a "laboratory ... [that] could be used as a
machine to carry out experiments, to alter behavior, to train and correct
individuals" (Foucault 1979: 203). It is a "privileged place for experiments on men, and for analyzing with complete certainty the transformations that may be obtained from them" (*ibid.*: 204). "Thanks to its
mechanisms of observation," Foucault reflects, the Panopticon "gains
in efficiency and in the ability to penetrate into men's behavior; knowledge follows advances of power, discovering new objects of knowledge
over all the surfaces on which power is exercised" (*ibid.*: 204). But while
many would understand in narrow terms the new "object" that is created to be the "gender disordered" child of the late twentieth century,
Foucault's advancement of the analysis of power/knowledge clarifies

that the objects must be taken to be more widely dispersed, that no one, in fact, escapes the objectification that comes, in the nineteenth century, to be centred around the notion of sexual identity.

Normalizing sex(uality)

Foucault most famously elaborated on this expression of power/knowledge in the first volume of *The History of Sexuality* (tellingly titled in French as *La Volenté de Savoir*, "The Will to Knowledge"), the book that immediately follows *Discipline and Punish*. In *The History of Sexuality* Foucault makes the remarkable claim that "the 'question' of sex" becomes in the late nineteenth century the most important question "in both senses: as interrogation and problematization, and as the need for confession and integration into a field of rationality" (1990a: 69). A whole host of technologies are born to regulate what becomes understood as a person's (sexual) "essence", the truth of an individual, who he or she "really" is. The most salient of these technologies is confession, first religious (as mandated by early Christianity), then psychological (in the nineteenth-century science of psychoanalysis) and finally political, as the mandate to produce information becomes the ground for what became known as population control.[4] What unites these different technologies is the concern with identifying (and so, Foucault explains, what in fact turns out itself to create, as a category, or object of understanding) a whole variety of "perversions" born during this time, different ways to violate the multiplying rules governing the important distinction between licit and illicit, normal and abnormal.

Of all the technologies, medicine comes to play the most important role in the development of "the norm", dictating, for example, what constitutes normal marital relations. Children's sexual activity also became an object of keen interest and concern, not only because of a perceived need to "detect" violations of new norms, but, as we saw in the example of the case of Nathan, to be on the alert for problems with parents' rearing of their children:

> Wherever there was the chance that [masturbation] might appear, devices of surveillance were installed; traps were laid for compelling admissions ... parents and teachers were alerted, and left with the suspicion that all children were guilty, and with the fear of being themselves at fault if their suspicions were not sufficiently strong ... [parents'] conduct was prescribed and their pedagogy

recodified; an entire medical-sexual regime took hold of the family milieu. (Foucault 1990a: 42)

Further, a whole class of deviant individuals comes to be identified at this time. Among the zoophiles (those who engage in sex with non-human animals), auto-monosexualists (those who are only able to experience erotic pleasure by themselves), gynecomasts (men with atypically large breasts), presbyophiles (those who engage in sex with the elderly) and dysparauenistic women (those for whom sexual intercourse is painful), perhaps the most lasting category of individual is "the homosexual", a new species of individual "born" in 1870 (*ibid.*: 43).[5]

In the late-twentieth-century diagnosis of the gender dysphoric child there is embedded a whole history of power/knowledge that involves a complex of elements that come to be designated in Foucault's work by the term "normalization". Normalization, the institutionalization of the norm, of what counts as normal, indicates the pervasive standards that structure and define social meaning. Norms are at once everywhere and nowhere. They are obvious when we are talking about the sorts of standards against which one can be tested with respect to intelligence or body mass, for example. But they are less conspicuous when they are unspoken, what we may even take to be natural or understand as our own (what Foucault would see as their "internalization"), as is often the case with norms concerning gender.

We may think that medicine has always played the role it has in shaping our understanding of the norm, but Foucault's earlier history of medicine, *The Birth of the Clinic*, suggests otherwise. In the ancient period, conceptions of health were understood not in terms of a single standard against which one should be measured, but rather in terms of the harmonious functioning of the individual. The role of medicine was to provide "techniques for curing ills" (Foucault 1975: 34). This view of medicine persisted into the eighteenth century, at which time, according to Foucault, medicine begins to fashion a concept of "the *healthy man*, that is, a study of the *non-sick man*, and a definition of the *model man*" (*ibid.*). At this point, medicine assumes a "normative posture, which authorizes it not only to distribute advice as to healthy life, but also to dictate the standards for physical and moral relations of the individual and the society in which he lives" (*ibid.*). This is a crucial change in the understanding of medicine, by the profession and by the public at large, paving the way for the shift that will take place from a focus on *health* understood as qualities specific to an individual, to *normality*, a standard imposed from without.

In the example of Nathan, and of his parents, there is an obvious effort to correct the behaviour that is regarded as abnormal. The techniques described by the case study – enforcing "good" behaviour with reward and punishing bad behaviour with being ignored, asking him to regulate himself with a wrist counter – exemplify the sorts of practices Foucault characterized in *Discipline and Punish* with respect to the operation of the Panopticon. For Foucault it is not accurate to describe the aim of these practices in terms of "repression". Instead, the aim of the panoptic expression of power/knowledge is to enforce a standard that it is at the same time trying to establish by comparing individuals against one another, measuring their differences and then asserting the truth of the standard it "discovers" as the rule (1979: 182–3). Practices such as these exemplify why Foucault makes use of this composite term, power/knowledge: the expression of each term, power and knowledge, are at every point implicated with one another.

Power/knowledge and resistance

In looking at the operation of power/knowledge, it can be difficult to remember that for Foucault power should not be understood solely in the negative terms of repression or constraint. In *Discipline and Punish*, Foucault insists that:

> we must cease once and for all to describe the effects of power in negative terms: it "excludes," it "represses," it "censors," it "abstracts," it "masks," it "conceals." In fact, power produces; it produces reality; it produces domains of objects and rituals of truth. The individual and the knowledge that may be gained of him belong to this production. (1979: 194)

While many seek to resist the effects of normalizing power that have wrought so much harm (arguably to us all, albeit in different ways, and to different effect), for Foucault the very effort of resistance must be understood itself as an expression of power. In the first volume of *The History of Sexuality*, Foucault returns to the exemplary case of homosexuality to make this point:

> There is no question that the appearance in nineteenth century psychiatry, jurisprudence, and literature of a whole series of discourses on the species and subspecies of homosexuality, inversion, pederasty, and "psychic hermaphroditism" made possible a

strong advance of social control ... but it also made possible the formation of a "reverse" discourse: homosexuality began to speak in its own behalf, to demand that its legitimacy or "naturality" be acknowledged, often in the same vocabulary, using the same categories by which it was medically disqualified.

(1990a: 101)

What does Foucault mean by "reverse" discourse? If the "normalization" of the homosexual by nineteenth-century medicine marked the production of a new conception of abnormality, and with it the abnormal individual, twentieth-century resistance to this process must likewise be understood in these terms, but in reverse; as an effort, in other words, to recast normalcy, to understand *as normal* this new person the homosexual. The recasting of normalcy would mean making use of the medical category, not in the sense of the one constricting norm against which all of us should be judged, but to understand homosexual orientation in the "older" sense of the individual standard of health that continues to be active in, and provide validation of, current conceptions of normality. (Even as there are clear standards of health of all kinds, it still makes sense for us to talk about what is healthy "for me".) This normalizing power that "made up" the "homosexual person" as an object of psychiatric medicine also produced "improbably", "spontaneously", as Foucault puts it (*ibid.*: 96), the previously unthinkable concept of "gay pride", which led to the depathologization of homosexuality in the United States in 1973.

The story of the depathologization of homosexuality, of its removal as a diagnosis from the handbook of psychiatric disorders called *The Diagnostic and Statistical Manual of Mental Disorders* (DSM), is remarkable in many ways (among them: it was the first, and to date the only, time that a diagnosis was removed from the DSM as a result of a vote by the membership of the American Psychiatric Association) (Bayer 1981). But it is also notable because the first edition of the DSM that did not include homosexuality as a diagnosis (DSM III, published in 1980) introduced Gender Identity Disorder (GID) of children as a diagnosis. The "risk" of what are characterized as untreated "problems" of gender identity, according to the most influential researcher responsible for the diagnosis, is the eventual assumption of a homosexual identity (Rekers *et al.* 1977: 4–5).[6]

There are at least two lessons to be learned from the replacement of homosexuality with GID. One lesson concerns the role of children in the "society of normalization", something that Foucault addresses in some detail in the first volume of *The History of Sexuality*. For the purposes of understanding the operation of power/knowledge, it is a lesson in how resistance, expressed as a "reverse discourse", can itself be resisted: psychiatry found, in the diagnosis of GID, a new way to pathologize (or maintain the pathologization of) homosexuality, a new way, in other words, to make it known as an object of psychological intervention, to dictate its truth and to manage the treatment of those so labelled, both medically as well as socially.

As a new revision of the DSM is currently in preparation (scheduled for publication in 2012) there has been a great deal of controversy about the diagnosis of GID, with many activists and mental health practitioners, as well as some academics, arguing in favour of removing the diagnosis, just as homosexuality was removed more than two decades ago. And yet, removal of the diagnosis could inhibit those mental health practitioners who have made use of the diagnosis to treat the distress that gender nonconforming, or "gender variant", children may experience as a result of familial or societal intolerance, a form of counter-attack that validates gender variant behaviour. This approach to treatment is itself a form of resistance to the "usual" understanding of the diagnosis of mental disorder, which locates the problem in the individual so diagnosed. And while many, perhaps even most, practitioners continue to see GID in the terms dictated by the DSM, which perceives mental disorders "in" the individual, there are those who understand the problem to lie instead in the hostile conditions that gender variant children may face. The implicit rationale of those who approach treatment of gender variation in this way is similar to that made about a variety of forms of disability (is the problem in the bodies of those with disabilities, or in the material conditions that make mobility or communication difficult?).[7] What some mental health practitioners have done in their practice is turn psychiatric treatment on its head, seeing a child whose gender behaviour does not correspond neatly with her assigned sex as suffering not from a gender identity disorder, but rather as a victim of an intolerance of gender variation that should instead be the focus of intervention.

Seeing the diagnosis in this way would mean, practically speaking, that it should be cast differently (for example, using terms like "Gender Variance" rather than "Gender Identity Disorder", which is an unnecessary and furthermore misleading term, because it suggests that psychological identity is the problem that needs to be corrected). Rather than remove the diagnosis, another possibility could be to rename and reformulate the diagnosis to better reflect the life goals and distress experienced by individuals, and furthermore direct treatment toward the most appropriate means of alleviating distress and promoting flourishing.

Beyond the change of name, an interesting and promising recommendation may be to make use of complementary diagnostic codes known as "V-codes". V-codes are defined in the *International Classification of Disorder* (ICD, a global handbook with which the DSM is meant to correspond) as "other conditions that may be a focus of clinical attention" (World Health Organization 2004). Some V-codes are diagnoses that have not yet been formally established as diagnoses through appropriate research (and in this sense it would seem that GID as it stands would qualify). Other V-codes are "conditions" that are located *outside the individual*, but that nevertheless affect the individual's functioning or well-being. An "Acculturation Problem" (V62.4), for example, can include a variety of problems adjusting to a new culture, a problem that is cast not as "the individual's" problem; an "Occupational Problem" (V62.2), which the DSM conservatively describes as "job dissatisfaction", could include distress as a result of working in a hostile environment where again, the problem cannot be understood properly to belong to an individual. With respect to GID in children, probably the most typical problem would be described as a "Parent–Child Relational Problem" (V61.20), but it could also include a "Phase of Life Problem" (V62.89). Including V-codes in the very structure of the diagnosis would provide a more accurate picture of the problems that gender variant children face, and furthermore indicate to practitioners that the object of treatment needs to be differently understood.[8] The use of V-codes in the case of GID could (indeed, would) entail disciplinary effects, but rather than seeking to activate these effects in the life of an individual subjected to treatment, these effects could promote – among therapists and society at large – a different story to tell about sexual difference.

The possibility of making use of V-codes in the diagnosis of GID is one that is consistent with Foucault's analysis of power/knowledge as a pervasive apparatus from which there is no escape, but that can at the same time be resisted or "reversed". Possibilities such as these become the focus of Foucault's attention in his later, "ethical" works.

Conclusion: power/knowledge and technologies of the self

After the first volume of *The History of Sexuality*, Foucault does not explicitly make use of the term "power/knowledge". Yet the focus on "technologies of the self" in Foucault's ethics provides what could well be understood as an elaboration of the concept of power/knowledge in the "positive" terms that are only suggested in the middle work.

He is still interested in the notion of subjectivity (*assujettissement*), both in the sense of "making a subject" and "making subject to". He is also concerned with disciplinary practices. Rather than focusing, as he does in *Discipline and Punish*, on how disciplinary practices promote normalization, he is far more concerned with how these practices can be put to work to resist normalization. At this point in Foucault's analysis he turns to the subject's relationship to her self, that is, her own subjectivity.

One of the most important ways that knowledge is constituted is through the asking of questions. Investigation of the kinds of questions that can be asked within a given historical period was arguably the focus of Foucault's earlier, archaeological works, and the use to which particular questions could be put and to what effect, the focus of the genealogical works. In the later, ethical works, Foucault turns to the kind of knowledge resulting from reflection, "an exercise of oneself in the activity of thought", or *askesis* (1990a: 9). Practices of thought that could be promoted in gender variant children, their parents and the mental health workers charged with their care could include a reframing of the questions posed. Interrogating "the problem" of gender variance, for example, could provide an opportunity, as Foucault recounts, to "learn to what extent the effort to think one's own history can free thought from what it silently thinks, and so enable it to think differently" (*ibid.*). Seeing the diagnosis of Gender Identity Disorder not as a disorder located in the individual, but as a larger problem of intolerance and the suffering it causes would indeed exemplify how this exercise of thought could, as Foucault remarked in an interview, "show people that they are much freer than they feel, that people accept as truth, as evidence, some themes which have been built up at a certain moment during history, and that this so-called evidence can be criticized and destroyed" (1988: 10).

Our understanding of madness, standards of "health", "normal" sexuality: all of these, Foucault finally argues, are consequences of a complex operation of power/knowledge of which his own works are also a part. His aim, in narrating the histories that make up his work, is not to uncover "the timeless and essential secret ... behind things" but rather to expose the greater secret: the "secret that they have no essence or that their essence was fabricated in piecemeal fashion" (1977: 142). With his own projects, he is interested, as he put it in an interview, in exploring "the possibility of a discourse that would be both true and strategically effective, the possibility of an historical truth which could have political effect" (1980f: 64).

Notes

1. One way power/knowledge manifests itself in Foucault's early work is in the closely related concept of the *episteme*, elaborated in *The Order of Things* (1973). An *episteme*, the prevailing order of knowledge particular to a historical period, accounts for the understanding of how things are connected in the overall "field" of understanding or knowledge; it describes the conditions under which what is taken to be knowledge is possible.

2. Parents of children with GID have themselves been diagnosed with different psychopathologies, and become themselves "cases" for further investigation (see e.g. Coates 1990).

3. The incidence of the disorder has ranged over the years. At the outset it was understood as very rare, affecting perhaps 1 in 100,000 children (Rekers *et al.* 1977: 4–5); by 1990 clinicians had concluded that it "may occur in two percent to five percent of the general population" (Bradley & Zucker 1990: 478), a finding revised by these same authors nine years later, who liken its frequency to a disorder such as autism, itself a diagnosis with an estimated incidence rate that has steadily increased over the past decades (Zucker & Bradley 1999: 24). For Foucault these differences would indicate changing historical needs to justify diagnosis and treatment.

4. Interventions by the state in matters such as population control are an example of what Foucault called "biopower". For discussion of this distinctive form of power, which must also be seen as an expression of power/knowledge, see Chapter 3 on biopower in this volume.

5. For a detailed treatment of the history of the "invention" of homosexuality, see Katz (1995).

6. Later in the development of the diagnosis, perhaps even greater risk of untreated GID is the assumption of a transsexual identity (Bradley & Zucker 1990: 482).

7. See, for example, Fine & Asch (1988).

8. This could also be seen in light of the idea of "exteriorizing" a problem faced by an individual or a family, a process that allows the emergence of a different meaning, "the development of an alternative story", as the psychologist Michael White, himself a close reader of Foucault, has put it (see e.g. White & Epston 1990: 39).

PART II

Freedom

PART II

Freedom

FIVE

Foucault's conception of freedom
Todd May

The concept of freedom is an elusive one in philosophy. It lies at the *centre* of at least two very different sets of philosophical problems. One concerns the metaphysical status of human beings. The other concerns their political status. And, to make matters more complicated, Michel Foucault's perspective on freedom lies within neither set of problems. It does, however, interact with and complicate them. What I propose to do here, then, is to approach Foucault's own approach to freedom in three stages. First, I will discuss the two notions of freedom that characterize traditional philosophy. Then I will turn to Foucault's conception of freedom, showing how it interacts with those traditional notions. Finally, in order to get a better sense of all this, I will briefly contrast his conception of freedom with that of another subtle thinker of freedom, Maurice Merleau-Ponty.

We might call the two traditional conceptions of freedom *metaphysical* and *political*. The term *metaphysical* is somewhat loaded, however, so it might be best to be clear about what we mean by it before we proceed. Metaphysics has been thought to concern the ultimate nature of reality. It concerns what there is, or what the first or founding principles are of what there is. In that sense, it can also be characterized by the term *ontology*. One area of focus in metaphysics has been with the relation of mind and body. This is because if reality ultimately is made up of two different kinds of stuff – mental stuff and physical stuff – the question of their relationship becomes a central one, as it has been at least since Descartes. And among the questions that this question concerning the relationship between mind and body raises is whether or not the mind can control the body. That question has evolved into the question of free will, a question we will return to in a moment.

The loaded character of the term "metaphysics" emerged over the course of the twentieth century under the influence of the thought of Martin Heidegger. For Heidegger, the entirety of Western philosophy is characterized by what he called metaphysics. Metaphysics, in his use of the term, is related to but not the same thing as metaphysics as we have just seen it. For Heidegger, the ultimate question for thought is that of Being. The problem, in his eyes, is that Being has been interpreted throughout most of Western philosophy in terms of beings. Being has been thought of as just another type of being. So, when we ask about the nature of reality, when we ask what there is, we wind up asking what kinds of beings there are. This approach neglects the question of Being itself. So when Heidegger uses the term "metaphysics", he is referring to a particular approach to philosophy that has forgotten philosophy's ultimate question, that of Being, in favour of questions about beings.

Heidegger's use of the term "metaphysics" has been enormously influential, particularly in the thought of recent French philosopher Jacques Derrida and his followers. For the purposes of this essay, however, we can leave this use to the side. What we mean by metaphysical freedom does not have to do with the question of Being or of beings, but with that of free will. (Philosophers influenced by the Heidegger/Derrida trajectory may accuse me of engaging in metaphysics in their sense. That is a debate that will have to await another occasion.)

What, then, is metaphysical freedom? It is something that human beings may or may not have. Those who endorse the idea of metaphysical freedom have very different views of what that freedom consists in, but all agree that whatever it is, it involves something that resists our being determined. To understand metaphysical freedom, then, one must understand the doctrine of determinism. What, then, is determinism? It is the view that human beings are in control of none of their actions or thoughts. Whatever we do, its source can be found outside of our conscious control. There are many different types of determinism. Calvinists adopt a religious view called *predestination*. This is the view that God has determined everything that is going to happen, and that human life is merely a playing out of God's script. Genetic determinists think that everything about who we will be and how we will react to things has been coded into our genes. Alternatively, behaviourists hold that our environment wholly shapes who we are; we are nothing more than the products of positive and negative reinforcement. What all these views have in common is the idea that people do not control any aspect of their lives. They are the product of forces over which they have no influence.

Those, by contrast, who hold that there is metaphysical freedom deny that human life is entirely determined. Here there are many different views, not only in what metaphysical freedom might consist in, but in how much of it we actually have. Some, though very few, philosophers hold that we are entirely free in every decision we make. Most hold a less radical doctrine. What characterizes all views of metaphysical freedom, however, is simply the denial that we are entirely determined. Humans, unless they are psychologically damaged, have some conscious control over their thought and their behaviour.

Political freedom is distinct from metaphysical freedom. Political freedom concerns the liberties one does or does not have as a member of a particular society. Freedom of speech, for instance, is a political freedom. People in the UK (at least informally) and (decreasingly so) in the US have it; people in Burma do not. Political freedom is not, as metaphysical freedom is, a doctrine about human nature. It is instead a characterization of particular elements in a society.

Metaphysical and political freedom are conceptually distinct. One can imagine people possessing one kind of freedom without having any of the other. On the one hand, one could be metaphysically free without any type of political liberty. For example, let us assume that people are not entirely determined in their behaviour. Someone who was being held as a political prisoner would, under that assumption, be metaphysically but not politically free. On the other hand, if we assume that people are entirely determined in their behaviour, then in a society that afforded many political liberties they would be politically but not metaphysically free.

This conceptual distinction is characteristic of the philosophical tradition. Perhaps, however, it is a little too neat. Perhaps it serves not so much to clarify concepts as instead to obfuscate reality. After all, cannot one imagine, for instance, that a sustained lack of political freedom in a society would limit the kinds of things people would be able to do, even if they were suddenly liberated? Behaviourists argue that we are entirely determined by our environment. We do not have to go quite that far to recognize that what we call our metaphysical freedom might be constrained by environmental factors, among them a lack of political freedom. After all, we have observed over the past several decades the difficulty people have in exercising political freedoms when they have been held for generations under conditions of political subjugation.

The theorist of metaphysical freedom might argue here that a lack of political freedom does not compromise the existence of metaphysical freedom. Their claim would be that metaphysical freedom is something all humans possess. People who are politically liberated do not gain or lose any of their metaphysical freedom. They are simply displaying an ignorance of how to utilize this metaphysical freedom in the service of their newly gained political freedom.

There is something about this response, however, that seems to miss the point. If we want to know what people's lives are like, what they can and cannot do, then it is perhaps not entirely helpful to be told that, regardless of their particular conditions, they are metaphysically free. What most people are interested in is not whether they are unconstrained in some abstract sense, but what options they might have in a more concrete one. That is to say, if people have been reinforced to be a certain way over a long period of time, the claim that they do not have to be will ring empty if all that is meant is that there is something about being human that is not entirely subject to those reinforcements. What would be of more interest to them would be to understand the character of their particular constraints, how those constraints affect who they are and what they do, and what they might do to liberate themselves from them.

It is at this precise point that the thought of Michel Foucault becomes relevant in thinking about freedom. Foucault does not defend any form of metaphysical freedom. Neither does he deny metaphysical freedom. He is often taken to be doing the latter, because he describes a number of constraints that have bound us. However, the constraints he describes, as he insists over and over again, are not metaphysical constraints but historically given ones. They are constraints that can be overcome. The overcoming of these constraints, however, is not a metaphysical or philosophical exercise. It is a political one. To put the point another way, Foucault neither defends nor denies metaphysical freedom. He assumes something like it in order for political resistance to take place. However, his interest does not lie there but rather in the question of the specific constraints that are part of our historical legacy. He would like to know what they are, how they came to be that way, and what their effects are. It is only then that we can liberate ourselves from them. As he writes in one of his last published works, "After all, what would be the passion for knowledge if it resulted only in a certain amount of knowledgeableness and not, in one way or another and to the extent possible, in the knower's straying afield of himself?" (Foucault 1990b: 8).

Foucault did not publish any books on freedom. He has no sustained reflections on freedom, either metaphysical or political. When he invokes the term or the concept of freedom, it is almost always in a context of a discussion of some other matter. Nevertheless, one can fairly say that, from one end of his career to the other, the question of freedom motivates his work. Not the question, "Are we free?" Instead, the question, "How are we historically constrained and what might we do about it?" And, although Foucault had little to say about the second part of this question, he was very clear about his role regarding the first part. His role was not to tell us what to do: that is, to offer up a new set of constraints. Rather, it was to help us (and himself) understand our particular historical constraints and, moreover, understand that those constraints are nothing more than historical. In that vein, he once wrote,

> There is an optimism that consists in saying that things couldn't be better. My optimism would consist in saying that so many things can be changed, fragile as they are, more arbitrary than self-evident, more a matter of complex, but temporary, historical circumstances than with inevitable anthropological constraints.
>
> (1990d: 156)

Up to this point, we have been discussing freedom in a very general way. However, if Foucault's approach is a fruitful one, we need to move from broad philosophical reflections on freedom to situated, historical analyses of our particular situation. That, of course, is what Foucault's writings do. In order to see the implicit role freedom plays in these works, let us briefly consider an example. *Discipline and Punish* is Foucault's history of the rise of prisons, especially (although not solely) in France. It describes the transition from torture to rehabilitation, passing through a phase that has one foot in each. During the period of torture, crimes were punished only sporadically, but severely. Every crime was considered an offence against the sovereign, an offence that was quite literally an attack against the sovereign's body politic. This offence had to be countered by an overwhelming punishment against the body of the criminal, one that would re-establish the power and standing of the sovereign. Thus, torture.

Torture was, in many ways, an ineffective method of punishment. It was costly, unevenly applied, and often generated sympathy for the criminal. With the rise of capitalism and the corresponding focus on property crimes, a more efficient system of punishment was needed. Foucault tells a complex story about the rise of the prison as a single method of dealing with this problem. For our purposes, what is relevant in this story is the emergence of a gradual shift of focus from crime to criminal. Instead of punishing crimes, a system arose that treated crimes as expressions of criminality. What needed to be treated, then, was the criminal behind the crime. Doing that required more advanced techniques of surveillance and intervention, which had been developing independently of the penal system in monasteries, hospitals and the military. These techniques were merged in the closed environment of the prison, where one could constantly monitor and intervene on the body of the incarcerated. The prison was the place where what Foucault calls *docile bodies* were created, bodies that were both efficient in performance and obedient to authority.

What was forged in the prison did not remain there. Techniques of surveillance and intervention have diffused throughout society. The former are more in the news these days, with the emergence of technologies such as surveillance cameras all over London and wiretapping in the United States. The latter have spread more quietly but no less effectively. From human resource departments in every mid-size to large corporation to the profusion of school counsellors and social workers, families and individuals are constantly exposed to psychological monitoring dedicated to ensuring conformity to appropriate social roles.

There has been much discussion about the contemporary status of this system of surveillance and intervention, a system Foucault labels *discipline*. Some, most notably the philosopher Gilles Deleuze, have argued that we have entered a new, post-disciplinary phase (Deleuze 1995). Our concern, however, is with the question of how freedom is implicated in this historical study. In order to see this, we must recognize first that what Foucault describes in *Discipline and Punish* is the rise of a set of historical constraints on people's behaviour. These constraints work in a way that is often neglected by traditional political philosophies. They do not operate by stopping people from doing something that they might otherwise be tempted to do. Instead, they create people to be certain kinds of ways, and by doing so make them into docile bodies.

The concept of power will be discussed in more depth in other essays in this volume. For the moment let me say only that what Foucault offers with *Discipline and Punish* and others of his historical analyses is what might be called a positive rather than negative view of power. On this view, power works not by restraint but by creation. Power does not place a limit on our liberty; it makes us be certain kinds of people. It does so on two levels. First, it trains our bodies to be oriented toward particular kinds of behaviour. Second, and perhaps more important, it makes us think of ourselves in certain kinds of ways. For example, the profusion of psychological monitoring and intervention that Foucault describes in *Discipline and Punish* creates a society in which people think of themselves as psychological beings. As a result, they consider their unhappiness as psychologically rooted and in need of psychological cure. Rather than questioning the character of the society in which they live, they instead question themselves. It is they rather than the social arrangements that must change. This, in turn, reinforces those social arrangements by deflecting any criticism of them back onto those who are dissatisfied. All problems become psychological rather than social or political in origin.

Power, in this case, works by what might be called *con*straint rather than *re*straint. But, like restraint, constraint works to limit one's options. By making someone into, say, a psychological being, it creates a conformity and blunts the possibility of either social resistance or experimentation with other forms of living. Moreover, it does so more effectively than restraint would. When one is restrained, one still desires that which is forbidden. However, when one is constrained, one is moulded to desire only that which is considered appropriate to desire. One is not simply blocked from attaining what one wants; one does not even consider alternatives to what are presented as the available social options.

What does all this have to do with freedom? Recall the concept of metaphysical freedom. If we are metaphysically free, then we can control some of our thought and/or behaviour; we are not controlled by some force or another outside of us. What Foucault recounts in *Discipline and Punish* is a force outside of us that is influencing how we think, how we act, and in fact who we are – at least at this point in our history. The difference between the force he describes and the forces that concern metaphysical freedom is that his are historical rather than metaphysical. He does not describe a type of force (God, the environment, genes) that necessarily controls human thought and behaviour. He depicts a historically contingent set of practices that have come to have influence over *our* behaviour in *this* particular period. Because of this, there is no reason to believe that, if we understand our historical legacy, we cannot change it.

That is why Foucault says, in the citation above, that "so many things can be changed". He has the view, inherited from the Enlightenment, that so many people see him as rejecting: if we understand our situation then we have a chance at changing it. This perspective tacitly embraces the idea of metaphysical freedom, although it does not argue for it and it does not seek to establish its particular character or limits. One can see this idea when Foucault writes that,

> One must observe that there cannot be relations of power unless the subjects are free. If one or the other were completely at the disposition of the other and became his thing, an object on which

he can exercise an infinite and unlimited violence, there would not be relations of power. In order to exercise a relation of power, there must be on both sides at least a certain form of liberty.

(1994: 12)

As can readily be seen, Foucault's approach to freedom as something that concerns changing our present is politically inflected. This raises the question of what it has to do with political freedom. Political freedom, recall, is a matter of what liberties we are afforded in a particular society or social arrangement. One might say, at a first go, that Foucault describes ways in which particular societies and social arrangements impinge upon liberty. This would not be entirely mistaken. Foucault does describe ways in which alternative ways of living are constrained by who we are made to be and how we are made to think about ourselves. However, there is something misleading about this way of putting things. It seems to presuppose a model of conceiving power and liberty that is not Foucault's model. In order to see this, we need to take a moment to describe that model.

For traditional liberal political theory, there is a tension between state power and liberty that must be balanced. If the state has too much power, then it unfairly curtails an individual's right to create one's life as one sees fit. On the other hand, if liberty is unbounded, then people themselves could interfere with one another's right to pursue a life of their choosing. Therefore, the role of liberal political theory is to figure out the particular balance between state power and liberty, the balance that will best avoid these two extremes. (Liberal political theory has other tasks as well; here we are looking only at its role *vis-à-vis* political freedom.) On this view, state power is an external constraint placed upon individual liberty; the question is, how much and where should it be applied?

This is a view of power as negative, as restraint. As we have seen, however, Foucault's treatment of power in *Discipline and Punish* and elsewhere does not operate with a negative view of power. To be sure, he does not deny that negative power exists, and particularly at the level of the state. However, much of the way power operates, in his view, is not at the level of the state and its various repressive apparatuses, but closer to the ground. It inhabits our daily practices, moulding us into particular kinds of compliant beings.

To the extent that Foucault's writings capture a real mode of power's operation, we must modify the traditional liberal view of liberty. It can no longer simply be an issue of how much restraint can be placed on which kinds of actions. It must also concern how we have come to be who we are, and what we can do about it. Therefore, political liberty is not just a matter of being left to do what one pleases. It is also, and more pointedly, a matter of understanding how we have been moulded in ways that certain things please us rather than others. And beyond that, it is a matter of understanding what else might be available to us. We might put all this somewhat schematically by saying that political freedom no longer simply concerns what we might be free from, but more significantly what, given current constraints, we might be free for.

Foucault captures this idea in a citation that will also allow us to deepen our view of his conception of freedom:

> I would like to say something about the functions of any diagno-
> sis concerning the nature of the present. It does not consist in a
> simple characterization of what we are but, instead – by follow-
> ing lines of fragility in the present – in managing to grasp why
> and how that-which-is might no longer be that-which-is. In this
> sense, any description must always be made in accordance with
> these kinds of virtual fracture which open up the space of freedom
> understood as a space of concrete freedom, i.e. a space of possible
> transformation. (1990c: 36)

Here we can see clearly the themes that we have isolated in Foucault's approach to freedom: constraint as a historical matter, the contingency of that constraint, and freedom as concrete rather than abstract. Moreover, in using the phrase "a space of possible transformation", Foucault captures the idea that freedom is not simply a matter of being left alone but also a matter of re-making ourselves into what we would like to be: freedom *for*, not just freedom *from*. Based on this citation, we might define Foucault's concept of freedom as that which we can make of ourselves from within the parameters of a particular historical situation.

If we define freedom this way, we need to be careful to understand this definition of freedom the right way. First, we should not think that there is a pre-given set of things that we can make of ourselves in a given particular historical situation. It is not as though there is what we might call a "truth" of what we can become, and that once we understand our historical situation, we can discover that truth. Such a view would violate Foucault's project of historicizing those aspects of ourselves that we think of as permanent or unchangeable. It would reify our possibili-ties in what is in reality a fluid historical situation.

Second, and related, we should not assume that we can come fully to understand our historical situation. If who we are is the product of a complex interaction of practices, then at least aspects of the forces

MICHEL FOUCAULT: KEY CONCEPTS

that shape us are likely to elude our comprehension. *Discipline and Punish*, for instance, is not an account of the whole of who we are. It is an account of only one aspect of who we are. The first volume of *The History of Sexuality* is another, and the lecture series Foucault gave on governmentality (2007, 2008c) yet another. Moreover, who we are changes with the changes in our practices. So it is even more difficult to get a grasp on who we are at a particular moment. We always risk understanding who we just were, rather than who are now.

The upshot of this is that, for Foucault, freedom is a matter of experimentation. To open up "a space of concrete freedom" is not to figure out who we might be and then go there; it is to try out different possibilities for our lives, different "possible transformations", to see where they might lead. To live freely is to experiment with oneself, not always knowing whether one is getting free of the forces that have moulded one, nor (and we will return to this in a moment) being sure of the effects of one's experimentation. It is to try to create a life from within a space of uncertainty, having some knowledge of how one has been made to be.

Our situation, then, is this. If we construct histories like Foucault's, histories which give us accounts of different aspects of the forces that have influenced us to be who we have become, then we have a partial knowledge of how we came to be that way. From there, we can decide which among those forces are acceptable to us, and which are, to use Foucault's term, *intolerable*. (Foucault's histories give accounts only of intolerable forces, since those are the ones we are most likely to want to change.) In seeking to overcome the intolerable forces, we must experiment with who we might become, not knowing entirely whether we are indeed escaping them. That is something we can only find out later, after our experiments are under way. We are, then, neither helpless in the face of what moulds us nor certain of how and what we can do about it. We are somewhere in between. That is where our freedom lies, and indeed that is what our freedom is.

Since we can only experiment without certainty as to the results of our experiments, we must always be vigilant. We do not know in advance where our experimentation will lead us. We might wind up either re-creating intolerable forces or creating new ones. Therefore, we cannot stop doing the kinds of histories Foucault engages in, nor resting content with his. The history of who we are is an ongoing project. Otherwise put, the effects of our freedom are as uncertain as our freedom itself. We must never assume that the "space of possible transformations" we exploit will necessarily lead us to a better situation. Freedom is not the same thing as liberation. Whether our freedom is liberating or not is something that is not guaranteed to us. It can only be approached through experimentation and historically informed reflection.

In order to get a better understanding of Foucault's conception of freedom, it might be useful to contrast it with that of a French philosopher from the generation preceding Foucault's. Maurice Merleau-Ponty also has a notion of situated freedom, one in which we are free but not entirely free. Seeing the differences between the two conceptions of freedom may sharpen our grasp on Foucault's own approach.

Merleau-Ponty constructs his concept of freedom in contrast to that of his contemporary Jean-Paul Sartre. Sartre's view of freedom is that we are radically free in the metaphysical sense. There is nothing that is not in our power to decide. Sartre, at least in his early works, rejects all notions of a psychoanalytic unconscious or hidden historical forces that make us be who we are. In pure existentialist fashion, Sartre posits that our choices are solely our own. We must take full responsibility for them. Merleau-Ponty does not embrace this radical view of freedom. For Merleau-Ponty, one of the forces that we cannot control but that makes us who we are is the body. Corporeality – which it is the core project of Merleau-Ponty to understand – gives us our first interactions with the world through perception, and our first understanding of the world. The living body, rather than being an inert substance through which sensations pass, is instead the source of our primal engagement with the world. We might be able to alter that engagement in certain ways, but our embodiment ensures that there will be aspects of our living over which we do not have complete control. There is a certain unconscious aspect to our lives that will always elude us, the aspect that runs through our corporeal interaction with the world. Further, as Merleau-Ponty points out, that interaction is not properly described in terms of a body on the one hand that interacts with a world on the other. It is more intimate than that. The interaction is instead better characterized as that of a body/world complex.

This position leads to a view of freedom far less radical than Sartre's. For Sartre, the body is simply an inert object manipulated by consciousness. If consciousness is unconstrained, then freedom of consciousness would be absolute. Sartre, of course, recognizes that consciousness is in some way embodied, so that even if one freely decides, say, to fly, that does not mean that one will actually be able to fly. But the decision itself is radically free. Merleau-Ponty's analysis of corporeality erases Sartre's radical distinction between mind and body. As Merleau-Ponty shows, the body already engages in perceptual interpretation before one consciously reflects on it. (He uses examples of visual illusions to make his point. Illusions are already seen *as* something before conscious

81

reflection attempts to correct them.) If this is true, then there is no radical freedom. Embodied creatures are constrained by their body/ world engagement. This does not mean that one cannot reflect on that engagement. But one always does so as an already embodied being.

The freedom of that reflection and of one's behaviour is, for Merleau-Ponty as for Foucault, a form of situated freedom.

> We choose our world and the world chooses us ... freedom is always a meeting of the inner and the outer ... and it shrinks without ever disappearing altogether in direct proportion to the lessening of the *tolerance* allowed by the bodily and institutional data of our lives. (Merleau-Ponty 1962: 454)

Our freedom is had within and through the constraints set by our bodies and our world. Those constraints can allow greater or lesser room for action: greater or lesser tolerance. But without bodies and historically given institutional frameworks, there would be no freedom, because there would be nothing through which (i.e. the body) to enact it and nothing about which (the world) it would concern.

There are ways in which Merleau-Ponty's conception of situated freedom is similar to Foucault's. Both of them acknowledge the importance of our embodiment, and they recognize the body's exposure to the world and its practices. Moreover, in both approaches that exposure opens out on to limitations on one's freedom. What distinguishes them is the level of analysis on which these recognitions rest. Merleau-Ponty's situated freedom is a metaphysical freedom. He offers a general philosophical account of the human body in its intertwining with the world. That account shows how mind and body as well as body and world form a single whole. From that he derives the conclusion that, contra Sartre, all human freedom must be situated. There can be no radical freedom because there is no aspect of our being that can stand outside our encrustation into the world. All freedom is the freedom of an embodied consciousness embedded in the world and its history.

Foucault does not need to deny any of this. Neither, however, does he need to embrace it. His approach is constructed along a different register. His question is not the metaphysical one of what the nature of human freedom is. Rather, his question is the more political one of what freedom we might have under particular historical conditions, namely *our* historical conditions. The situated freedom he is interested in is not the freedom of one situated as a human body in the world; it is the freedom of our situation. In the citation above, Foucault emphasizes that a diagnosis of the nature of the present must characterize that present in such a way as to show its fragility, its fractures. The fragility of the present is not due to humans' possession of metaphysical freedom, although, as we have seen, he does seem to assume some form of metaphysical freedom. It is due, rather, to the contingent structure of history.

History does not unfold according to a pre-given or transcendental framework. It is largely the product of dispersed practices that intersect with and influence one another in ways that cannot be predicted in advance and that conform to no transcendent pattern. (This does not mean that one cannot find patterns within history; it means that one can only see them after they have created themselves through the interaction of contingent practices.) Situated freedom arises as a result of this contingency of history. The issue for one interested in one's freedom, then, is not the metaphysical question of who one is and where one's freedom lies, but rather the question of where one's particular history has deposited one, and how that history might be intervened upon. For Foucault, in short, situated freedom is a historical and political concept rather than a metaphysical one.

Foucault's approach to freedom, then, like the approach of many aspects of his work, is at once philosophical and historical. As a philosophically oriented concept, it takes history in a more sophisticated direction than most historians are capable of. As a historically inflected concept, it raises questions to traditional philosophical analyses. Foucault's writings ask to be read along both of these axes, each one in conversation with the other. If we allow ourselves to engage in this two-level conversation, we may become more aware not only of the particular philosophically inflected way in which we often view the world, but also of the historically contingent and malleable character of that way. In other words, we may come face to face with our freedom.

present in such a way as to bring its 'necessity'. The tracing of the 'unsaid' is not just to inform its possession of an explicit relation, although, as we have seen, he does seem to assume some form of mediation. If telling, it telling rather to the contingent affinities of history.

Historical personhood, according to it, is grounded upon a third framework. Its largely a proper understanding to advance an interest or within influence one another in ways that cannot be predicted in advance, and that constitute, into non-complex patterns, of his does not imply that one cannot find patterns within changing rules that one can only see them: one may have created themselves through the interactions of normalising of practice. Locating how an agent creates of the changing environment in a 'theatre' to be interconnected in the formation, is not the mainly visual question of who one is and whole one is free to do, but rather the much more about one's particular interest he depended upon, and how that mainly might include interpretation too. For him, rather than simply being born as a historical being one is much rather than a manipulated one.

Foucault's approach to freedom, then, like the approach to many aspects of his work, is at once philosophical and historical. As a philosophically oriented attempt at telling history of a self, architects and directors in their most interviews are capable of a fundamentally full and complex, it raises questions of traditional philosophical analyses, crucially seeking not to be read along both: to they give each one in conversation with the other, if we allow whether its conveyed in this two-level conversation we may become more aware not only of the particular philosophically inflected ways in which we often view the world, but also of the universally significant and valuable character of that way. In other words, we may come face to face with our freedom.

SIX

Freedom and bodies
Johanna Oksala

The critical impact of Michel Foucault's philosophy is not based on the explicit theories or judgements he makes, but rather on the approach that he adopts to analysing our present. While science and much of philosophy aim to decipher from among the confusion of events and experiences that which is necessary and can be articulated as universal law, Foucault's thought moves in exactly the opposite direction. He attempts to find among the apparent necessities that which upon closer philosophical scrutiny turns out to be contingent, historical and culturally variable. Everything, especially those things that we are convinced do not have a history, is scrutinized.

This method is also utilized regarding Foucault's conception of the body. He does not present a theory of the body anywhere, or even a unified account of it, and his conception of it has to be discerned from his genealogical books and articles. Yet his philosophical approach to it is distinctive. The body is central for understanding the influence of history and the mechanisms of modern power. Its intertwinement with practices of power means that it has a central role in practices of resistance too: it is capable of displaying a dimension of freedom.

According to Foucault, we believe that the body obeys only the necessary and universal laws of physiology, and that history and culture have no influence on it. In reality, bodies are shaped by society: they are used and experienced in many different ways and their characteristics vary according to cultural practices. They are moulded by rhythms of work, eating habits and changing norms of beauty. They are concretely shaped by diet, exercise and medical interventions. In short, they too have a history.

In his most widely read books, *Discipline and Punish* (1975) and *The History of Sexuality, Volume I* (1976), Foucault aims to bring the body into the focus of history by studying its connections with techniques and deployments of power. His understanding of the body is further elaborated in numerous interviews and articles. I will focus here on the central texts in which he discusses it in order to present a coherent and cohesive account of Foucault's understanding of the body, paying particular attention to its relationship to both power and freedom. In order to illustrate the body's relationship to power, I will discuss his analyses of the prison, as articulated in *Discipline and Punish*, and of sexuality, as articulated in Volume I of *The History of Sexuality*. In order to illustrate how the body is implicated in resistance and the practices of freedom, I again draw upon *The History of Sexuality*, as well as Foucault's analysis of the life of the hermaphrodite, *Herculine Barbin*. I conclude the chapter by discussing the ways in which Foucault's work has influenced emancipatory efforts by queer and feminist theorists.

It should be kept in mind that Foucault never intended his views on the body to form a unified theory. His genealogies are best understood as a toolbox, a flexible and varied methodological approach that draws from a multiplicity of sources and is applicable to a variety of questions. However, one of the key ideas that unites them is that genealogies are always crucially "histories of the body": they typically question all purely biological explanations of such complex areas of human behaviour as sexuality, insanity or criminality.

Docile bodies

In an early and definitive article on his genealogical method, *Nietzsche, Genealogy, History,* Foucault follows Nietzsche in insisting that the task of genealogy is to focus on the body. Nietzsche had attacked philosophy for its denial of the materiality and vitality of the body, for its pretentious metaphysics that deals only with abstractions such as values, reason and the soul. Genealogy must be "a curative science", charting the long and winding history of metaphysical concepts in the materiality of bodies (Foucault 1984b: 90). Rather than contemplating what is understood as high and noble, genealogy will focus on the things nearest to it: the body, the nervous system, nutrition, digestion and energies (*ibid.*: 89). Foucault writes polemically that the philosopher needs the genealogy of the body to "exorcise the shadow of his soul" (*ibid.*: 80).

In this text Foucault also presents his most extreme formulations of the body as completely shaped by history and culture. He seems to deny that there is anything universal and ahistorical about it that could be understood as its stable and fixed core: "nothing in man – not even his body – is sufficiently stable to serve as the basis for self-recognition or for understanding other men" (*ibid.*: 87).

Foucault's aim in this discussion of Nietzsche's conception of the body as a historical construct is not to develop some kind of extreme social constructivist theory of the body, however. He does not consider the body here as an object of a theory, but rather as essential to his genealogy in two different ways. The first is political or ethical: Foucault wants to use genealogy to study the history of the very things we believe do not have a history. As Gary Gutting writes, "whereas much traditional history tries to show that where we are is inevitable, given the causes revealed by its account, Foucault's histories aim to show the contingency – and hence surpassability – of what history has given us" (1994: 10). Foucault's point is thus not to argue for an extreme view of the body as a cultural construction, but to place under suspicion and subject to further scrutiny all claims of its immutable being: essences, foundations and constants.

The second way in which the body is essential to Foucault's genealogy is methodological: he wants to bring the body into the focus of history and study history through it. Foucault's genealogy is methodologically distinct in that it criticizes the idea of power operating by the ideological manipulation of minds: the idea that those in power are trying to brainwash people into believing things that are not true. Foucault's aim is to show the inadequacy of such a conception of power by revealing the material manipulation of bodies.

Foucault's illustration of how power operates through the manipulation of bodies is done in a powerful manner in his first major work of the genealogical period, *Discipline and Punish*. The book charts the genealogy of the modern prison institution and brings under scrutiny the connection between power and the body by analysing the ways in which the bodies of prisoners are consciously manipulated. It also demonstrates effectively Foucault's idea of the essential intertwinement of body and power: bodies are not given, natural objects, but assume their shape and characteristics in cultural practices of power, including punitive practices.

Discipline is a historically specific technology of power that emerged in the eighteenth century and operates through the body. It consists of various techniques, which aim at making the body both docile and useful. Bodies of prisoners, soldiers, workers and schoolchildren were subjected to new kinds of discipline in order to make them more useful for mass production and at the same time easier to control. The functions, movements and capabilities of these bodies were broken down into narrow segments, analysed in detail and recomposed in a maximally effective way. The human body became a machine the functioning of which could be optimized, calculated and improved. Foucault argues that in the seventeenth century a soldier, for example, still learnt his profession for the most part in actual fighting in which he proved his natural strength and inherent courage. But by the eighteenth century a soldier had become a fighting machine, something that could be constructed through correct training. Foucault tells us:

> The human body was entering a machinery of power that explores it, breaks it down and rearranges it … It defined how one may have a hold over others' bodies, not only so that they may do what one wishes, but so that they may operate as one wishes, with techniques, the speed and the efficiency that one determines. Thus discipline produces subjected and practiced bodies, "docile" bodies. (1979: 138)

Hence, a novel aspect of modern disciplinary power is that it is not external to the bodies that it subjects. Although the body has also in the past been intimately tied to power and social order, Foucault claims that disciplinary power is essentially a modern phenomenon. It differs from earlier forms of bodily manipulation, which were violent and often performative: public tortures, slavery and hanging, for instance. Disciplinary power does not subject the body to extreme violence, it is not external or spectacular. It does not mutilate or coerce its target, but through detailed training reconstructs the body to produce new kinds of gestures, habits and skills. It focuses on details, on single movements, on their timing and rapidity. It organizes bodies in space and schedules their every action for maximum effect. This is done in factories, schools, hospitals and prisons through fixed and minutely detailed rules, constant surveillance and frequent examinations and check-ups. Bodies are classified according to their best possible performance, their size, age and sex. Unlike older forms of bodily coercion, disciplinary power does not destroy the body, but reconstructs it. Individuals literally incorporate the objectives of power, which become part of their own being: actions, aims and habits.

In prisons, for example, disciplinary technologies subject prisoners by manipulating and materially inscribing their bodies. Their bodies are separated from others in practices of classification and examination, but also concretely and spatially. They are manipulated through exercise regimes, diet and strict time schedules. These processes of power operate through the bodies of prisoners, but they are also essentially objectifying: through processes of classification and examination the individual is given a social and a personal identity. He or she becomes a delinquent, a person with a distinct identity. Disciplinary power thus constitutes delinquents through concrete bodily manipulation and discursive objectification. These two dimensions strengthen each other. On the one hand, concrete bodily manipulation made discursive objectification possible, resulting in the birth of sciences such as criminology and criminal psychiatry. The development of these sciences, on the other hand, helped the development and rationalization of disciplinary technologies in prisons. The two dimensions furthermore link together effectively through normalization. Scientific discourses produce truths that function as the norm: they tell us what is the normal fat percentage, cholesterol count or number of sexual partners for a certain sex and age group, for example. Modern power operates through the internalization of these norms. We modify our behaviour in an endless attempt to approximate the normal, and in this process become certain kinds of subjects.

This process of normalization is illustrated in *Discipline and Punish* in which Foucault analyses the strategies used by disciplinary power for the subjection of criminals. Where prisoners are concerned, disciplinary power does not aim at repressing their interests or desires, but rather at reconstructing these desires as normal. This is not done by the ideological manipulation of their minds, but on and through their bodies. The aim of disciplinary techniques is to inscribe the norms of the society in the bodies of criminals by subjecting them to reconstructed patterns of behaviour. The prisoners must subject themselves to power to the extent that its aims become their own inner meaning of normal. Foucault formulates this complete subjection poetically by turning around the old philosophical and religious idea that the body is the prison of the soul:

> The man described for us, whom we are invited to free, is already in himself the effect of a subjection much more profound than himself. "A soul" inhabits him and brings him to existence, which is itself a factor in the mastery that power exercises over the body. The soul is the effect and instrument of a political anatomy; the soul is the prison of the body.　　　　　　　　　(*Ibid.*: 30.)

The "soul" of the prisoner – that which is supposed to be the most authentic part of him and, therefore, a key to his emancipation – is in fact an effect of the subjection of his body.

Sexual bodies

Foucault's next major work, *The History of Sexuality, Volume I*, thematizes the body through the question of sexuality. It puts forward his famous account of the discursive constitution of sexuality. Although the book is a historical study of the emergence of modern sexuality in the nineteenth century, Foucault's criticism targets contemporary conceptions of sexuality as well. The prevalent views in the West on sexuality in the 1960s and 1970s held that there was a natural and healthy sexuality that all human beings shared simply by virtue of being human, and this sexuality was presently repressed by cultural prohibitions and conventions such as bourgeois morality and capitalist socioeconomic structures. Because it was essential to have an active and free sexuality, repressed sexuality was the cause of various neuroses. The popular discourse on sexuality thus fervently argued for sexual liberation: we had to liberate our true sexuality from the repressive mechanisms of power.

Foucault challenges this view by showing how our conceptions and experiences of sexuality are in fact always the result of specific cultural conventions and mechanisms of power and could not exist independently of them. Sexuality, like delinquency, only exists in a society. The mission to liberate our repressed sexuality is thus fundamentally misguided because there is no authentic or natural sexuality to liberate. To free oneself from one set of norms only meant adopting different norms in their stead, and that could turn out to be just as normalizing. Foucault wrote mockingly that the irony in the deployment of sexuality is "in having us believe that our 'liberation' is in the balance" (1990a: 159).

In order to challenge the accepted relationship between sexuality and repressive power Foucault had to reconceive the nature of power. His major claim is that power is not essentially repressive; in fact, it is productive. It does not operate by repressing and prohibiting the true and authentic expressions of a natural sexuality. Instead it produces, through cultural normative practices and scientific discourses, the ways in which we experience and conceive of our sexuality.

The sexual body is an essential component of this process. In a much-quoted passage Foucault writes:

> We must not make the mistake of thinking that sex is an autonomous agency which secondarily produces manifold effects of sexuality over the entire length of its surface of contact with power. On the contrary, sex is the most speculative, most ideal, and most internal element in a deployment of sexuality organized

by power in its grip on bodies and their materiality, their forces, energies, sensations, and pleasures.   (*Ibid.*: 155)

Foucault thus claims that sex is an essential element in the strategy through which power holds a grip on our bodies. But what exactly does Foucault mean by sex in this passage? The French word *sexe* is ambiguous because it can refer to the categories of male and female in the sense of sex organs – anatomy and biology that differentiates males from females – or it can refer to a natural function, a biological foundation or principle in the body that belongs in common to both men and women, or to the activity of having sex. This ambiguity is essential for Foucault's argument, however, because he attempts to show that rather than being a natural entity, "sex" in fact refers to a completely arbitrary and illusory unity of disparate elements.

Foucault begins his discussion of sex in the end of *The History of Sexuality* by anticipating an objection. He invents an imaginary opponent who claims that his history of sexuality only manages to argue for the cultural construction of sexuality because he evades "the biologically established existence of sexual functions for the benefit of phenomena that are variable, perhaps, but secondary, and ultimately superficial" (*ibid.*: 150–51). The imaginary critic thus raises a question about a natural and necessary foundation of sexuality in the body: even if the manifestations of sexuality are culturally constructed and variable, there must nevertheless be a biological foundation in the body, a pre-cultural, embodied givenness which cannot be bent at will. There must be something purely natural – biological organs, functions and instincts – that causes the culturally varied manifestations of sexuality.

Foucault responds to his opponent by, first, denying that his analysis of sexuality implies "the elision of the body, anatomy, the biological, the functional" (*ibid.*: 151). On the contrary, what is needed is an analysis, which would overcome the biology/culture distinction (*ibid.*: 152). The aim of his genealogical histories is precisely to show how history and bodies are bound together in complex ways in the development of modern forms of power such as disciplinary power. He explicitly argues that his analysis of sexuality as a discursive construct does not deny the materiality of the body and the biologically established existence of sexual functions (*ibid.*: 150–51). The purpose of his study is, in fact, to show:

how deployments of power are directly connected to the body – to bodies, functions, physiological processes, sensations, and pleasures; … what is needed is to make it visible through an analysis in which the biological and the historical are not consecutive to one another … but are bound together in an increasingly complex fashion in accordance with the development of the modern technologies of power that take life as their objective. Hence, I do not envisage a "history of mentalities" that would take account of bodies only through the manner in which they have been perceived and given meaning and value; but a "history of the bodies" and the manner in which what is most material and most vital in them has been invested. (*Ibid.*: 151–2)

Foucault thus accepts that ontologically there is some kind of materiality: there are such things in the world as bodies, organs, somatic locations, functions, anatomo-physiological systems, sensations and pleasures. What he does deny, however, is that this materiality corresponds to the idea of sex in an unproblematic way. In other words, there is no natural or necessary referent for the notion of sex. In scientific discourses on sexuality the notion of sex came to refer to something that in reality did not exist as a natural unity at all. It was a pseudo-scientific object like hysteria or monomania, which we now think refer to purely fictitious unities of disparate symptoms. The term sex is then placed inside inverted commas in Foucault's text because it becomes suspect. He brackets the accepted meaning of the notion in order to be able to study its genealogy: how the idea of "sex" took form in the different strategies of power, and what role it played in them.

Foucault notes three theoretical benefits that the idea of sex produced: it made it possible to group together different kinds of elements – anatomical features, behavioural patterns and fantasies, for example – and make use of this fictitious unity as a causal principle of explanation for different forms of sexuality. Second, the idea of sex gave the sciences of sexuality a proximity to biological sciences of reproduction, which functioned as a guarantee of their quasi-scientificity. Third, because sex was something biological and natural, power could only appear as something external to it.

Foucault, in contrast, refutes the idea that sex is a given, biological foundation and as such the "other" with respect to power. For him, the idea of a natural and foundational sex is a normative, historical construct that functions as an important anchorage point for power. Foucault's aim in analysing the sexual body is to study how the scientific idea of "sex" took form in the different strategies of power, and what role it played in them. The idea that "sex" is the scientific foundation, the true, causal origin of one's gender identity, sexual identity and sexual desire makes it possible to effectively normalize sexual and gendered behaviour. Through scientific knowledge about one's true sex it is possible to evaluate, pathologize and correct one's sexual and gendered behaviour by viewing it as either "normal" or "abnormal".

Bodies, pleasures and freedom

Foucault's analysis of power attempts to describe the historical limits that are imposed on us, but it is also an experiment with the possibility of modifying and crossing them: relations of power always incorporate relations of resistance and points of recalcitrance. We cannot step outside the networks of power that circumscribe our experience, but there is always a possibility for thinking and being otherwise within them. To be free does not mean that everything is possible, but neither is the present way of thinking and being a necessity. Freedom refers to the contingency of structures and limits – including the limits of our present field of experience.

This is also true about sexual experiences. Foucault does not view the sexual body only as a docile and passive object of dominant discourses and techniques of power. It also represents the possibility of resistance against such discourses and techniques. In an important passage of *The History of Sexuality*, Foucault writes:

> We must not think that by saying yes to sex, one says no to power; on the contrary, one tracks along the course laid out by the general deployment of sexuality. It is the agency of sex that we must break away from, if we aim – through a tactical reversal of the various mechanisms of sexuality – to counter the grip of power with the claims of bodies, pleasures and knowledges, in their multiplicity and their possibility of resistance. The rallying point for the counterattack against the deployment of sexuality ought not to be sex-desire, but bodies and pleasures.   (1990a: 157)

What Foucault suggests in this paragraph is that it is in the body that the seeds for subverting the normalizing aims of power are sown. The body is a locus of resistance and freedom (see also Foucault 1980a: 56). The body is never completely docile and its experiences can never be wholly reduced to normative, discursive determinants. The sexual body is always discursive in the sense that it is an object of scientific discourses and disciplinary technologies. Nevertheless, it is also a body acting in the world and experiencing pleasure. And a distinction must be drawn between discourse and experience, even if we accept that language forms the necessary limits of our experience and thought. Even if we believe that it is only possible to experience something that we have words for and that language makes intelligible for us, the experience itself is still not reducible to language.

The ontological distinction between experience and discourse – the experience of something and the linguistic description or explanation of this experience – is crucial for understanding the resistance of the body. The body represents a dimension of freedom in the sense that its experiences are never wholly reducible to the discursive order: embodied experiences and language are imperfectly aligned because experience sometimes exceeds language and sometimes it is completely inarticulate. Bodies are capable of multiplying, distorting and overflowing their discursive determinants and of opening up new and surprising possibilities that can be articulated in new ways.

While *The History of Sexuality, Volume I* already suggests the possibility of understanding bodies and pleasures as a locus of resistance, the book that followed it in 1977, *Herculine Barbin: Being the Recently Discovered Memoirs of a Nineteenth-Century French Hermaphrodite*, is equally important for understanding Foucault's view of the resistance of the body. Herculine Barbin was a hermaphrodite who lived at the end of the nineteenth century, at the time when scientific theories about sex and sexuality were gaining prominence. She was designated as female at birth, but grew up with an ambiguous awareness of her bodily uniqueness. As an adult she decided to confess her anatomical particularity to a priest and as a consequence was scientifically reclassified as a man by doctors. She/he was incapable of adapting her/himself to the new identity, however, and committed suicide at the age of thirty. She/he left behind memoirs recounting his/her tragic story, which Foucault discovered in the archives of the Department of Public Hygiene. He edited them and they were published together with the medical and legal documents related to the case as well as an introduction written by him.

The way the book is compiled is significant. It effectively juxtaposes Herculine's memoirs and thus the first-person, lived account of the hermaphrodite body with the third-person, legal and medical accounts of it. It is clear that Herculine's own account cannot be understood as the authentic or authoritative description of her embodiment as it is clearly shaped by the narrative conventions as well as the cultural conceptions of hermaphrodites of her time. But neither can the third-person legal accounts and medical diagnosis be accepted as the "true" account. The tragedy of Herculine's experience is exactly the result of the fissures and disjunctures – as well as the necessary correspondence and overlapping – between the subject's experience of his or her body and the dominant scientific and legal discourses on its true sex.

The form of the book, not just its content, is thus highly significant for Foucault's attempts to show that while our embodiment is never independent of dominant discourses and practices of power, it is not reducible to them either. Bodies always assume meaning through a complex process in which competing discourses, conceptualizations and practices intertwine with private sensations, pleasures and pains.

How to use Foucauldian bodies?

As noted earlier, Foucault conceived of his books as toolboxes that readers could rummage through to find a tool they needed to think and act with. It is therefore pertinent to conclude by asking how his conception of the body has been and can be appropriated by contemporary thinkers attempting to understand and change current ways of living our sexuality.

Foucault's understanding of the historical constitution of the body through the mechanisms of power has influenced feminist theory profoundly: it has provided a way to theorize the body in its materiality while avoiding all naturalist formulations.[1] It has also given tools for understanding the disciplinary production of the female body. Feminists have appropriated Foucault's ideas about power and the body to study the different ways that women shape their bodies – from cosmetic surgery to dieting and eating disorders – and analysed these everyday practices as disciplinary technologies in the service of patriarchal, normalizing power. These normative feminine practices train the female body in docility and obedience to cultural demands, while at the same time they are paradoxically experienced in terms of "power" and "control" by the women themselves (see e.g. Bartky 1988; Bordo 1989).

Foucault's historicization of sex has also profoundly influenced feminist theory. Judith Butler (1990) has effectively appropriated Foucault's thinking on the relationship between subject, power and sex for the question of gendered subjects. She has followed Foucault in arguing that there is no true sex behind gender identity that would be its objective cause and biological foundation. Instead, gender identity is constructed as a normative and regulatory ideal in the networks of power and knowledge. Individuals perform gender by repeating behaviour that approximates this ideal. While their behaviour is understood to be the inevitable and natural consequence of their sex, Butler argues that it is actually a performance without any natural and foundational cause. Feminine behaviour, for example, is not the result of a true and foundational female sex, but the reverse is true: the idea of a true and foundational female sex is the result of feminine behaviour. The idea of a stable gender core is a fiction that is upheld by a constantly ongoing performance.

Not only did Foucault influence feminist thinkers, his views on the sexual body have also influenced gay and lesbian studies. His conception of sexuality has, to a large extent, founded a new theoretical approach to sexuality called queer theory.

The main idea behind the queer conception of sexuality is that the identities of gay and lesbian – as well as of heterosexual – are not natural, essential identities, but are culturally constructed through normative discourses and power relations regulating the "healthy" and "normal" expressions of sexuality. This does not mean that homosexuality does not "really" exist. As in the case of woman, just because something is constructed does not mean that it is not real. People are defined and they must think and live according to such constructions. The aim of sexual politics, however, cannot be simply to find one's true identity through a scientific study of the various aspects of the sexual body. Sexual bodies as well as the sexual identities they are supposed to cause and found are constructed through the oppressive power relations that our politics must attempt to challenge and to resist.[2]

The goal of queer and feminist politics therefore has to be more complicated than simple liberation from power and the affirmation of one's homosexuality or gender identity: practising freedom entails questioning and even denying the identities that are imposed on us as natural and essential by making visible their cultural construction and dependence on the power relations that are operative in society. Rather than thinking in terms of stable binary categories such as man and woman, heterosexual and homosexual, we should study their constitution and the ways in which sexuality emerges as a complex construction only in relation to them.

While a shared focus on bodies has opened up important connections between feminist theory, queer theory and Foucault's thought, it has been argued that Foucault understands the body as too docile and culturally malleable, and that his conception of it is thus one-sided and limited for feminist purposes (see e.g. Bordo 1989, 1993; Bigwood 1991; McNay 1991; Soper 1993). The opposite charge has also been made. Judith Butler, for example, criticizes Foucault's understanding of the body in *The History of Sexuality* for a return to "a non-normalizable wildness" (1997: 92). She claims that while Foucault advocates the critical historicization of sexuality and sex in *The History of Sexuality*, he does not extend it to the sexed body, but naively presents bodies and pleasures as the site of resistance against power.

I have attempted to show, however, that Foucault's conception of the body provides fruitful tools for theorizing the body *both* as an effect of power *and* as a locus of resistance and freedom. Bodies are both docile and anarchic. They are not reducible to a collection of biological facts, but provide possibilities for experimentation and a variety of pleasures. They are always inevitably intertwined with mechanisms of power, but they also open up the realm of creative politics and personal experimentation. They open up a realm of freedom in the sense that they break and disturb every totality, but this ream of freedom must not be understood as some absolute and mystical outside to power. Foucault emphasizes that the "virtual fractures" for thinking and being otherwise "which open up a space of freedom" must be understood in terms of concrete practices capable of transforming our present (1990c: 36). We must try to rearticulate the possibilities opened up by the indeterminacy and ontological contingency of our bodies in ways that are conducive to concrete political transformation of our present. Foucault's message to us is that sexuality should be understood as a practice or a way of being that provides possibilities for being otherwise, rather than as a psychological or biological condition that we must reveal the truth about. It should be transferred from the realm of biological necessity to the realm of practices of freedom.

Notes

1. For feminist appropriations of Foucault, see, for example, Butler (1990), Braidotti (1991), Sawicki (1991), McNay (1992), McWhorter (1999), Oksala (2005).
2. On Foucault and queer theory, see, for example, Halperin (1995).

SEVEN

Freedom and spirituality

Karen Vintges

Spirituality is an idiosyncratic concept in the work of Foucault, which might best be characterized as an "intensity without a 'spirit'".[1] To understand Foucault's specific concept of spirituality, we have to take into account some basic themes of his oeuvre, especially of his later work, that is, his books, interviews and lectures since 1976. In this chapter I will first analyse the way in which Foucault uses the concept of spirituality in his early work, a utilization that is inspired by surrealist writers. For this analysis I rely heavily on the work of Jeremy Carrette, who in his book *Foucault and Religion* (2000) devotes a chapter to this topic. In the second section of the chapter I briefly discuss Foucault's analysis, as found in his "middle" (1970–76) works, of dominant forms of subjectivity in the modern West. This discussion lays the ground for the chapter's third section, which analyses the "exit" status of the concept of spirituality in Foucault's final works. Here I show that spirituality constitutes an ethical self-transformation as conscious practice of freedom. In a fourth section, I discuss Foucault's epistemological claims regarding the relation between spirituality and truth. In the next two sections I analyse his concept of "political spirituality" and argue that this concept offers us a new normative perspective for cross-cultural politics. In a concluding section I illustrate Foucault's idea of spirituality as freedom practice by going into the emerging discourse of Islamic feminism.

Beyond the body/soul dualism

As Carrette shows, Foucault in his early (pre-1970) work only once talks about spirituality. In a debate on the "new novel" and surrealism, Foucault comments on certain surrealist experiments which he witnessed in which people tried to let the body speak. "(R)eference is constantly made", Foucault states,

> to a certain number of experiences – experiences, if you like, that I will call, in quotation marks, "spiritual experiences" (although "spiritual" is not quite the right word) – such as dreams, madness, folly, repetition, the double, the disruption of time, the return, etc. These experiences form a constellation that is doubtless quite coherent. I was also struck by the fact this constellation was already mapped out in surrealism.   (Foucault 1999b: 72)

Foucault shared with the surrealists an interest in "a new space of thought created by a radical critique of rationality and certainty", without, however, taking on board the wider surrealist fascination with religious ideas (Carrette 2000: 56). Through the work of semi-surrealist authors such as Artaud and Klossowski, Foucault tries to think beyond the body/soul dualism of Western, Christian and Cartesian traditions, and to conceive of what Carrette calls a "spiritual corporality", and a "reordering of spiritual concepts into the body" (ibid.: 54).

Whereas surrealism incorporated occult and gnostic influences in its fascination for transgression and its attempt to overcome "all control exercised by reason" (ibid.: 50), Foucault's interest in "spirituality" concerns modes of experience that are rooted in the body and that transgress rational or conscious thought. As we will see, Foucault will retain this element of "spiritual corporality" in his later works but will also add something else to it, since he then is no longer satisfied with the idea of resistance against the rationalist or logo-centric order as primarily a bodily expression (Thompson 2003).

Critique of normality

In his middle work, Foucault at length discusses and criticizes dominant forms of subjectivity in modern Western society. His works of the 1970s unmask the claim of Western Enlightenment that it brought progress for humanity and society through reason. "'The Enlightenment,' which discovered the liberties, also invented the disciplines" (Foucault 1979:

222). Originating in the nineteenth century, these disciplines – pan-optic, controlling, discursive institutions such as prisons, schools and medical and welfare institutions – applied power techniques, such as surveillance, training and examination, to individual bodies in order to generate rational self-control. The idea that reason makes self-control possible leads to the application of disciplinary techniques not only by institutions, but also by individuals themselves, as a means of gaining such control. In this way, an internal "core self" is established and the autonomous subject is born.

The human sciences play a major role in the disciplines, classifying and categorizing people, surveilling their behaviour, and treating them where their behaviour is deemed abnormal. Sciences like psychiatry, biology, medicine and economics and, later, psychoanalysis, psychology, sociology, ethnology, pedagogy, criminology, in all their practical dimensions – such as buildings, therapy rooms, intake procedures, exams – codify what is rational and what is not, what is normal and what is not, and what is human and inhuman. Through this regime of political rationality, the subject form of the rational autonomous individual has since the Enlightenment become *the* norm in Western culture.

However, to Foucault, the political rationality that characterizes Western societies creates not only a prison for so-called abnormal people (criminals, sexual perverts, madmen, etc.) but for the "normal" ones too, and his compassion clearly lies with both (White 1996).[2] Whereas in *Discipline and Punish* Foucault analyses at length the surveilling power techniques that are applied to the body and that generate rational self-control, in the first volume of *The History of Sexuality* (1990a) he discusses an inner subjectification at an even deeper level. Discourses such as psychology, psychiatry, pedagogy and medicine force people, on behalf of an inner Truth that has to be revealed, to talk about their supposedly hidden sexual feelings, thus allocating a sexual identity to each of them. To know oneself has become an endless task of turning inward at yet deeper levels. The psy-sciences in general and Freudian psychoanalysis in particular are Foucault's *bêtes noires* in his middle work. Through them the modern Western subject has become a supposedly authentic, deep self which is compelled time and again to confess its inner feelings. The deep self to Foucault is a prison house *a fortiori*.

Spiritual practices

Foucault's historicizing of the Western subject leads him to ancient Greek and Hellenist forms of subjectivity in his final works. In his

1981–82 Collège de France course, *The Hermeneutics of the Subject* (2005a), he clearly points out that the ancient saying "you have to know yourself" (*gnothi seauton*) was grounded in something other than the search for one's inner truth. It was interwoven with the "care of the self" (*epimeleia heautou*), a tradition which we seem to have forgotten since modernity.

The label "care of the self" is, from 1976 onwards, used by Foucault to articulate ancient practices which aim for self-improvement in relation to an ethical way of life. Ethics in antiquity was a strong structure in itself, relatively autonomous in regard to other structures. It consisted of vocabularies that were intended as guides for the concrete shaping of oneself as ethical subject. The striving for self-knowledge concerned one's position and one's behaviour, so as to be able to transform oneself "in order to attain a certain state of happiness, purity, wisdom, perfection, or immortality" (Foucault 1997d: 225). Here we have a subject that is not the deep self of the disciplines but rather a more superficial self, which strives for the ethical coherence of its acting. Through constant practising or "ascesis", by way of "technologies of the self" such as writing exercises, meditation and dialogue with oneself, one tries to create an "ethos". This personal ethics (the word ethos meaning literally "character" in Greek, referring to one's personality) is not only a matter of thought; instead, it is "a mode of being for the subject, along with a certain way of acting, a way visible to others" (1997e: 286). It is in this context that Foucault again uses the concept of spirituality.

The work of Pierre Hadot, classicist and colleague of Foucault at the Collège de France, is of importance here. Hadot, in his approach to classical philosophy, emphasizes the fact that philosophy in antiquity for a large part consisted in "spiritual exercises". To indicate that ancient philosophy was a way of life that engaged the whole of existence, Hadot considers the term "spiritual" the most appropriate:

> It is … necessary to use this term, I believe, because none of the other adjectives we could use – "psychic," "moral," "ethical," "intellectual," "of thought," "of the soul" – covers all the aspects of the reality we want to describe … the word "thought" does not indicate clearly enough that imagination and sensibility play a very important role in these exercises. (1995: 81–2)

In his later work Foucault, clearly inspired by Hadot's approach, uses the concept of "spirituality" in a similar vein, namely to indicate the transforming of one's mode of being, not just of one's thinking:

By spirituality I mean – but I'm not sure this definition can hold for very long – the subject's attainment of a certain mode of being and the transformations that the subject must carry out on itself to attain this mode of being. I believe that spirituality and philosophy were identical or nearly identical in ancient spirituality. (1997e: 294)

Whereas Foucault here equates spirituality and ancient philosophy as such, in his 1982 lectures *The Hermeneutics of the Subject* the concept of spirituality is linked to the concept of care of the self: "going through the … different forms of philosophy and the different forms of exercises and philosophical or spiritual practices, we see the principle of care of the self expressed in a variety of phrases" (2005a: 12). Carrette rightly identifies in the later Foucault an overlapping and merging of ethics and spirituality as each pertains to a "mode of self-formation" or a "mode of being" (Carrette 2000: 136, 138). Spirituality in the later Foucault parallels his definition of ethical self-transformation through ascesis which involves one's whole way of life. It is in this sense that we find a spirituality without a spirit, without an incorporeal supernatural being or immortal soul, in Foucault's work.

As with his early surrealist-inspired notion, the concept of spirituality opposes the Cartesian body/soul dualism. It explicitly involves the bodily dimension, be it this time in a normative context, that is, in the form of an ethos which is a *lived ethics* and as such involves bodily elements, acts and behaviour.

The winning of an ethos, through a care of the self, clearly is something Foucault puts forward as an exit from the impoverished self-techniques of modern man, which are over-determined by surveilling and scrutinizing disciplines and governing practices. "In the Greek and Roman civilizations, such practices of the self were much more important and especially *more autonomous* than they were later, after they were taken over to a certain extent by religious, pedagogical, medical, or psychiatric institutions" (Foucault 1997e: 282, emphasis added). Care of the self in antiquity used to be the framework for the knowledge of oneself instead of the other way around, as it is in Western modernity where a care of the self only occurs through the concern for truth (*ibid.*: 295). We can conclude that the concept of spirituality in Foucault's final works points to this tradition of ethical self-transformation through ascesis, as an autonomous dimension of life. We then deal with practices of ethical self-transformation which are not dictated by moral rules or codes, but which come down to "practices of freedom", since people can freely create themselves as ethical subjects. These ethical self-practices are "not something invented by the individual himself. They are models that he finds in his culture and are proposed, suggested, imposed upon him by his culture, his society, and his social group" (*ibid.*: 291). However, through these models, tools and techniques one can acquire and freely create a personal ethos, visible in one's acts and way of life.

When asked whether the care of the self in the classical sense should be updated, Foucault answers: "absolutely", but adds that in modern times this of course will lead to something new (*ibid.*: 294). The "growth of capabilities" of modern man should be disentangled from the dominant power regime (1997g: 317). Whereas in antiquity the care of the self was linked "to a virile society, to dissymmetry, exclusion of the other" ("all that is quite disgusting!"), "couldn't everyone's life become a work of art?" (1997e: 258, 261). Foucault's normative horizon is that freedom practices should be developed as much as possible by as many persons as possible.

Foucault emphasizes that acquiring an ethos in antiquity always took place in different philosophical schools and groups, in which people through spiritual practices trained themselves in acquiring an ethos (2005a: 113). Occasionally he talks about religious groups as well, for instance when he discusses the Therapeutae group in *The Hermeneutics of the Subject* (*ibid.*: 116). He also refers to the autonomous ethical spiritual dimension in a religious context, discussing certain strands of Christianity, for instance when he states:

> during the Renaissance you see a whole series of religious groups ... that resist this pastoral power and claim the right to make their own statuses for themselves. According to these groups, the individual should take care of his own salvation independently of the ecclesiastical institution and of the ecclesiastical pastorate. We can see, therefore, a reappearance, up to a certain point, not of the culture of the self, which had never disappeared, but a reaffirmation of its *autonomy*. (1997f: 278, emphasis added)

Note that once again Foucault emphasizes the relatively autonomous realm of ethical spiritual self-formation. Also, more importantly, note that according to him this realm can exist in religious contexts as well (Vintges 2004). The concept of spirituality does not refer to religion as such, as Carrette (2000) implies in several places, but to practices of free ethical self-transformation, which can be found inside as well as outside religious frameworks.

Spirituality and truth

In addition to taking the form of free ethical self-transformation through self-techniques, the issue of spirituality also appears in Foucault's later work in relation to truth. In *The Hermeneutics of the Subject* he argues that "spirituality" is:

> the search, practice and experience through which the subject carries out the necessary transformations on himself in order to have access to the truth. We will call "spirituality" then the set of these researches, practices, and experiences ... [which are for the subject ...] the price to be paid for access to the truth.
>
> (2005a: 15)

Before Descartes, knowledge was based on this type of spirituality. The "Cartesian moment", however, marks the beginning of the modern age of the history of truth, where knowledge and knowledge alone is the condition for the subject's access to truth. Moreover, for Descartes such access is possible without the individual "having to change or alter his being as subject", that is, without the need of transforming the structure of one's subjectivity in substantial ways (*ibid.*: 17).

Foucault acknowledges that we can recognize a "false science" by its appeal to (the necessity of) such a transformation. However, he then states that in "those forms of knowledge (savoir) *that are not exactly sciences, and which we should not seek to assimilate to the structure of science*, there is again the strong and clear presence of at least certain elements, certain requirements of spirituality" (*ibid.*: 29, emphasis added). Marxism and psychoanalysis are two forms of post-Cartesian knowledge that still demand an initiation and transformation of the subject in its very being. However, both forms of knowledge have tried to conceal this, instead of openly acknowledging the necessity of ethical self-transformation, that is, spirituality as a condition of access to truth (*ibid.*). Foucault seems to imply that philosophers should not try to assimilate their form of knowledge to the structure of science, but instead should have an eye for the relation of spirituality to truth.

Perhaps to avoid any suggestion of privileging a philosophical type of knowledge which is based on initiation as closure, Foucault in his next years' lectures specifies his preferred notion of "spirituality as access to truth" by analysing the concept of *parrhēsia*. The word *parrhēsia* means "saying everything". A "*parrhēsiastēs*" is the speaker who says everything he has in mind, even if it is something which can endanger his life – for instance if it is something different from what the king, or the majority of the people, believe. Foucault analyses at length how courageous truth-telling is part of the ancient tradition of spirituality as access to truth. In *Fearless Speech*, a collection of lectures delivered in Berkeley during the summer of 1983, Foucault defines the verbal activity of *parrhēsia* as follows: "In *parrhesia*, the speaker uses his freedom and chooses frankness instead of persuasion, truth instead of falsehood or silence, the risk of death instead of life and security, criticism instead of flattery, and moral duty instead of self-interest and moral apathy" (2001: 19–20).

In these lectures Foucault once more outlines the ancient Greek ideal that one's whole way of life is important: the true *parrhēsiastēs* is a person "of moral integrity", a person "of blameless principle and integrity", whose acts and thoughts are in accordance (*ibid.*: 69). In his studies on *parrhēsia* Foucault wants to trace "the roots of what we can call the critical tradition of the West". He wanted to construct a "genealogy of the critical attitude in Western philosophy" (*ibid.*: 170–71). His emphasis on the *parrhēsia* aspect of ancient spirituality might well be his implicit answer to the possible objection that, at least since Descartes, knowledge has become democratic and open instead of the prerequisite of a certain privileged group, and critical instead of based on persuasion. Foucault's work on *parrhēsia* is intended to articulate a democratic, open spiritual basis of knowledge for present purposes: a philosophical attitude of critique which is about one's whole way of life and in that sense "spiritual", an attitude which he identified as the core value of Western Enlightenment (1997g) and which he practised in his own work and life.[3]

Political spirituality

Foucault's concept of spirituality as free ethical self-transformation through ascesis is political through and through in that it is an exit, a critical alternative to the "normal" Western subject formations of the rational autonomous individual and the deep self, the products of the power/knowledge regime of Western modernity. This is the reason why Foucault invokes the concept of "political spirituality" when he speaks about "the will to discover a different way of governing oneself through a different way of dividing up true and false – this is what I would call 'political *spiritualité*'" (1991b: 82, quoted in Carrette 2000: 137). Foucault is expressing the need to detach our subjectivity from Western modernity's political rationality.

He sympathized with any resistance against this true/false regime of subjectivity, a resistance he also identified in the 1978 Iranian

Revolution, which started as a revolution against the attempt to modernize Islamic countries in a European mode. In the last lines of his article "What Are the Iranians Dreaming About?" Foucault puts forward the "possibility we have forgotten since the Renaissance and the great crisis of Christianity, a *political spirituality*" (2005b: 209). In another article on this subject, Foucault talks about Shi'ism as a form of Islam that differentiates between "mere external obedience to the code" and "the profound spiritual life". In revolutionary Iran at that time identification with the Islamic tradition combined with "the renewal of spiritual experiences", that is, the "desire to renew their entire existence" (2005c: 255). When invoking a "political spirituality", it is the dimension of freedom practices opposing truth regimes, and involving the whole of peoples' ways of life, that Foucault has in mind, and once more we find that he locates this dimension within religious contexts as well.

A cross-cultural concept of freedom

We have seen that in his final works Foucault refers to practices of free ethical spiritual self-transformation not only in secular contexts, but in religious ones as well. He refers not only to certain strands in Christianity and Islam, but also in Asian religion. Liebman Schaub discusses whether there is a counterpart to Foucault's hopelessly trapped "Western man", in the form of a hidden discourse in Foucault's work, which can be designated as an "Oriental subtext" (Liebmann Schaub 1989). Foucault concealed its presence since he wanted to avoid his work being stigmatized as "religious" or "metaphysical", and since he did not want to offer any anthropological model, that is, any absolute truth concerning the human condition.

According to Liebmann Schaub, Foucault's non-Western counter-discourse is to be found in his style rather than in overt opposition to the Western, "normalized" way of life. She, however, only analyses the early Foucault, focusing on his notions of transgression and his ideas on the disappearance of the rational autonomous subject. She argues that Foucault's unsettling style is informed by Buddhism. He wants to show the essential insufficiency of language for expressing truth, in other words that wisdom is beyond words. It is through his style, which criticizes Western civilization as a whole, that he has been a "teacher" and a "moralist".

However, if we turn to Foucault's later work, in which Eastern – and Western – philosophies are approached from their practical, ethical side, we find that Foucault *does* offer a positive alternative to the "normal-ized" Western ways of life, through his new concept of spirituality as free ethical self-transformation through ascesis. Foucault, during his visit to Japan in 1978, showed great interest in the practice of Zen Buddhism. He took lessons and afterwards said to his teacher: "I'd like to ask you just one question. It's about the universality of Zen. Is it possible to separate the practice of Zen from the totality of the reli-gion and the practice of Buddhism?" (1999b: 113). He also remarks that whereas Zen and Christian mysticism cannot be compared, the *technique* of Christian spirituality and that of Zen are comparable. Foucault's question and remark show his interest in ethical spiritual self-techniques as a cross-cultural phenomenon. He not only explored Zen in 1978 but also Islam, as we have seen from his articles in which he described the Iranian Revolution in terms of a spirituality which opposed Truth regimes and possesses the potential to inspire new politi-cal forms. What I see in these texts is not a right or wrong judgement on the Iranian Revolution,[4] but the search for a new concept of freedom which is cross-cultural in that it can take into account a diversity of moral frameworks, including religious ones.

Paraphrasing Liebman Schaub, and together with Bernauer (2004), I would conclude that an "Oriental Subtext" runs through all of Foucault's work. Bernauer asks whether an oriental influence is to be seen in Foucault's radical interrogation of Western individualism and whether his notion of self-stylization was influenced by Asia, more specifically his visits to Japan in 1970 and 1978. I suggest that this influence has been the background to his reconceptualizing of freedom in other terms than the ones of individual rational autonomy, in terms namely of spirituality as ethical self-transformation through exercises, which involve the creation and invention of one's whole way of life. His oriental interest, in my view, has inspired this normative horizon of freedom practices for all, as a cross-cultural alternative to the dominant concept of freedom of Western liberalism.

The emerging discourse of Islamic feminism

The emerging discourse of "Islamic feminism" illustrates the topical-ity of Foucault's new concepts. Since the 1990s, new perspectives and practices are developing that demonstrate that Islam and "gender jus-tice" are not inherently incompatible. These perspectives and prac-tices also criticize both Western feminism and liberalism for imposing Western concepts of freedom and autonomy on believing Muslim women, as well as Islamic fundamentalists for claiming that women in the Islamic world are already able to live their lives to the fullest.[5] Believing Muslim women in, for example, Egypt, Malaysia, Indonesia, Iran and Morocco do contest structures of male domination in the Islamic world by arguing for gender equality and gender justice in new interpretations of the moral source of Islam, the Qur'an. Scholars such as Leila Ahmed, Amina Wadud and Asma Barlas refer to the dynamic and diverse history of Islam for their reinterpretations of the Qur'an and Islamic historical traditions. They highlight the egalitarian Spirit of Islam's ethical spiritual message, and the active role of women in the history of Islam. Other studies show the active role of women in Islamic societies today, demonstrating that Islamic women are in no way the passive, oppressed creatures that many Western feminists hold them to be. In Muslim-majority countries there are women's organizations that have a feminist agenda (such as Malaysia's "Sisters in Islam").

This new emerging discourse of Islamic feminism can be analysed as a political spirituality, that is, as a practice of free ethical self-transformation which opposes the Truth regime of Western liberalism as well as the fundamentalist type of Islam. These women are freely but ethically transforming themselves through all kinds of self-techniques, on the collective and individual level, such as veiling in new contexts, educating themselves in interpreting the Qur'an, practising mixed gender prayer, and inventing themselves as modern, believing, Muslim women. The emerging discourse of Islamic feminism shows that Western feminists who contend that feminism should be based on secular liberalism's fundamentals should enlarge, if not revise, their concept of freedom, so as to escape the limits that are imposed on all women.[6]

When asked about the state of the art of Western philosophy, Foucault said:

> European thought finds itself at a turning point ... (which) is nothing other than the end of imperialism. The crisis of Western thought is identical to the end of imperialism ... There is no philosopher who marks out this period. For it is the end of the era of Western philosophy. Thus, if philosophy of the future exists, it must be born outside of Europe, or equally born in consequence of meetings and impacts between Europe and non-Europe.
>
> (1999c: 113)

Foucault, through his new concept of spirituality without a spirit, in the sense of free ethical self-transformation through self-techniques, has offered us new concepts of freedom and equality which criticize

Western modernity[7] as well as other Truth regimes, and which offer a cross-cultural normative perspective. In my view Foucault was ahead of his time in that he felt that we have to change our concepts to make sense of the culturally pluralist world we live in.

Notes

1. I borrow this phrase from Jeremy Carrette (2000: 60; see also 162–3, n.72).
2. Many argue that Foucault's work *Discipline and Punish* lacks any normative perspective. Explicit phrases, however, clearly show Foucault's rejection of the disciplines as domination, for instance where he speaks of the development of the disciplines as the "dark side" of the establishment of the egalitarian juridical framework (Foucault 1979: 222) and of the "malicious minutiae of the disciplines and their investigations" (*ibid*.: 226).
3. Discussing Kant's text "What is Enlightenment?" Foucault points out how Kant's answer "sapere aude" ("dare to know") refers not only to "institutional, ethical and political" conditions, but to a "spiritual" condition as well. Kant's answer involves as well an appeal to an "act of courage to be accomplished personally", by man, "by a change that he himself will bring about in himself". Western Enlightenment is a spiritual attitude to Foucault. He argues that it is "not faithfulness to doctrinal elements but, rather, the permanent reactivation of an attitude" that may connect us with the Enlightenment (1997g: 306, 312).
4. My view here is contrary to Afary and Anderson (2005), who fiercely attack Foucault. For a critique of their view see Honig (2008). We have to take into account that in 1978 many people considered the Iranian Revolution to be primarily an anti-colonialist revolution. The enthusiasm of this anti-imperialist uprising is what Foucault tries to describe in a few journalistic articles, wherein he discusses how people were "spiritually" involved, in that their whole way of life was at stake, and speaks in terms of a "political spirituality", opposing Truth regimes and producing something new. Foucault responded to the violence that marked the post-revolutionary power struggle in Iran by distancing himself from its outcome in the form of simply another regime of Truth. In journalistic articles published in April and May 1979 he supported the rights of the individual against the "bloody government of a fundamentalist clergy" (Foucault 2005d: 265).
5. For an overview see Dubel and Vintges (2007).
6. Okin 1999 has been very influential in the debate on feminism and multiculturalism. As the title indicates, Okin argues that multiculturalism is bad for women, and that only Western liberalism has a place for women's rights. Instead I would argue that Western liberalism in its own way puts limits on women, in that they have to adapt themselves to the ways of life, and subject form, of the Western autonomous rational individual.
7. "The political, ethical, social, philosophical problem of our days is not to try to liberate the individual from the state, and from the state's institutions, but to liberate us both from the state and from the type of individualization which is linked to the state. We have to promote new forms of subjectivity through the refusal of this kind of individuality which has been imposed on us for several centuries" (Foucault 1982a: 216).

EIGHT

The practice of freedom
Eduardo Mendieta

Freedom has a history

Freedom is one of the most intractable philosophical problems in the Western philosophical tradition. Indeed, there is a way in which the history of Western philosophy can be written in terms of the different attempts that have been made to define freedom. The history of ethics, without question, has been determined by how freedom has been defined. In the West, since the ancient Greeks, what we take to be human, or rather, the humanity of humans, has been defined in terms of freedom. Humans are free animals, the argument goes, whereas other animals are unfree because they are determined by instinct. Yet what is this freedom that marks the boundary between human and non-human animals? How does it relate to reason? How does it relate to our passions and emotions? How does it relate to our imagination? Are we free if we submit to a putatively rational norm? Is this not a form of subjugation that constrains freedom? Are we free if we choose our will contrary to what is alleged to be a commandment of God? Are we free if we have been condemned to damnation by an original sin that had nothing to do with us? Are we free if we abandon ourselves to our pleasure and seek to live on the razor's edge of pleasurable danger? And, perhaps most importantly, has freedom been construed or defined in the same way across different historical periods? That is to say, was the freedom of the Egyptian peasant the same as that of the Greek and Roman citizens, the same as that of a slave in an American plantation, the same as that of a citizen in the European Union? If ethics has a history, freedom must have a history, too (Patterson 1991). The history of freedom then turns out to be a history of ethics, as well as a history of the different ways in which we have conceived what it means to be a subject, an agent, and a free person.

In this chapter I am going to offer a way of reading and understanding Michel Foucault's work as an extremely original analysis of freedom. My reading of Foucault's work will illustrate that his work has been profoundly misunderstood when he has been read exclusively as a thinker of domination, subjugation, subjection, discipline, normalization and power. I will show that Foucault's work can be understood as an exploration of freedom, as so many attempts to understand the ways in which freedom is not a given, an *a priori*, primordial and foundational right of a subject, but is instead an achievement, a practice, a vocation, an ascesis, a way of being. We are not born free. We make ourselves free through practices of caring for ourselves, of governing, relating ourselves to ourselves through others, for either love or hate of others is a way of relating to ourselves. Freedom is thus not a state of being, but a way of being in relation to ourselves, to others and to our world. Freedom is a praxis. Additionally, I will seek to show that freedom is not unitary and ontologically stable, but rather that it is relational and generative. Freedom is not a given aspect of human nature, nor is there a human nature. We produce our humanity by generating modalities of freedom, ways of relating to ourselves, to truth, and to our historical period, or present. If there is freedom, it is always creative freedom. Thus, I hope to show that Foucault has been one of the most important contemporary philosophers of freedom.

In this chapter I will follow Foucault's own way of characterizing his work as gravitating or revolving around three major axes, each marking a particular period or stage of his work. Thus, there are the axes of knowledge, power and ethics. These axes have been the focus of particular approaches or methods of investigation: archaeology, genealogy and hermeneutics. Yet Foucault himself resisted and contested the attempt to see a succession of methods or problems within his work. In his view, his work is held together by one central motif, the subject, or more precisely "practices of the self" (1997c, 2005a, 1997a). In contrast to reading his work as an analysis of power, we should understand it as a genealogy of the subject. A genealogical analysis seeks to understand how something could become an object of preoccupation, concern, debate and admonition. Instead of assuming the givenness of an object of analysis, genealogy aims to show how a series of practices, institutions and structures constituted the object of study. Additionally, for Foucault, a genealogical study is in turn a history of our present; it is an investigation of our own contemporaneity or contemporary times. We are the ones asking how this particular object of analysis was constituted and how that constitution informs our own ways of being and relating. To understand Foucault's work in this way, however, also means that we have to recognize how central the question of freedom is to this project. Genealogy is a technique of analysis that renders what we took to be natural, ontologically stable, historically immutable into something that is historically contingent, produced, mutable and thus open to transformation, revision, abandonment and challenge. Genealogy, it could be said, is a science of freedom, of creative freedom that opens up horizons of being by challenging us to exceed, to transgress, to step over the limit established by existing modes of subjectivity and subjectivation.

Foucault's genealogies of the modern subject aim to draw out the ways in which freedom is a practice and not a given, an *a priori*, something antecedent to the subject. I will show in the following that Foucault developed this generative understanding of freedom through original readings of key figures in the Western philosophical canon. I will focus on three key figures that Foucault studied closely in his published works, and in his lectures at the Collège de France during the last decade of his life, namely Socrates, Augustine and Kant. I will show that through his readings of each one of these figures Foucault challenges us to see each of them in a new light, in the light of the history of freedom and the subject.

Socrates or democratic freedom

Socrates is undoubtedly one of the most important figures in the Western philosophical canon. He is also the exemplar of what Foucault called "philosophy as a way of life" (2005a). He died after having been sentenced to death by his fellow Athenians. Socrates had been charged with "corrupting the youth" and for "impiety". Socrates chose to die rather than escape and thus betray his Athens. Socrates died for his convictions: he did not want to betray Athens or his philosophical calling. For this reason, Socrates is also a martyr of philosophy as a way of life (see Hadot 1995).

In many of Plato's dialogues, in particular those dealing with virtue, we encounter a Socrates who argues that knowledge, courage and justice are virtues (*Gorgias, Laches, Protagoras, Sophists*). These Platonic dialogues have left us with a philosophical problem, however. Are knowledge, courage and justice one or separate virtues? If knowledge and courage are virtues, should this not entail that we should also be just, that is to say, moral? If courage and justice are forms of knowledge does this not entail that we should act correctly? In the history of Western philosophy in general, and within the history of the appropriation of Plato's work in particular, Socrates' moral theory has been treated as both a form of moral intellectualism and as moral *eudaimonia* (Vlastos 1991). Moral intellectualism is a form of moral cognitivism, which argues that morality is a form of knowledge, that we can discover what is the right thing to do if we set out to question our reasons for doing the just and moral. Moral *eudaimonia*, on the other hand, argues that morality is the pursuit of the happy, content, fulfilled life. It should be noted that for the Greeks, *eudaimonia*, or happiness, was not related to pleasure or narcissism, but was rather about attaining a beautiful and admirable life. Thus, the pursuit of the happy, admirable, life is the pursuit of virtues that are linked to knowledge.

For Socrates, morality is a form of knowledge. If we know what is the right thing to do, can we fail to do it, and if so, why? This has been called the problem of the weakness of the will, or *Akrasia*. Socrates, in Plato's *Protagoras*, already diagnosed this problem when he postulated: "no one willingly chooses the bad" (358d). Evidently, if one knows what is the good and the bad, one will choose what leads to happiness, which is coeval with knowledge. Yet this is contrary to our mundane experience. Even extremely moral Greeks failed to choose what was the good, over what was the bad, notwithstanding their mental lucidity. We do not always choose what is rationally the best, and we sometimes chose what is patently the immoral. In the philosophical canon, thus, we have these two different, even incompatible images of Socrates. On the one hand, we have a Socrates committed to the moral life as a form of knowledge, and on the other, a Socrates that submits to the injustice and evident "ignorance" of his fellow Athenians. Socrates himself chose injustice over justice, despite his own knowledge of this injustice.

Foucault dealt with Socrates in several of his last works, in particular in Volume II of *The History of Sexuality* (1990b), his 1981–82 lecture course at the Collège de France, *The Hermeneutics of the Subject* (2005a), and his course at Berkeley in the autumn of 1983 (2001). Foucault develops a very original reading of Socrates by reading Xenophon, Plato and Plutarch jointly as sources on Socrates' character and way of life. What emerges in these readings, spread out over these different texts produced over six or seven years, is a Socrates who is a champion of a technology of living (*tekhnē tou biou*) that is coextensive with the care of the self (*epimeleia heautou*) (Foucault 2005a: 86). By reading specifically the Platonic dialogue *Alcibiades*, Foucault demonstrates that Socrates is articulating the art of living as an art of taking care of oneself. This taking care of oneself is a relationship to oneself that has political implications. One cannot govern, or rule over others, if one has not taken care of oneself. What Socrates articulates in the *Alcibiades*, thus, is a circle: "from the self as an object of care to knowledge of government as the government of others" (2005a: 39). Socrates, furthermore, will show how this caring of the self constitutes the philosophical life. Philosophy thus is an ethos, or way of life, that challenges us to live rightly by taking care of ourselves; not so that we can behold ourselves in a narcissistic way, but precisely so that we can properly govern others. Here it becomes discernable how the self is not already given. It is not an irreducible substance, some hidden gem, to be discovered or excavated. The self is to be fashioned through vigilance, courage and perseverance so that one may be worthy of governing others.

There is a link, according to Foucault, between caring for the self and speaking the truth. While truth-telling can be dangerous to both oneself and others, from a Foucauldian perspective whoever speaks the truth does so because they are caring for themselves and, in doing so, caring for others. Socrates' experiences illustrate this point, and Foucault returns to the figure of Socrates in later texts and lectures, specifically from the perspective of *parrhēsia*, which is translated by him as frank, truthful, unconstrained speech: in a word, fearless speech (2001: 11–13). In his 1983–84 lectures at the Collège de France, titled *The Courage of Truth*, Foucault now treats Socrates as a person who speaks frankly, freely and fearlessly: a *parrhēsiastēs* (Flynn 1997: 268). Socrates is the speaker of truth. The central text in this reading is the *Apology*, the dialogue in which Plato reconstructs Socrates' trial. In the *Apology* we encounter the famous lines, "the unexamined life is not worth living" (*Apology* 38a). Yet Foucault focuses on the way in which Socrates challenges the Athenian polity by turning his defence, his *apologia*, into an indictment of the way in which Athenians have failed to take care of themselves. Socrates has spoken the truth, he has engaged others in dialogue in the agora, the public square. He has done so because not to have spoken the truth would have been a failure to himself and others.

In Foucault's analysis, then, the Platonic dialogues *Apology*, *Alcibiades Major* and *Gorgias* address how the art of living calls for a coordination between caring for the self and speaking truthfully so as to be able to live beautifully, or ethically, in a democracy. Socrates is someone who both exemplifies and challenges us to give a rational account of ourselves (Foucault 2001: 97). This giving a rational account of oneself by having the courage to speak the truth is what Foucault calls Socratic and democratic *parrhēsia* (*ibid.*). Frank and fearless speech may be dangerous to democracy, but it is also indispensable for its health. Without speaking frankly and fearlessly, we cannot properly take care of ourselves, and thus are not able to engage properly in the art of living rightly. What Foucault said about Epictetus could also be said about Socrates. Indeed, Epictetus is the culmination of a process that Socrates had inaugurated. "The care of the self, for Epictetus, is a privilege-duty, a gift-obligation that ensures our freedom while forcing us to take care of ourselves as the object of our diligence" (Foucault 1986: 47). To take ourselves as an object of care requires that we become *parrhesiasts*, speakers of truth, and in this way we could govern ourselves and others.

Freedom is produced through these techniques of the self, *parrhēsia* and *epimeleia heautou*, fearless speech and the care of the self. Freedom here is agonistic and creative, it results from not submitting to an external power but generating a power that is exercised over oneself so that one can be worthy of exercising it over others. This agonistic freedom, a freedom that results from a contest with oneself and with others, is thus also a democratic freedom, inextricably produced within and for a democratic life. We are never free alone, but only in the company of those before whom we give an account of ourselves by speaking fearlessly.

Augustine or ethopoetic freedom

Augustine may be said to be the first Christian philosopher, and surely the first major Christian theologian within the West. Along with Boethius, Augustine is a key figure in the articulation of Greek and Roman thinking into a distinct form of Christian philosophy. His *Confessions* remains one of the most influential works of this unique form of spiritual exercise (Augustine 1991). Augustine is also credited with having formulated a very original answer to the question of why there is evil in the world, even if God is both almighty and all-beneficent.

In several works, such as *The City of God*, *On Free Choice of the Will* and *Concerning the Nature of Good, Against the Manicheans*, Augustine formulated his theodicy. Theodicy, which literarily means God's Justice (*theo*, God, and *dyke*, justice), is an answer to the question of the existence of evil. Augustine argued that evil is not a substance, but a privation, an absence, or diminution of the good. Against the Manicheans, he argued that evil could not be a separate substance, entity or being.

This would be a heresy, as it would challenge the Christian monotheistic doctrine of God's omnipotence. Evil, thus, is not a thing, but a non-being. It is not itself a principle, but a turning, a negation, a privation of some prior or primordial good. In his famous *On Free Choice of the Will*, Augustine argues that evil is a product of the human will turning away from God's goodness (Augustine 1993). The will turns away from goodness towards evil, not because it is itself evil, but because it lets itself be turned by what Augustine calls *libido*, or inordinate desire. This inordinate desire has always been called or translated as concupiscence. How do we allow ourselves to be led astray by concupiscence? In Augustine's view, we bring evil into the world because we aspire to terrestrial or temporal things instead of aiming for that which is eternal and truly good. We bring evil into the world because we fail to be vigilant over our carnal desires and inclinations. We allow that which is superior and more perfect, our will and mind, to be subjugated to that which is inferior and finite: the flesh.

For Foucault, Augustine occupies a pivotal role in the transformation of the technologies of the self from late antiquity to the medieval and early modern periods. At one point Foucault planned to publish five additional volumes of *The History of Sexuality* with the introduction that was published in 1976. Volume II was to be called *Flesh and the Body* and it was supposed to deal with the problematization of the flesh in early Christian thinking. The others would have been called: *The Children's Crusade*; *Woman, Mother, Hysteric*; *Perverts*; and finally, *Population and Race* (Davidson 1994: 117). Foucault published only two more volumes: *The Use of Pleasure* (1990b) and *The Care of The Self* (1986). This is worth noting because we can speculate that the projected Volume II would have dealt extensively with Augustine. For Foucault, Augustine marks the transition in late antiquity from a pre-occupation with desire that is distributed among different techniques: from diet, to physical exercise, to with whom and when to have sex to a "doctrinal unification" that made it possible to put together under one theoretical overview questions of death and immortality, with questions of desire, sex, marriage and the "conditions of access to truth" (1990b: 253–4). Sex, concupiscence, desire became a privilege point of access to the subject, or rather, the subject is now formed around the specific relations that are to be had with one's desire, body and flesh. With Augustine, what had been dietary and medical concerns become the litmus test of the sinfulness and salvation of the subject. Indeed, the flesh that seems to have its own will is now deciphered as emblem of humanity's sinfulness. As Foucault put it: "Sex in erection is the image of man revolted against God. The arrogance of sex is the punishment and consequence of the arrogance of man" (1997c: 181–2). This flesh revolted against God became in Augustine the problem of the relationship between one's desire and one's will. This problem will command a "permanent hermeneutics of the self" (*ibid.*: 182).

There is another treatment of Augustine in Foucault's writing that is perhaps more interesting and provocative, and that is to be found in some lectures from 1982 titled "Technologies of the Self". In these lectures Foucault approaches Augustine from the standpoint of the use of writing techniques and exercises to take care of the self. The care of the self was not just a dietary, medical and philosophical concern; it was also the object of writing. One wrote in order to take care of one's self.

> The self is something to write about, a theme or object (subject) of writing activity. That is not a modern trait born of the Reformation or of Romanticism; it is one of the most ancient Western traditions. It was well established and deeply rooted when Augustine started his *Confessions*. (*Ibid.*: 232)

Indeed, the *Confessions* could be said to encapsulate and epitomize this ancient practice of diary writing. In his lecture course from 1981 to 1982, *The Hermeneutics of the Subject*, Foucault discusses Augustine in relation to Plutarch's exemplification of writing about the self as a technology of the self. Writing was a tool to say and discover something about yourself in such a way that you could become different. These forms of personal and private writing bring us close to a form of knowledge that transforms us. The ancient Greeks had several words for this type of transformational knowledge: *Ēthopoios* or *Ēthopoiein* (ethopoetic). With the former word the Greeks referred to something that has the quality of transforming a person's being. With the latter, they referred to that which produces, changes and transforms an ethos, a way of life, a code of conduct (Foucault 2005a: 237). With these words, and cognates, the Greeks marked a type of knowledge that is decisive and transformative of the self. There is knowledge that is superfluous and insignificant, but there is knowledge that can transform a person irreversibly. The knowledge produced by this hermeneutics of the self must lead to the sacrifice of the self, so that a new self may be born (see also Foucault 1997a: 227–31).

The different techniques of writing that were available to the Greeks, and which Augustine brought to a new level, were ethopoetic technologies of the self. They aimed at transforming the subject by providing a material vehicle for a vigilant and relentless analysis of the self, not simply to restrict and domesticate it, but to transform it. This writing was a technology of the self that called forth a transformative hermeneutics of the self. Personal writing was the medium for an ethopoetic knowledge. In these techniques of writing about the self, about oneself, Foucault discerned a mechanism for the production of new ways of being. Through them a freedom to be a different self is practised. Ethopoetic knowledge is coupled with an ethopoetic freedom, a freedom that transforms us and grants us the power to proclaim truths about ourselves that may lead others to transform themselves. We wrote, and continue to write, in order to become different, and by becoming different we practise a transformative freedom.

Kant, or critique as freedom

Modern moral philosophy begins with Immanuel Kant. He provided a philosophical analysis of how morality can be based on reason alone, and can thus dispense with religion, convention and even physical nature. Kant showed that to be moral is the mark of the rational being, and how the rational determination of the will is all that is required for a philosophical justification of morality. For him, rational beings alone can be free, so long as they submit their will to rational adjudication. Kant's most famous book of ethical theory, *Groundwork for the Metaphysics of Morals*, enigmatically pronounces: "Nothing in the world – indeed nothing even beyond the world – can possibly be conceived which could be called good without qualification except a *good will*" (Ak: 393). It is much later that we learn why Kant believed this to be the case. A good will is "absolutely good which cannot be bad, and thus it is a will whose maxim when made into a universal law, can never conflict with itself" (Ak: 437). A good will cannot be bad because it is a will determined in accordance with universality. A good will, therefore, is not determined by anything external to it, whether it be obedience to God, deference to tradition, or submission to our desires or inclinations. What motivates individuals to determine their will in accordance with universal law is not something that Kant addresses in this book. Nor does he think it is appropriate to do so at the level of the grounding or justification of morality. How and why people may act in accordance with the moral law is part of the doctrine of virtue, which is the second part of Kant's moral philosophy. One would have expected that if Foucault were to have approached Kant's moral philosophy, he would have chosen to focus on Kant's doctrine of virtue, or how it is that we direct our will and mind to choose that which is the moral. Yet he did not. He focused instead on Kant's philosophy of history.

It could be said that Kant was one of the philosophers with whom Foucault dealt most throughout his career. As a young scholar, he translated Kant's *Anthropology from a Pragmatic Standpoint*, and wrote an accompanying commentary (2008a). He also dealt with Kant in his *The Order of Things* (1973), and devoted many key essays throughout the late 1970s and early 1980s to him (Foucault 1997a). He dealt with Kant extensively in his last lecture course at the Collège de France (Foucault 2009). In it Foucault engages Kant specifically concerning his answer to the question *Was ist Aufklärung?* (What is Enlightenment?). Kant's famous text, "An Answer to the Question: What is Enlightenment?", published in a newspaper, begins with the memorable lines:

> *Enlightenment is the human being's emancipation from its self-incurred immaturity. Immaturity* is the inability to make use of one's intellect without the direction of another. This immaturity is *self-incurred* when its cause does not lie in a lack of intellect, but rather in a lack of resolve and courage to make use of one's intellect without the direction of another. "*Sapere aude!* Have the courage to make use of your own intellect!" is hence the motto of enlightenment.   (Kant 2006: 17)

Answering more directly the question what is Enlightenment? Kant writes, "If it is asked, then, whether we live an *enlightened* age, then the answer is: no, but we do live in an age of *enlightenment*" (*ibid.*: 22). As Foucault underscored, enlightenment here is a process in which the entire human race is involved; it is also something that is ongoing, and it is something that involves a change in our relationship to our reason (1997a: 105–10).

Kant's "What is Enlightenment?" is part of a long tradition in which thinkers are trying to decipher the signs of the times as heralds or ciphers for either a past that is fulfilling itself, or something that is about to unleash a future that is expected. Yet, for Foucault, Kant's text steps outside this tradition when he does not seek to place his age within either a divine plan or the logic of a rational plan of history. Kant does not subordinate the age of enlightenment to another period; nor to something that is dawning or inchoate.

Kant defines *Aufklärung* in an almost negative way, as an *Ausgang*, an "exit," a "way out." In his other texts on history, Kant occasionally raises questions of origins or defines the internal teleology of a historical process. In the text on *Aufklärung*, he deals with the question of contemporary reality alone. He is not seeking to understand the present on the basis of a totality or of a future achievement. He is looking for a difference. What difference does today introduce with respect to yesterday?

(Foucault 1997a: 104–5)

In other words, according to Foucault, Kant's answer to the question of enlightenment is an attempt to formulate the radical character of the present with respect to the task that it presents to us as contemporaries, as children of our own time. Foucault translates Kant's question into a question about how we can differentiate what is new with respect to what has come before. In this way, then, enlightenment turns into critique. We do not live in an enlightened age, avers Kant, but we do live in an age of enlightenment: "If it is asked, then, whether we live in an *enlightened* age, then the answer is: no, but we do live in an age of *enlightenment*" (Kant 2006: 22). We are exiting, departing, abandoning a self-imposed tutelage, to use the other word used to translate *Unmündigkeit* (immaturity), by means of the critical use of our reason, by daring to criticize, to know. Enlightenment is that contemporary moment when humanity makes use of reason without the tutelage, the guidance, the submission or derogation, of anyone. Enlightenment is the critical use of reason. Critique is indispensable to enlightenment for it is through critique that we can discern what is a legitimate or illegitimate use of reason. Critique guides reason, leading it to enlightenment. As Foucault put it: "The critique is, in a sense, the handbook of reason that has grown up in Enlightenment; and, conversely, the Enlightenment is the age of critique" (1997a: 111).

The challenge from Kant to Foucault is whether we can discern a philosophical ethos that would relate to our own time in a parallel way to how Kant's critique related to his own age of enlightenment. Foucault's own text "What is Enlightenment?" is a response to that call. In it, Foucault provides both negative and positive characterization of what he calls a philosophical ethos that may be proper to our age. The positive sketching of this philosophical ethos is what concerns us here, for it is in this sketch that Foucault refers to the development of a "historical ontology of ourselves". Foucault explains that this philosophical ethos may be characterized as a *"limit-attitude"* (1997a: 124). If for Kant criticism was about analysing limits, for Foucault criticism, critique, has to be turned into a positive question. In other words, criticism should not be about demarcating limits but, rather, about transgressing them (see Simons 1995). Criticism, in Foucault's philosophical ethos, turns into a meditation on transgression. "The point, in brief, is to transform the critique conducted in the form of necessary limitations into a practical critique that takes the form of a possible transgression" (1997a: 125). Criticism entails that instead of searching for invariant and transcendental structures that may apply to and hold the same value and significance for all humanity, we set out in a historical investigation into the processes and events that have led to the constitution of our way of being. Critique as a meditation on possible transgression becomes a critical analysis of the historical ontology of our ways of being. Here historical ontology entails precisely the questioning of who we are and how this "we" has emerged. A critical ontology of ourselves reveals the constructedness of our being, its contingency, its revocability and thus its transformatibility. Because we have become, we can also become different. A critical ontology of ourselves, as a genealogy of our modern selves, allows us to extract from the very contingency that has made us signs or ciphers of the possibility of becoming other than what we presently are. Critical ontology of the present unleashes what Foucault calls felicitously the "undefined work of freedom" (*ibid.*: 126).

In short, the Kantian project of a critique of contemporaneity, of our own time, calls for critique as the handbook of enlightenment. In our time, Foucault argues, critique must go beyond the merely negative aspect that Kant had given it. Critique must become positive by becoming a critical ontology of our present. In this way it can sketch the contours of a different time, a time in which we have become different in unexpected ways. The philosophical ethos of enlightened critique that Kant championed in his text from the late eighteenth century is transformed by Foucault in the late twentieth century into the philosophical ethos of critical historical transgression. The new philosophical ethos that corresponds to the critical ontology of ourselves is "a historical-practical test of the limits that we may go beyond, and thus as work carried out by ourselves upon ourselves as free beings" (*ibid.*: 127). We may meet Kant's call to dare to use our reason, to live in an age if not enlightened at least of enlightenment, by working on our limits, those limits distinctly drawn out by a critical ontology. It is this critical labour of transgressing our historical contingency that gives form to "our impatience for liberty" (Bernauer & Mahon 1994: 155–6). We give shape to our freedom by engaging in a transgressive critique of our time. We practise our freedom by critiquing the historical shape our humanity has taken. Here, however, freedom is produced, given shape by engaging our time, our day, our own historical period in its brilliant contingency. Freedom is produced in a critical engagement with history, and in this way it cannot but be historical, and thus have a history. Still, Foucault shows that freedom is practised and given shape through this use of reason to unmake the solidity and putative inevitability of history.

The truth of freedom and the freedom of truth

The guiding thread in the present chapter has been that if we follow the different axes along which Foucault structured his investigation, we are able to discern distinct and original discussions of freedom. In one of the first lectures at what was to be his last lecture course at the Collège de France, Foucault characterized his work in a slightly new way. He said: "Basically, I've always tried to articulate among modes of veridiction, techniques of governmentality and practices of the self"; Foucault then noted that by moving towards an analysis of veridiction, or the practices of producing truth, techniques of governmentality, or technologies of government of oneself and others, and the practices of the self, or how one makes oneself into a subject, he in fact has pursued a:

> *triple theoretical displacement* of the theme of knowledge (*con-naissance*) toward that of veridiction, of the themes of domination toward that of governmentality, and of the theme of the individual toward that of practices of the self that it seems to me one can study the relations between truth, power and subject without reducing them one to another.
> (Foucault quoted in Flynn 1997: 262)

Evidently, there is a thread that links these three axes: freedom. But when freedom is related to each one of these axes, we see a different aspect of it emerge.

Perhaps we can use Flynn's word, prismatic (Flynn 1997), and talk about prismatic freedom: freedom that is refracted differently as it passes through the fields of veridiction, governmentality and techniques of the self. I have shown in this chapter that while freedom may be primordially creative freedom, when it relates to the games of truth, what Foucault calls veridiction, freedom becomes ethopoetic; when freedom relates to governmentality, it is transgressive; when freedom refers to the techniques of the self, it is agonistic. Freedom is never one, it is never stable, it is never an *a priori*, nor is it ever a transcendental. It is always contingent, it is always to be practised, it is always discursive and relational, it is intransigent and recalcitrant. It is always to be achieved, sustained, preserved and wrested from the games of power in which it always circulates like blood in a living organism. Wherever we look in human history, we see the evident truth of freedom, but wherever it has been practised, it has produced its own truth, the truth that:

> If societies persist and survive, it is because behind all the consent and the coercion, beyond the threats, the violence, and the persuasion, there is the possibility of this moment where life cannot be exchanged, where power becomes powerless, and where, in front of the gallows and the machine guns, men rise up.
>
> (Afary & Anderson 2005: 263–4)

Subjectivity

Subjectivity

NINE

Foucault's theory and practice of subjectivity

Edward McGushin

Everyone, at some point, has heard that seemingly ubiquitous advice: *just be yourself*.[1] Keep it real, be true to yourself, be your own person, find yourself, express yourself, be confident in yourself, have self-esteem, follow your own path, and so on. On the one hand, this guidance seems completely natural: are we not all trying our best to be ourselves? Yet, on the other hand, the directive, *be yourself*, sometimes sounds strangely hollow: after all, who else could I possibly be but myself? Of course, everyone is familiar with the many ways in which we fail to be ourselves. We all know the pressures and impulses to conform, to mask, to deny ourselves. We say what we think others want us to say; we act the way others want us to act. We lie to ourselves, betray ourselves, forget ourselves, let ourselves down, and neglect ourselves. On top of all this we live at a time of rapidly advancing technologies for the chemical manipulation of moods and the genetic engineering of physical and mental traits. Faced with the capacity to transform one's mood, memory, longevity, or sexuality through chemical or genetic manipulation, what could it possibly mean to "just be yourself"?

And yet in the face of all these obstacles we still seek out and prize the true, authentic self and the true, authentic life. This struggle to be true to oneself is one of the most defining characteristics of modern life. Movies and music, literature and reality television all portray it. It is the central motif of commercial advertisements and brand marketing, psychology, ethics and politics. If we stop to think about all this we are faced with a strange, unsettling realization. All this focus on the true self reflects a desire for a higher, truer life; a yearning for something more that could be called an "ethic of the self" or an "ethic of authenticity"

(Taylor 1992). Yet at the same time, the fact that we seem to need all of this constant encouragement to be our true selves also implies that our predominant way of being is false, that for the most part we fall short of truly being ourselves, that *we are not our selves*. As Jean-Paul Sartre (1989) put it, a human being is not a cauliflower. A cauliflower never has to confront the problem of what it means to be a cauliflower; it never has to make a choice about how it will live its life; it will never be challenged about its choice. A cauliflower is just what it is, fully defined and determined by its essence as a cauliflower. A human being, on the other hand, at a profound level is strange and unfamiliar to him or herself, at once far from and yet bound to the *self*.

Resolutely facing this paradoxical task of being ourselves is what Michel Foucault calls the "care for the self" (*souci de soi*).[2] He defines our "subjectivity" as what we make of ourselves when we do devote ourselves to taking care of ourselves. We can begin to understand precisely what Foucault means by the care for the self and subjectivity by examining more carefully what the quest to be true to oneself entails. Each of those very common pieces of advice – be true to yourself, express yourself, or discover yourself – refers to ways of forming a relationship of the self to itself. For example, when I express myself, I am both the self who is *doing* the expressing and the self who is *being* expressed. My self as expressive agent is related to my self as object expressed through the very activity of self-expression (whatever that activity might concretely entail). When we speak of self-discovery or self-expression, we have a tendency to get caught up in the content delivered in each of these activities and hence neglect their relational character. In the activity of seeking and discovering my self, my attention is entirely directed towards the self as that object being sought, as that substance or essence that I discover and come to know. In self-discovery and self-expression our interest is in the self that is being expressed. If we attend to the expressive act or gesture it is usually in order to make sure that it is properly suited to the content being expressed. In other words, we tend to see the act of discovery or expression as a mere vehicle for the manifestation and communication of the self being expressed. On closer examination, however, it becomes clear that discovering and expressing are what we might call *relational* activities. In other words, they are activities that form, maintain, or intensify relationships. What makes *self*-relational activities distinctive and strange is that the terms being related are essentially identical. Self-discovery and self-expression form a relationship of the self to itself. But this implies that the self is in some sense other than itself.

How does this work? The self-relational activity forms a relationship by establishing a difference within an identity. For example, in the activity of finding oneself, the self divides itself into (a) a subject actively seeking and (b) an object passively being sought. Of course, the activity of relating these two terms is nothing other than the self actively seeking, discovering and expressing itself. But for the self to become both active agent and passive object, it must actively divide itself through some activity of self-relating. In other words, it is the activity of seeking and discovering that makes or *constitutes* the self as both an active seeker and sought after object.

Care of the self is what we do when we set out to do the hard work of forging a relationship to ourselves. The resulting subjectivity is the concrete form of activity that defines the relationship of the self to itself. Subjectivity in this sense is the real basis of the self as both agent and object. In other words, Foucault argues that the self or subject is not a self-standing being, some sort of essence or substance, that exists within us whether we look for it or not (1996b). It is brought into existence as the upshot of some form of relational activity. What is more, subjectivity, as a dynamic, active relationship, can take on a number of different forms (1996a: 440). For example, someone may believe, as did the Cynics and Nietzsche, that they can only discover who they truly are by facing great hardships or dangers. Or someone might think, like the Stoics or Descartes, that self-discovery is the work of quiet, solitary introspection. Still another, following the lead of Socrates, might hold that self-discovery is only possible through provocative dialogue with others where individuals examine and challenge each other's most cherished beliefs. Each of these activities of self-seeking produces a different kind of active agent and makes manifest a different self-substance or self-object. In each of these cases, it is the *activity* through which the individual takes on this dynamic relationship to herself that establishes who she truly is. When we lose sight of this we start to accept a static, fixed idea of who and what we are, and then we are inclined to neglect the development of the active relationship, which is the real life and heart of subjectivity.[3] Rather than assuming that facing hardships allows me to *discover* my true qualities, my true self, I need to recognize that actively facing hardships is what *makes* me into a certain kind of self.[4]

Because Foucault holds that subjectivity is the relationship of the self to itself and that this relationship is composed of and formed by a variety of possible activities, he does not produce a theory of the subject or the self that would tell us who and what we truly are – he does not tell us what kind of substance we are or what our essence is. Rather, Foucault's work simultaneously carries out two tasks. First he presents us with a careful description and analysis of a few of the many various forms of subjectivity that Western civilization has produced since the time of the ancient Greek philosophers. Second, and at the same time, he puts into practice a distinct form of subjectivity. In other words, Foucault's works are activities through which he gave form to his own subjectivity and established a certain way of being a philosopher. In order to better understand Foucault's theory and practice of subjectivity, and to see how it might help us in our quest to become ourselves, let us turn to a brief survey of the elements or material that we address when we try to form a relationship to ourselves.

Disciplinary subjectivity

When I look into myself I find thoughts and feelings, hopes and desires, memories and fantasies. I recognize my own power to perceive and to think, to focus and to choose. I distinguish my body, with its features and processes, from my mental or psychological life. As a consequence, I may wonder whether I am wholly a material substance or if I am an immaterial substance somehow connected to and dependent on this material body to perceive and move around in the world. But even if my true self (mind or soul) is distinct from my body, this self is bound to and responsible for its actions in the world.

My life from moment to moment, day to day, is composed of a series of interconnected experiences in which I find myself involved in relationships and engaged in projects that connect me in various ways to objects, persons, places and values that do not belong to my self. In fact, most of my inner life takes place as a result of and with respect to my actions, relationships, contact, or interaction with objects, persons, places and values that exist outside and independently of my self, that are *other* than me. I form opinions about the things I have seen and done, about what I have felt, desired and hoped. I make judgements, deciding that some things are good and others bad, that I like some and not others. In addition to judging things and forming opinions, I deliberate and choose. It seems that at every moment I am faced with the possibility of choice, although much of the time things keep moving forward and taking me with them without my having to make a stand. But I believe that I am free to do one thing rather than another. Finally, I try to explain and understand all of these things and formulate an account of them, sometimes going as far as elaborating systematic theories about the world.

I spend my time doing things: going to school, eating, sleeping, hanging out with friends, killing time, entertaining myself, working, wondering what I am doing on earth. Sometimes it can seem as though my life is made up of a fairly random string of events, one after the other. At other times I recognize that there is a certain order to much, perhaps most, of what I do. At those times I can see that my life is composed of projects and tasks. I usually act in order to attain some end. And usually that end is really just the means to some other end. For example, I go to school to get an education and I get an education in order to get a good job and I get a good job in order to make good money so that I can support myself and maybe a family and so on.

I might believe in God and have faith that there is some purpose to all of this. But maybe I believe that there is no God and you just do these things and then die. Most likely, whether I believe in God or not, I generally find myself trying to, or at least hoping to, make the most of my time before I die. And when I think of this I realize that death itself lends a certain urgency and order to the things that I do. I do not live on this earth forever, and I cannot stop the passage of time. My life has a direction, a flow towards the future, from birth, through childhood and adolescence to adulthood, to old age and death: that is, if I do not die sooner. Even in the prime of my life, part of what defines me and makes me who and what I am is that I am a fragile, vulnerable, mortal being. I will absolutely die one day, but I *could* die at any moment. My body is vulnerable to harm from external objects, but its own internal processes could go awry and cause me to suffer or die. My inner life, my mental and emotional life, is in some respects even more vulnerable to outside events and forces than is my body: other people influence how I see myself, they can lead me to feel inadequate, strange, misunderstood, abnormal or evil. My vulnerability is intensified because I seem dependent on objects and people other than myself. In other words, my interactions with the world around me are not indifferent; they are necessary and urgent. I need food, shelter and companionship. My interaction with other people is especially urgent and consequently fraught with dangers. I find myself constantly seeking the affirmation and approval of others, I want them to recognize me, value me for who I am. I realize that this recognition is terribly important to me – I crave love, respect, honour. And yet the more I crave these things the more difficult they become, the more I seem to be at the mercy of others and how they see me. At the same time I realize that they crave the same sorts of things as I do, sometimes they even seem to want that recognition and love to come from *me*.

This brief and rather simplistic pastiche is sufficient to illustrate the complexity of the struggle to be true to oneself, to discover oneself, to express oneself. Sorting through the elements of which life and self seem to be composed I wonder precisely how I might even begin to discern and discover my self in them and to live a life that is authentic and true. However, the need for real self-examination loses its intensity when I realize that I can go through life with a minimal attention to these facts and without much reflection on how best to understand and live them. Life, as it turns out, has largely been laid out before me. I am daily encouraged and instructed, gently nudged, or firmly pushed in the proper direction. It is easy enough simply to absorb, sponge-like, much of what I need to know to survive in the world. It is easy enough to follow the path, robot-like, that I have been set upon. For example, I go to school and write down what my teachers say and study it. But what I learn is more than just the content of the lesson. Whether I am studying maths or history, biology or economics, by getting up, brushing my teeth, getting dressed, eating breakfast, making it to class on time, sitting in my place and focusing on the lesson, I learn many other things than maths or history, biology or economics. I learn how to wait and listen. I learn how to defer gratification. I learn how to measure myself in quantitative terms: I am smart if I get a certain number on my exams, if I do certain things before others do them. I learn the importance of these quantitative evaluations and to consume them with passion and anxiety – the letter C is first met with a desire to do better, then with frustration and resentment, and finally with quiet resignation. Grades, evaluations, pay-cheques, commodities tell me who I am, how I am doing, what I am worth.

Television and entertainment amuses me and gives me a chance to feel things, but it also trains me by forming my imagination, by helping me form concrete images of what I love and desire, what I hate, who I want to be and how I need to act. Marketing does the same things, just less effectively. Thanks to all of this programming I know how to party and hang out, what to wear and what to listen to, how to talk and who to talk to. Whether I am in class, hanging out with my friends, at work, with my girlfriend or boyfriend, watching a movie, playing video games, I am always getting the message, sometimes directly and explicitly and sometimes indirectly and implicitly: here's how to be yourself! The pattern of my life, the form of my self, is mostly pre-established and already waiting for me.

This ready-made character of life comes from what Foucault calls disciplinary power or governmentality.[5] As I pass through all of the institutions (schools, workplaces, households, government agencies, doctors' offices, entertainment venues, etc.) that give form to my life, I find myself caught up in an intricate web of compulsion and choice, desire and necessity. I interact with experts and authorities who are there to help me become a well-adjusted, happy, healthy, productive member of society. Psychologists and medical doctors, for example, have carefully worked out all of the minute stages of psychological and physical development and have devised marvellously precise instruments for measuring our lives and selves in terms of these stages. The market and the entertainment industry have worked hard to construct a world of commodities that help us know and express our true selves through the products and brands that we consume, the music we listen to, the movies we watch. These industries, authorities, experts and institutions guide me by pushing me to discover, maximize and express my self: "the chief function of disciplinary power is to 'train' … Discipline 'makes' individuals" (Foucault 1979: 170). All of these authorities and institutions train me to be me.

Central to this training process is the way it focuses attention on me (and you and everyone else) as an object of both control and knowledge. Discipline is a form of power that carefully watches, examines, records and measures. It does this in order to help me reach my full, productive potential. But in so doing it regulates my behaviour and structures my time so that I can get the most out of it. It organizes everyone's time and behaviour so that it can compare us all to each other and get an idea of what kind of growth and development is normal. The end result is "calculable man" – a highly disciplined animal, very capable but also very "docile" (*ibid.*: 193; 135–69). This process is what Foucault calls "normalization" (*ibid.*: 177–84). The process of normalization has continued to become more pervasive and more intensive even as it becomes less obvious or intrusive.[6] Surveillance is more and more subtle (security cameras capture me in public places, spyware watches me on the Internet, my boss can audit my computer activity at work, my cell phone can be overheard easily, marketers register my behaviours and choices and target me with custom designed advertisements). Less and less of life is free and unstructured – new communication technologies may free me from the cubicle, but they do so by making every place part of an interconnected network so that I am always at the office. Children's lives are more regimented, disciplined and governed than ever before: from the scientific design of developmental toys, to the structured, organized and supervised "play" groups and developmental activities that occupy more and more of their time.

In all of these examples, I am not governed in a way that represses or oppresses me. Rather, discipline makes me more productive, it trains me and develops my capacities for living, making it very hard to resist since it seems to be on my side, it provides me with resources to live my life. Yet, while all of these things shape me, give form and order to my life, and help me form an idea of who I am and how I am supposed to feel things and do things, I sometimes get the sensation that this is not really who I am.

It is in this disciplinary context that we often decide to look within for that true self, the self that has not been moulded or made to conform, that has not been disciplined. But even at this moment, we are governed or trained to relate to our self in certain ways. The very idea that there is a true self within, waiting beneath the surface, is, as we have noted already, a very particular kind of relationship of the self to itself. Foucault calls this kind of subjectivity "hermeneutic" or "confessional" because it is formed through the activities of self-interpretation (hermeneutics is the art of interpretation) and self-expression (confession is the art or practice of expressing and communicating that which is difficult but necessary to say). Foucault's point is that hermeneutics and confession do not discern and express the inner truth. Rather by practising these activities we become a specific kind of self:

> The confession has spread its effects far and wide. It plays a part in justice, medicine, education, family relationships, and love relations, in the most ordinary affairs of everyday life, and in the most solemn rites; one confesses one's crimes, one's sins, one's thoughts and desires, one's illnesses and troubles; one goes about telling, with the greatest precision, whatever is most difficult to tell ... *Western man has become a singularly confessing animal.*
> (1990a: 59, emphasis added)

The hermeneutic and confessional subject falls into the trap we noted above. By focusing on the self who is revealed through interpretation and confession, we fail to see the way in which these very activities themselves are what define us and make us into the kind of person we are. While discipline arranges and orders our lives, hermeneutics and confession give form to our subjectivity.

Subjectivity and care of the self

In response to the disciplinary form of life and the hermeneutic, confessional form of subjectivity, Foucault proposes an alternative way of thinking about and giving form to our lives and selves. As we have seen, for Foucault subjectivity is not some *thing* we *are*, it is an activity that we *do*. Subjectivity is relational, dynamic and restless, potentially unruly and unpredictable. But if subjectivity is an active becoming, rather than a fixed being, then the quest to discover or find oneself – in the form of an essence or substance – is futile. What is more, by focusing our attention on this self and our energy on trying to "express" it, we neglect our subjective becoming, which is taken over by the processes of disciplinary training and normalization.

In order to describe and analyse subjectivity, Foucault turns to a framework he calls "care of the self", which is his translation of an expression that appears regularly in the works of ancient Greek and Roman philosophy (*epimeleia heautou*). Foucault juxtaposes care of the self with the confessional self and the hermeneutic self. Hermeneutic and confessional subjectivity is dominated by the imperative: "know yourself". In the ancient world, on the other hand, subjectivity was based on the imperative: "take care of yourself". Foucault tries to show that the framework of care of the self makes possible a fuller, richer way of thinking about, and actively becoming, ourselves. For ancient philosophers subjectivity was not a form of self-knowledge, rather self-knowledge was pursued only to the extent that it was necessary in order to take care of oneself. The pursuit of self-knowledge was only one possible element, and not always the most important one, in the more fundamental effort to take care of oneself. So if care of the self is not completely defined by self-knowledge, what else might it involve? The care of the self is composed of what Foucault sometimes calls the "technologies of the self" or the "arts of living".

When Foucault speaks of the "technologies" or "arts" of the self or of life, he is drawing on the Greek term *technē*, the etymological source of our word technology. The term "*technē*" is usually translated as know-how or craft or art. *Technē* is the kind of knowledge that allows someone to accomplish a specific task or produce a specified outcome. Ancient philosophers often thought of philosophy as the *technē tou bio* – the art of living (Foucault 2005a: 177–8). Philosophy was conceived of as the art or craft of producing a noble, beautiful and true life (for ancient Greeks goodness, beauty and truth are regularly thought of as identical). In this framework the self is understood to be a work of *technē*, of art.

Foucault's notion of the technologies or arts of the self, and the arts of living, has little to do with a fairly common, and essentially modern conception of the artist and her relationship to her work of art. We often think of art in terms of self-expression, again falling back on our presupposition about the substantial, foundational self. When we give in to this tendency we miss the dynamic genesis of art and artworks. We fail to appreciate how artists actually work to produce an art object and we fail to comprehend how artists actually *become* artists. For Foucault, art or *technē* is realized in creative labour or work (the Greeks called this kind of labour *poiesis*, the root of our word "poetry"). In order to produce an object or an outcome it is necessary to perform certain very precise and well-ordered activities, activities that require a certain amount of know-how. For instance, an artist needs to know how the particular paint she is using will take to the surface she is painting on because the way that the paint adheres to or is absorbed by a surface will shape the look of the painting. If the artist begins with an idea of the painting to be accomplished but has no knowledge of how to mix her paints, or what kind of paint to use on which kind of surface, she will not be able to realize her idea, she will not be able to create the work. The know-how of the artist is not the kind of knowledge that can be learned primarily through study; it is not essentially "theoretical" knowledge. Of course, learning the chemical science behind oil-based paints and their adhesion to wood surfaces may be useful, but studying chemistry does not result in art. In order to acquire art the artist needs to experiment with and experience the look and feel of the paint on the surface – no study of chemistry can provide this kind of know-how. Only by mixing the paint, choosing a particular brush and surface, and applying the paint to the surface can the artist begin to develop the art – *technē* – that is necessary to produce a painting, to produce a work of art. One learns to paint by painting.[7]

The artfulness of the work derives from these very precise activities and the know-how (*technē*) that both makes them possible but also, and importantly, comes from them. Of course, painting is more than the mere study of paints and surfaces. In addition to all of the other concerns that go into the artfulness of the painter, there are those key elements that we as spectators tend to focus on: the form or style of the painting and its content or "meaning". A completed work of art is the realization of what we call the artist's "vision", "intent" or aesthetic "idea". In the self-expression view of art we presume that vision, intent or idea express who the artist truly is. The painting is then seen as a kind of confession of the artist and its meaning is discerned through a hermeneutic that would discern, operating behind the manifest content, the hidden motive, the vision, intent or idea that reside in the self (soul, heart, mind) of the artist. But form, style and content are just as much the *upshot* of the actual labour of art as they are its directives and sources. The ability of an artist actually to see, imagine or conceptualize the completed work is the consequence of having learned the possibilities of the medium through the concrete practice of painting. Certainly, we all gain some capacity to envision a work of art that does not exist by looking at possible subjects of art and especially by studying the works of others. But we do not have a realizable aesthetic vision or idea until we have actually learned the real possibilities of the medium we wish to work in, and these can only be learned through the practice of painting. Intent, idea and vision are the results of practice and art, not the causes of it. The vision of the artist is itself transformed, deepened, expanded or intensified by the actual labour. In effect the artist is a work of art just as much as the object she produces. It is through rigorously practising the activities of the art that we acquire something like vision and become capable of a real, meaningful, realizable artistic idea or intent.

How does this discussion of art apply to the relationship of the self to itself? How does the self give form to itself and its life as works of art? Foucault discovers many examples of arts of the self and arts of living in the works of ancient philosophers. For Foucault the study of these practices can provide us with a resource of all sorts of techniques that we might adapt and try out. In the following we will briefly summarize and examine a couple of the techniques for taking care of the self developed by ancient philosophers. This will give us a more concrete idea of what the arts of the self and of living might look like. We will also consider how Foucault's work itself is composed of arts of the self that he practises in order to form a certain kind of relationship to himself, to become a particular kind of philosopher.

First, let us look at a couple of examples of the ancient practice of the examination of conscience. For example, here is how Foucault describes the way Marcus Aurelius begins his day with an anticipatory examination of conscience:

> This examination does not at all involve going back over what you could have done in the night or the day before; it is an examination of what you will do ... It involves reviewing in advance the actions you will perform in the day, your commitments, the appointments you have made, the tasks you will have to face: remembering the general aim you set yourself by these actions and the general aims you should always have in mind throughout life, and so the precautions to be taken so as to act according to these precise objectives and general aims in the situations that arise.
> (2005a: 481)

The relation to oneself that is formed by this technique is not principally one of confession or interpretation. Rather, it is a form of preparation and memory. I must remember my goals and my principles,

I must be prepared for the events of the day so that I will not forget what I am trying to achieve. In a similar vein, Foucault discusses a form of self-examination that can be found in the work of Seneca. In this example, Seneca takes some time at the end of the day to recollect and record what he has done that day. Once again, his primary aim and focus in this activity is not to discern the hidden motive at work in what he did, nor is he primarily intent on judging his actions (although he does employ juridical language for describing the process). There is no sense of a self lurking behind his actions and giving them meaning. First and foremost his activity is a kind of "accounting" or administrative activity, adding up the balance sheets and seeing how he has done that day. He also describes this art as a kind of inspection of his actions that day to see if he has done everything as well as he could have and to learn how he might avoid mistakes and improve in the future. As with the morning examination of Marcus Aurelius, the evening examination of Seneca is:

> primarily a test of the reactivation of the fundamental rules of action, of the ends we should have in mind, and of the means we should employ to achieve these ends and the immediate objectives we may set ourselves. To that extent, examination of conscience is a memory exercise, not just with regard to what happened during the day, but with regard to the rules we should always have in our mind. (*Ibid.*: 483)

The examination of conscience in both Marcus Aurelius and Seneca is an art for the *formation* of subjectivity, for the formation of the self. It is not an attempt to discover a pre-existing substance or essence, but rather part of an effort to *become* a certain kind of individual, to give a distinctive form to one's life, to shape, deepen, intensify and cultivate the relationship of the self to itself. These techniques of self-examination are ways of taking care of oneself in the sense that they assist one in the activity of becoming the self that one wants or needs to be. Marcus Aurelius and Seneca both take up the material of life, all of those elements which we reviewed at the beginning of this essay: thoughts and feelings, actions and relationships, and so on. In face of the rush of events and actions, storms of emotion, the endless flow of thoughts, judgements, choices, they attempt to sculpt a form out of life and to shape the self-relation. The aim of the exercise is to make sure that I do not end up completely uprooted and carried away in the stream of events, never catching a glimpse of or getting a firm hold on what is worthwhile in life and what I might be able to make of my self. Foucault's purpose in turning to these philosophers is not to convince us to relive the lives of Stoic philosophers. Rather, the drift of his work detaches us from the hermeneutic and confessional practice of subjectivity; to show us that the self is not a substance or essence but a work of art; and to give us a taste of the many different arts, and consequently many different kinds of self, that can be practised. In this way his study provides us with new resources, techniques that we might use, even if we do not appropriate wholesale the Stoic life and the Stoic aims in life.

Not all of the arts of the self and of life are forms of self-examination. For example, one of the principal arts of the self in ancient philosophy involved the contemplation of nature and of external reality. The contemplation of nature can have a powerful, transformative effect on one's relationship to oneself and the way one lives. For example, Seneca practised a form of natural philosophy that allowed him to attain an elevated perspective from which he could look down on himself and his life (*ibid.*: 275–85). When we are caught up in the middle of things – the pressures of work or school, relationships, money, health, and so on – the day-to-day anxieties of life become all consuming. We find ourselves absorbed in our problems and concerns, obsessed with our work or our relationship, in ways that take a toll on us and can result in self-destructive behaviours and habits, the crushing anxiety that accompanies a life and self that is spinning out of control. But through the contemplation of the vastness and magnificence of the cosmos we elevate ourselves above and beyond the day-to-day world. Then looking down on it from above we are able to see it within this larger, truer, cosmic perspective. The world of our everyday preoccupations appears in truth as a brief moment in the vast infinity of time, hardly a speck of dust swallowed up in the endless expanses of space, completely insignificant in relation to the power and beauty of the heavenly bodies. Other ancient philosophers developed their own forms of the contemplation of nature, but in each case they serve as arts for the formation of the self: freeing the self from its fears or compulsions, calming the mind disturbed by pressing problems, reinforcing a will constantly bombarded by frivolous demands, distractions, temptations. For Foucault, this art of the self shows us that the practice of subjectivity does not necessarily entail turning our gaze inward, focusing on and essentializing the inner life. Rather, there are powerful arts of living that project us out into the world, further detaching us from our presuppositions about self-discovery and self-expression. Being true to ourselves may in fact involve focusing our attention on the natural world or history and society – in other words, turning outwards rather than inwards.

Becoming oneself

Foucault's study of care of the self and the arts of the self in ancient philosophy is not merely a record and analysis of these activities. In fact, it is clear that in this study Foucault, as in all of his philosophical activity, was engaged in the active practice of forming his own subjectivity. If we examine the trajectory of Foucault's own work, we see that through the labour of philosophical thought, Foucault developed an art of philosophical practice that served as the source of a certain vision and relationship to himself. He formed a distinctive way of being a philosopher. Here is one way he described his own efforts to fashion himself as a work of art:

> As for what motivated me, it is quite simple; I would hope that in the eyes of some people it might be sufficient in itself. It was curiosity – the only kind of curiosity, in any case, that is worth acting upon with a degree of obstinacy; not the curiosity that seeks to assimilate what it is proper for one to know, but that which enables one to get free of oneself. After all, what would be the value of the passion for knowledge if it resulted only in a certain amount of knowledgeableness and not, in one way or another and to the extent possible, in the knower's straying afield of himself?
> (1990b: 8)

Foucault's care of the self was composed of numerous arts – including but not limited to reading, thinking, writing, teaching – that allow him to "get free" of himself. Philosophy for Foucault was not primarily a form of knowledge or self-knowledge but rather "an exercise of oneself in the activity of thought" (*ibid.*: 9). What is the result of this kind of exercise?

> There is irony in those efforts one makes to alter one's way of looking at things, to change the boundaries of what one knows and to venture out a ways from there. Did mine actually result in a different way of thinking? Perhaps at most they made it possible to go back through what I was already thinking, to think it differently, and to see what I had done from a new vantage point and in a clearer light. Sure of having traveled far, one finds that one

is looking down on oneself from above. The journey rejuvenates things, and ages the relationship with oneself.   (*Ibid.*: 11)

Clearly getting free of oneself does not mean that one simply abandons oneself in order to become a completely new person, whatever that might mean. Rather, one gets some distance and perspective, one "looks down on oneself from above". But who is the self that one gets free of? The self Foucault gets free of is none other than the one formed by discipline, whose subjectivity is shaped by the practices of hermeneutics and confession. Discipline, confession and hermeneutics produce a self that lives a certain way, that sees itself and the world in terms of normalization, self-interpretation and self-expression. When Foucault "exercises" himself in the "activity of thought" he is attempting to "think differently", to detach himself from the disciplined, normalized self that he has become so far. The work or art of the self is the exercise by which Foucault establishes a relationship of distance from the self of discipline, hermeneutics and confession. But has he now arrived at his true self?

Just be yourself. Keep it real. Follow your own path. Foucault's account of subjectivity gives a whole new meaning to these words and helps us understand why the task they prescribe is so urgent but yet so difficult, ultimately endless. Being oneself is a matter of strenuous *trying* and determined artfulness, because the self is a continuous becoming, not a fixed being. Consequently, the art of becoming my self is always to some extent an art of no longer being what I was, an art that detaches the self from itself in order to form a new, deeper, wiser relationship to itself, which in turn will give way to its own self-distancing, sending me on my way towards unknown futures.

Notes

1. I would like to acknowledge Serena Parekh, Paul Bruno and Dianna Taylor for reading drafts of this chapter and giving me invaluable feedback and insight. This paper has also benefited greatly from the careful reading and incisive comments of two students at Saint Anselm College: Sara Kallock and Ryan Manley.
2. For example, see Foucault (1988, 1997e, 2005a).
3. Paul Bruno has helped me to see the particular danger that occurs here, a kind of divorce between the "fixed idea of who we are" and action/human agency. In other words, when we have a fixed idea of ourselves, our actions become meaningless in a way. No matter what we do, we are still the fixed person we have conceived for ourselves.
4. See Foucault's discussion of self-reflection as constitutive of the self as both knower and known (Foucault 2005a: 461–2).
5. See the chapters on power in Part I of this book.

6. For an excellent study of the spread and intensification of power since the death of Michel Foucault, see: Nealon (2008).
7. One of the key features of *technē* is its bodily character: it is acquired through embodied activities, situated and concrete investigations and experiments. Techné is embodied or bodily knowledge.

TEN

Subjectivity and truth

Brad Elliott Stone

Is there a relationship between subjectivity and truth in our contemporary age? Foucault's answer is "no". In this chapter, I seek to explicate Foucault's conclusion about the divorce of subjectivity and truth. Beginning with Foucault's account of the shift between ancient and modern philosophy,[1] I show in the first section that the modern, strictly epistemological understanding of truth removes us from the possibility of having an ethical relationship to the truth. This ethical relationship to the truth, however, was the heart of ancient philosophy, whose goal was not "knowledge" but human flourishing. The second section explores the role of truth in ancient philosophy. The third section turns to an explication of Foucault's account of *parrhēsia* as it was understood in ancient philosophy. *Parrhēsia* is the act of telling the truth out of one's moral duty, even in dangerous situations. I then offer examples of how *parrhēsia* was used in ancient philosophy, followed by a brief discussion of whether or not we can recreate a meaningful relationship between subjectivity and truth.

In the shadow of the Cartesian moment

Foucault's 1982 lecture course *The Hermeneutics of the Subject* continues his investigation into the connection between subjectivity and truth begun in the 1981 course *Subjectivity and Truth*.[2] In the 1981 lecture course, Foucault focused exclusively on Hellenic views of sexuality. In 1982, Foucault wants to ask the question of the relationship between subjectivity and truth in a more general way: "[i]n what historical form do the relations between the 'subject' and 'truth,' elements that do not usually fall within the historian's practice or analysis, take shape in the West?" (2005a: 2). How does the West relate subjectivity and truth, if at all?

One of Foucault's main arguments in his opening lecture in 1982 is that there is a discontinuity in the history of the relationship between subjectivity and truth. To show this discontinuity, Foucault discusses the radical difference between how the ancient thinkers understood the relationship between subjectivity and truth and how the modern thinkers understand it. Foucault returns to the old philosophical motto "Know yourself", *gnōthi seauton*. This hope for self-knowledge, central to the philosopher's quest, was always essentially coupled with another motto: "take care of yourself", *epimeleia heautou*. However, in the contemporary age, this coupling is no longer essential. For the ancient thinkers, one had to be a particular kind of person in order to know oneself, let alone know anything else of importance. In our age, however, knowledge is considered something that one can obtain regardless of the kind of person one is. This is where Foucault detects an archaeological (in Foucault's sense of the term) break in the history of knowledge. Foucault asserts that the ancient thinkers considered the care of the self "the justificatory framework, ground, and foundation for the imperative 'know yourself'" (*ibid.*: 8). That we can now claim self-knowledge without any ethical requirements would be for the ancients unintelligible.

The 1982 course focuses on the ancient methods of being the kind of person who could gain access to the truth. This will provide a preliminary answer to Foucault's key question: "Why did Western thought and philosophy neglect the notion of *epimeleia heautou* in its reconstruction of its own history?" (*ibid.*: 12). Why has contemporary thought claimed continuity with ancient thought through the quest for self-knowledge while being oblivious to the fact that the ancient thinkers had requirements for self-knowledge that modern thought does not bother to fulfil?

One possible explanation is the rise of Christianity with its emphasis on selflessness. The non-egoist principle of Christianity causes one to see the care of the self as too selfish. Also, the Judaeo-Christian belief in an omniscient God whose knowledge is distinct from God's moral goodness allows for a hope for God's kind of knowledge without having to care for oneself. Although this is a possible explanation, it does not give the strongest case. For Foucault, the stronger case is archaeological rather than historical.

For Foucault, Descartes' philosophy represents an archaeological event[3] in which the "concept" of self-knowledge had shifted. Foucault

describes what he calls "the Cartesian moment", a moment characterized "by philosophically requalifying the *gnōthi seauton* and by dis-
crediting the *epimeleia heautou*" (*ibid.*: 14). Foucault spends the rest
of the first hour of the opening lecture of the 1982 course on the
discontinuity in the history of the relationship of subjectivity and truth
evidenced by this moment. At the heart of the Cartesian moment is
the belief that self-knowledge is a given, a fact that Descartes nimbly
proves in the Second Meditation of *Meditations on First Philosophy*.
From this self-knowledge, one can then proceed, with certainty, to
knowledge of God, mathematics and even the physical world itself.
What is missing here, Foucault points out, is the ancient notion of the
care of the self.

What is missing at the core of Cartesian philosophy (and modern
thought since Descartes) is *spirituality*. Foucault uses this term in a
technical sense, not to be immediately confused with one's religious
practices (although that sense of spirituality will itself be a mode of
what Foucault means here by "spirituality"). Foucault defines spirituality as "the search, practice, and experience through which the subject carries out the necessary transformations on himself in order to
have access to the truth" (*ibid.*: 15). When philosophy is coupled with
spirituality, philosophy is "the form of thought that asks what it is
that enables the subject to have access to the truth and which attempts
to determine the conditions and limits to the subject's access to the
truth" (*ibid.*). Ancient philosophy was the pursuit of the kind of life
that would lead to knowledge, not just an analysis of what could be
known and how one could know it. The Cartesian moment, however,
allows for a philosophy without spirituality, removing the first part of
philosophy's definition (What enables the subject to have access to the
truth?) while retaining the second part (What are the conditions and
limits to the subject's access of truth?). This is a *point of diffraction*
(cf. Foucault 1972: 65) between ancient and modern thought: ancient
thought finds the second part of the definition unintelligible without the first part, while modern thought cleanly divides epistemology
from ethics.

The reason the ancients would find modern philosophy unintelligible, Foucault claims, is the Cartesian insistence that self-knowledge is
self-given, and that the right use of one's own already-in-place mental
powers can lead to truth. One of the postulates of spirituality presented by Foucault is that "the truth is never given to the subject by
right"; that is, "the subject does not have right of access to the truth"
(Foucault 2005a: 15). For the ancients, the subject's already-in-place
mental "powers" are precisely what need to be overcome! The second

postulate is that "there can be no truth without a conversion or a transformation of the subject" (*ibid.*). In order to access the truth, one must care for oneself and become a particular kind of person, a person who has correctly prepared oneself to be the bearer and speaker of the truth for which one has prepared. The third postulate of spirituality is that the truth, once accessed, "enlightens the subject" and "gives the subject tranquility of the soul" (*ibid.*: 16). Knowledge is not for knowledge's sake; rather, it is to bring about a particular kind of person.

Modernity does not accept any of these three ancient postulates. Foucault states the rules for accessing knowledge in the modern period. First, there must be an epistemological method that will lead one to the truth. Second, one must be sane, educated and willing to participate in the scientific community. Foucault laments that in the modern age "the truth cannot save the subject" (*ibid.*: 19) since there is no requirement that one modify one's life in order to access the truth that would in turn further modify that life. With the Cartesian moment, the philosopher's task is no longer defined in terms of care of the self, but is strictly in the purview of knowledge. As Foucault mentions in a later interview, in the post-Cartesian age, "I can be immoral and know the truth ... Before Descartes, one could not be impure, immoral, and know the truth" (Foucault 1997f: 279).

The rest of *The Hermeneutics of the Subject* describes the practices undertaken by the Greeks, the Hellenists and the early Christians in their quest to care for the self in order to obtain knowledge.[4] I will not explore them here because there are other chapters in this collection that will address them. However, I will remind the reader that there are discontinuities between the Greek, Hellenist and early Christian's respective understandings of the care of the self. For example, the Greeks saw care of the self as a pedagogical issue having to do with youths preparing to govern in the *polis*, whereas the Stoics saw care of the self as a medico-therapeutic method that covered one's entire lifespan. Of interest in this essay is the bigger archaeological shift between the period in which there was at least *some* expectation of a relationship between subjectivity and truth and our contemporary age, an age in which, as Foucault states in *The Order of Things*, "no morality is possible" (1973: 328).

Truth-telling in antiquity

For several years prior to his death, Foucault was obsessed with the question of truth-telling as a moral activity. After the Cartesian moment, truth simply became an epistemological matter, a mere question of whether statements corresponded to facts about the world (or, if one is a coherentist, whether all the statements about the world can be held without contradiction). Scepticism, which in the ancient world had to do with the limits of human understanding, became the epistemological standard bearer and pacesetter. In order to have knowledge, one had to be able to overcome the threat of scepticism. Descartes suggests that the way around scepticism is method. In his *Rules for the Direction of the Mind* and the Fourth Meditation, Descartes lays out a way to enumerate the parts of a problem correctly so that one can have a clear and distinct understanding. Nowhere in these rules will one find any moral requirements.

This Cartesian account of truth is quite different from what the Greeks called *parrhēsia* and the Latins called *libertas*. In *Fearless Speech*, the transcripts of his 1983 lectures at the University of California at Berkeley, Foucault defines *parrhēsia* as:

> verbal activity in which a speaker expresses his personal relationship to truth, and risks his life because he recognizes truth-telling as a duty … the speaker uses his freedom and chooses frankness instead of persuasion, truth instead of falsehood or silence, the risk of death instead of life and security, criticism instead of flattery, and moral duty instead of self-interest and moral apathy.
>
> (2001: 12)

This personal relationship to truth is missing from modern thought, so perhaps a potential way to "return to morality" would be to investigate what *parrhēsia* is, how it was used, and what hope there is for us in the modern age to reclaim it as a philosophical practice. Foucault begins his exploration of truth-telling in 1981 with the Collège de France lecture course *Subjectivité et vérité* (not yet published). This theme marks the rest of his lecture courses before his death: *The Hermeneutics of the Subject* in 1982, *Le Gouvernement de soi et des autres* in 1983 (published in French, not yet translated into English), and *Le Courage de la vérité: Le government de soi et des autres II* in 1984 (published in French, not yet translated into English).

Foucault claims that there are three ways in which ancient philosophy takes up *parrhēsia* as its governing principle. First, ancient philosophy was not separate from how one was to live one's life. Foucault says that we should interpret this unity of thought and life as "the general framework of the parrhesiastic function by means of which life was traversed, penetrated, and sustained" (Foucault 2008b: 315). *Parrhēsia* was key to the living of a philosophical life. The ancient thinkers concerned themselves not just with truth-telling (*dire-vrai*) but also with the true life (*la vraie vie*). The question of the true life, for the most part, is missing in the modern philosophical age.

Second, philosophy in the ancient period "never stopped addressing, in one way or another, those who governed" (*ibid*.: 316). The relationship between philosophy and politics, Foucault argues, was a dominant feature of antiquity. As he states, "philosophy is a form of life; it is also a kind of office – at once both public and private – of political counsel" (*ibid*.: 317). Although there have been post-Cartesian thinkers who have offered their truth-telling abilities to those who govern, it is no longer considered a necessary part of the philosopher's job description. This absence of political counsel would be very strange to Plato, for example, whose Philosopher King serves as the paradigm for the just city in *Republic*.

Third, the ancient thinkers did not limit their work to the classroom. Any audience could be the audience of a philosophical discourse, and any location could become a philosophical classroom. Philosophy was a public enterprise, never a subject taught in school to a select band of people or a solitary armchair contemplation of thought experiments; its goal was to improve people's souls. The philosopher had "the courage to tell the truth to others in order to guide them in their own conduct" (*ibid*.: 318). It is no surprise, then, that Socrates, upon being condemned for doing philosophy and asked what his punishment should be, responds by suggesting that, in exchange for his public service, he should receive lunch every day for a year just like a victorious Olympic athlete (*Apology* 36d–e). It would be a fitting reward for everything he had philosophically done for Athens.

Foucault laments that modern philosophy does not have ancient philosophy's parrhesiastic features. He states that "modern Western thought, at least if we consider it as it is currently presented (as a scholastic or university subject), has relatively few points in common with the parrhesiastic philosophy [of the ancients]" (2008b: 318). It is curious that Foucault uses the appositive phrase "at least if we consider it as it is currently presented". Could there be a way of thinking of modern philosophy that might reopen the possibility of morality? Perhaps, but we will need to do some work first. If we want to return to morality, we will need to investigate *parrhēsia* further and determine if there is anything in our age that might serve as a good substitute for it.

Telling the truth: *parrhēsia*

In *Fearless Speech* Foucault highlights five important characteristics of *parrhēsia*: frankness, truth, danger, criticism and duty. These characteristics will differentiate moral truth-telling from other forms of communication. We will address each in turn.

(a) Frankness. First, *parrhēsia* is *franc parler*, or as we would say, "telling it like it is". The *parrhēsiastēs*, the one who performs the act of *parrhēsia*, does not use rhetoric; she simply reveals whatever is in her mind on a given subject. As Foucault describes it, "the speaker is supposed to give a complete and exact account of what he has in mind so that the audience is able to comprehend exactly what the speaker thinks" (2001: 12). Because they worry too much about offending, most people often do not tell the truth; instead, they tell half-truths or flat-out lies. Frankness, however, shows the audience a couple of things: (i) that the speaker really believes what she is saying, and (ii) that the speaker believes in what she is saying enough that it should be said as if it were directly from her mind, unmediated by language.

Of note is that the truth-teller speaks for herself, completely revealing her cards in the process. This differs, Foucault claims in the 1984 lectures at the Collège de France, from the prophet, who indeed tells the truth, but "does not speak in his own name. He speaks for another voice; his mouth serves as an intermediary for a voice which speaks from beyond" (2009: 16). The unmediated frankness of the truth-teller, compared to the prophet's mediated, representative speech, gives the *parrhēsiastēs* moral authority and culpability. The truth-teller cannot advise interlocutors to "not kill the messenger". She lives and dies on what is said: the message and the messenger are one and the same.

(b) Truth. Frankness, however, is not sufficient for *parrhēsia*. It is not enough that someone really believes that what they say is true; what they say must actually be true. As Foucault writes, the *parrhēsiastēs* "says what is true because he *knows* that it is true; and he *knows* that it is true because it really is true ... his opinion is also the truth ... there is always an exact coincidence between belief and truth" (2001: 14). There is no conflict between the mind of the *parrhēsiastēs* and her heart: she believes in the truth that she knows, believes in her knowledge of the truth, and knows that her beliefs are true. The truth is judged by the bare conviction of the speaker. It is this conviction that makes the *parrhēsiastēs* tell the truth (the really true); it is not a "correspondence" between "the world" and the statements made by the

speaker. Scepticism is dismissed by Foucault as "a particularly modern [question] which ... is foreign to the Greeks" (*ibid.*: 15). So, although *parrhēsia* requires that the truth-teller tell the truth in an "epistemic" sense, the importance is not on the epistemic fact that the truth was said; rather, the importance lies in the moral power of the truth-teller.

(c) Danger. However, frank speech, even when spoken with conviction, is not sufficient to classify an utterance as *parrhēsia*. *Parrhēsia* occurs when the truth puts the truth-teller in some kind of danger. In the face of danger, liars lie. The *parrhēsiastēs*, however, tells the truth, usually to a person who is more powerful than she, a person who knows that what the truth-teller says is true. Hence there is an element of courage in *parrhēsia*. As Foucault tells us, "a grammar teacher may tell the truth to the children that he teaches, and indeed has no doubt that what he teaches is true. But in spite of this coincidence between belief and truth, he is not a *parrhēsiastēs*" (*ibid.*: 16). Simply put, there is no courage required to say that three is a prime number. A philosopher pointing out a tyrant's tyranny, however, is a different situation. The tyrant knows that he is a tyrant, so the philosopher is not saying something that the tyrant does not know. However, telling the tyrant that he is a tyrant puts the truth-teller in danger; nonetheless, although aware of the danger, the philosopher tells him anyway, and suggests ways for the tyrant to change his way of governing. In order for one to be a *parrhēsiastēs*, one must have something to lose in telling the truth. No risk, no *parrhēsia*.

In the 1984 lectures, Foucault reasserts that the *parrhēsiastēs* "is not the professor, the teacher, the how-to guy who says, in the name of tradition, *technē*" (2009: 25). Instead of *technē*, technical knowledge, the truth-teller proclaims *ethos*, a way of living one's life. This involves a risk unknown by the technician. The teacher knows no risk, Foucault claims, because he works in the context of shared values: heritage, common knowledge, tradition, friendship. The truth-teller, however, "takes a risk. He risks the relationship that he has with the one whom he addresses. In telling the truth, far from establishing a positive line of common knowledge, heritage, affiliation, recognition, and friendship, he can, to the contrary, provoke anger" (*ibid.*: 24). Truth-telling requires stepping outside of the alleged "shared values" held by the interlocutor. This "stepping outside" will be the grounds for the critical dimension of *parrhēsia*.

(d) Critique. *Parrhēsia* has to be more than just frank statements stated that causes the truth-teller to be potentially endangered. Truth-telling in a moral sense requires that the truth be something that the hearer

does not like. In other words, *parrhēsia* must have a dimension of criticism. The truth told by the truth-teller must force, even if just for a moment, the interlocutor to examine himself. It is at this point that courage is required. Given that the recipient of *parrhēsia* is usually in a superior position of power to the speaker, the recipient is tempted to unleash his power upon the truth-teller by punishing her, firing her, killing her, and so on. This is where most people fall short: afraid of the possible retaliation, the liar lies, converting what could be a moment of *critique* into a moment of *flattery*. The *parrhēsiastēs* frankly tells a critical, unflattering truth about the matter. *Parrhēsia* is the opposite of self-interested, cowardly, unhelpful flattery. The *parrhēsiastēs* speaks the truth with frankness in the face of danger in order to help those for whom violence is the easier solution.

(e) Duty. So far we have described *parrhēsia* in terms of frankness, conviction, danger, and criticism; what is missing is that which unites these principles. That connective feature is the sense of moral duty that accompanies the *parrhēsiastēs*. In the face of potential danger, the liar lies, and he justifies his action by appealing to the circumstances. This is a consequentialist response. But, akin to Kant, Foucault claims that *parrhēsia* is the result of a moral decision to tell the truth, even if doing so is dangerous. The truth-teller "is *free* to keep silent. No one forces him to speak, but he feels that it is his duty to do so ... *Parrhēsia* is thus related to freedom and to duty" (2001: 19). In order to tell the truth in the sense of *parrhēsia*, one must be free to not tell the truth, either by lying or by saying nothing. To tell the truth requires that the truth-teller have an ethical relationship with herself. The *parrhēsiastēs* "risk[s] death to tell the truth instead of reposing in the security of a life where the truth goes unspoken ... he prefers himself as a truth-teller rather than as a living being who is false to himself" (*ibid.*: 17).[5] Truth-telling is morally praiseworthy because it is done exactly when it would be easier not to do it.

This is what differentiates the truth-teller from the sage. In the 1984 lectures, Foucault points out that although the sage is like the truth-teller in so far as there is a unity of messenger and message (unlike the prophet), "the sage ... keeps his wisdom in retreat, or at least in an essential reserve. Basically, the sage is wise in and for himself, and he need not speak ... nothing obligates him to distribute, teach, or manifest his wisdom" (2009: 18). The *parrhēsiastēs*, in contrast, is morally obligated to speak. She cannot keep the truth to herself; she must proclaim the truth – she must speak *all* of the truth to everyone to whom it is addressed. *Parrhēsia* understood this way is a truth that cannot be kept hidden. The truth-teller un-conceals herself, the interlocutor, and the truth that is to be communicated.[6]

Uses of *parrhēsia* in ancient philosophy

In the Berkeley lectures in 1983, Foucault describes the use of *parrhēsia* in three different arenas: community life, public life and personal life. Foucault refers to the Epicureans in order to illustrate the use of truth-telling in community life. In Epicurean communities, *parrhēsia* was a collective, communal activity. At the heart of the communal use of truth-telling were the personal interviews done by advanced teachers. In these interviews, "a teacher would give advice and precepts to individual community members" (Foucault 2001: 113). There were also group confession sessions, "where each of the community members in turn would disclose their thoughts, faults, misbehavior, and so on ... 'the salvation by one another'" (*ibid.*: 114). In this communal model, *parrhēsia* was used "in house" for the purpose of spiritual guidance, either privately or in open groups.

To illustrate the public use of *parrhēsia*, Foucault turns to the Cynics. The Cynics used truth-telling as a means of public instruction. Foucault highlights three truth-telling Cynic practices: critical preaching, scandalous behaviour and provocative dialogue. We will address each in turn.

The Cynics, unlike the Epicureans, spoke to large crowds, usually composed of people who were outside of their community. Foucault states that preaching "is still one of the main forms of truth-telling practiced in our society, and it involves the idea that the truth must be told and taught not only to the best members of the society, or to an exclusive group, but to everyone" (*ibid.*: 120). Cynics told the truth to anyone, anytime, anywhere. The need to speak out against the institutions of society (the favourite target of Cynics) on the larger public scale exemplifies *parrhēsia* as frank, critical truth-telling done simply because "the truth has to be said", regardless of the risk.

The Cynics were the masters of frank risk-taking truth-telling. Scandalous behaviour, particularly personified in Diogenes the Cynic, was a public way to show the truth and the relationship one had to the truth. The most famous example of Diogenes involves Diogenes masturbating in the public square. When asked to give an account for his behaviour, Diogenes states that "he wished it were as easy to banish hunger by rubbing the belly" (*ibid.*: 122, quoting Diogenes Laertius, VI, 46; 69). The point here is clear: if eating, the removal of hunger, is allowed in the public square, then surely the removal of sexual desire, which is just as much *aphrodisia* as eating and drinking, should be allowed in public. That one considers masturbation shameful is strange given that one does not consider eating and drinking shameful.

The third Cynic practice was the use of provocative dialogue. This is often depicted as dialogues between Diogenes and Alexander the Great. One example from the texts is that Diogenes told Alexander to move out of his way because Alexander was blocking the sun. Another example would be Diogenes calling Alexander a bastard. To say such a thing to the emperor, especially in public, is indeed provocative. From Diogenes' point of view, Alexander just is not so great! Foucault points out that "whereas Socrates plays with his interlocutor's ignorance, Diogenes wants to hurt Alexander's *pride*" (*ibid.*: 126). In other words, the provocative dialogue is a unique variation of Socratic dialogue: by showing someone that they are not true to what they claim, the philosopher encourages the interlocutor to examine oneself and begin to take care of oneself.

Preaching, acting out and attacking pride: these were the three main categories of the public use of *parrhēsia* performed by the Cynics. Foucault would have more to say about the Stoics in the 1984 lectures at the Collège de France. This is because, as Foucault states, "the Cynic parrhesiastic game is played at the very limits of the parrhesiastic contract. It borders on transgression because the *parrhēsiastēs* may have made too many insulting remarks" (*ibid.*: 127).[7] The Cynics reappear as examples for Foucault because they take truth-telling to its absolute limit; *parrhēsia* is the *modus operandi* of the entire Cynic worldview. Perhaps no other group completely embodied *parrhēsia* in their own persons in the way that the Cynics did.

The final arena for the use of *parrhēsia* is in one's private life, including one's personal relationships. One needs truth-telling such that one is one's own interlocutor: pride and flattery are possible even with one's self. One needs *parrhēsia* in order to stay away from self-deception. The group that best represents this use of truth-telling is the Stoics, although Foucault would later add early Christians to the list.

At the heart of Stoic life was self-examination. This self-examination is not the same as confession in the later Christian period. Instead, self-examination was more of an administrative activity. As Foucault notes, Seneca does not account for "sins" but:

> mistakes ... inefficient actions requiring adjustments between ends and means ... The point of the fault concerns a *practical* error in his behavior since he was unable to establish an effective

> rational relation between the principles of conduct he knows and
> the behavior he actually engaged in.   (*Ibid.*: 149)

Seneca is only keeping track of his errors because those errors are frustrating his goal. If Seneca were to give up that goal, then there would be nothing to account for. In order to tell whether one is fulfilling one's goals, one must be able to give an honest, flattery-free account of oneself: this is the role of self-examination.

The second truth-telling practice that the Stoics used was self-diagnosis. Once again, Foucault warns us not to make self-diagnosis into what would later be thought of in terms of confession. Instead, self-diagnosis was a way to figure out where one's problem lies. Foucault reads from Seneca's "On the Tranquility of Mind", a letter in which Seneca responds to the self-diagnosis of Serenus, who had written to Seneca for moral advice. The self-diagnosis lays out Serenus' moral "symptoms", and leaves it to Seneca to make a moral "diagnosis". Serenus does this only because he wants tranquillity and needs help from Seneca on how to obtain it. When Serenus speaks of his "illness", he must be careful not to misrepresent himself, regardless of whether his description presents him in the most flattering light. In order for Seneca truly to help him, Serenus understands that he must say all – tell the truth – about his life, his likes and his dislikes.

The third practice is self-testing. Foucault discusses Epictetus' method of testing representations and sorting them into the categories of those things that are in one's control and those things that are not in one's control. It is important, as with self-examination and self-diagnosis, to be frank, critical and truthful about this sorting. In so doing, the practitioner gains a truth about himself that is free from flattery and self-deception. As Foucault says,

> The truth about the disciple emerges from a personal relation
> which he establishes with himself: and this truth can now be
> disclosed either to himself ... or to someone else ... And the dis-
> ciple must also test himself, and check to see whether he is able
> to achieve self-mastery.   (*ibid.*: 164–5)

Upon deciding on self-mastery, the disciple must be able to examine himself in order to be able to disclose to himself whether he is working towards self-mastery or not. Upon discovering any flaws in the plan or in its execution, the disciple diagnoses himself in order to give the master correct information in order to secure a correct "remedy" to flaws.

A return to morality?

Epicureans, Cynics and Stoics: these Hellenic schools of thought represent, as Foucault argues in 1983, "a genuine golden age in the history of care of the self" (2005a: 81). Although we are unable to "return" to these schools of thought owing to archaeological reasons, we can at least pose the question of how we as subjects became so divorced from truth as a practice of the self such that "subjectivity" and "truth" are merely placeholders for something now long gone. How can we return to morality? Can we reclaim truth as a *moral* activity, freed from mere epistemology?

We need to offer a few *caveats*. First, I am not suggesting that one can no longer take care of oneself through practices of the self. Weight Watchers, for example, employs many practices that would fit into the Stoic model of care of the self.[8] Other examples include the martial arts, meditation and, given my proximity to the beach, surfing. We are still engaged in something like practices of the self, as other contributors to this volume well illustrate. Second, I am not suggesting that one cannot tell the truth in dangerous situations. There are whistleblowers who risk job security in the name of truth. Protesters are often willing (and plan) to get arrested for the sake of their cause. There is also something akin to the use of *parrhēsia* in interventions and psychoanalysis. We indeed have practices *like* care of the self and *parrhēsia*, but they are discontinuous with their older meaning.

Foucault argues that it is impossible in the modern period for practices of the self to be of much use in helping one be a *parrhēsiastēs* and vice versa. The yogi, for example, will have a hard time claiming that doing yoga *justifies* her critique of the government (if she *were* even to offer such a critique). It would be difficult to understand that the government should believe her critique as true because of her moral character *as a result of doing yoga*. Additionally, how many people do yoga in order to gain the moral fortitude to access the truth and tell the truth to others? In the United States, yoga is done mostly for aesthetic purposes or for medical benefit. The spiritual dimension of yoga is often internal to the practitioner: stress release and better breathing. Yoga is not the action done in order to truly gain truth about the world; it is a relaxing form of exercise. This is not to suggest that exercise cannot be a practice of the self aimed at truth, but most people exercise for the sake of health and beauty – usually the latter – not for the sake of truth and knowledge. So we see a disconnect between truth and subjectivity here. Yoga, dieting and other practices of the self in today's society seem to have nothing to do with one's moral self. Yoga is done by the virtuous as expertly as the wicked, by the more intelligent as carefully as the less intelligent. One does not go to one's yoga instructor and seek solutions to serious problems; the yoga instructor is simply there to offer the class, not to live in community with the students.

In fact, when most people resolve for the New Year that they will "take better care of themselves", they usually always mean this in a strictly *medical* sense. One resolves to lose weight, lower their bad cholesterol, cut out junk food, and so on. In making those resolutions, one rarely adds to the list "become a morally better person by lowering my cholesterol". The modern period sees the body mechanically, so there is no automatic connection between one's moral self and the body as medical object. No student will believe that the knowledge taught by a given professor, for example, is true in virtue of the professor having a healthy body.

The more I discuss our modern "practices of the self", the clearer it seems that we do not "take care" of ourselves in the ancient sense at all. It might be best to say that we have self-disciplinary practices more than practices of the self *per se*. Therefore, *our* return to morality might entail being more self-conscious about how our self-disciplinary practices inform our desires to tell the truth. Let us resolve to be truth-tellers, and form ourselves in such a way that we live for the truth. But what is truth in today's world? Is it the kind of truth one should live or die for? We must therefore become more aware of what counts for truth at any moment. Perhaps the return to morality, the critique of truth and self-discipline is simply the Foucauldian project.

Notes

1. It is perhaps here that we see Foucault's greatest debt to Heidegger's "The Age of the World Picture" (Heidegger 1977: 115–54).
2. "Subjectivity and Truth" was a draft of his 1983 book *The Care of the Self*, the third volume of the *The History of Sexuality* (Foucault 1986).
3. Of course, it need not be *Descartes* who did this, but since that is the figure that most people would know, we go with him. Foucault does not ascribe agency to authors; therefore, we must be sure not to "blame" Descartes for the Cartesian moment we are about to describe.
4. Although Foucault runs out of time before giving a detailed account of early Christian practices, he gives many hints throughout the lecture course. His best accounts of early Christian (and later Christian) practices can be found in the essays "Technologies of the Self", "Sexuality and Solitude" and "The Battle for Chastity" from the same period of Foucault's work (Foucault 1997c).
5. Immanuel Kant, *Metaphysics of Morals*, Akk. 6:429, where Kant states that our duty to tell the truth is not a duty to others but a duty to ourselves as a moral being.

6. Foucault mentions in the 1984 lectures that *parrhēsia* is not about "epistemological structures", but rather *"des formes alèthurgiques"*, forms of unconcealment (Foucault 2009: 5; see Heidegger 1996: §44).
7. Note that the theme of transgression, a Foucauldian theme from the 1960s, reappears here. See "A Preface to Transgression" (in Foucault 1998: 69–87).
8. I am thinking primarily of the food journal, although there are other techniques. See Heyes (2006, 2007).

ELEVEN

Subjectivity and power

Cressida J. Heyes

> One must remember that power is not an ensemble of mecha-
> nisms of negation, refusal, exclusion. But it produces effectively.
> It is likely that it produces right down to individuals themselves.
> Individuality, individual identity are the products of power. [1]

"Subjectivity" and its cognates are philosophical terms that describe a
possibility for lived experience within a larger historical and political
context. "The subject" (*le sujet*) is not simply a synonym for "person";
instead the term captures the possibility of being a certain *kind* of person, which, for the theorists who tend to use it, is typically a contingent
historical possibility rather than a universal or essential truth about
human nature. These terms are especially philosophically important
for Michel Foucault, who, in his middle works *Discipline and Punish*
and *The History of Sexuality, Volume I*, develops a theoretical-historical
account of the emergence of the modern subject in the context of what
he calls "disciplinary power". This chapter draws on these texts to
elaborate how Foucault believes such subjects come into being and what
the implications are for us: the persons who, he argues, have inherited
a system of power that both creates our possibilities and constrains our
existence. I examine two related challenges to Foucault's account, and
then conclude by drawing on contemporary discourses of weight and
weight loss to show how his work can be applied to case studies beyond
those Foucault himself discussed.

In French, the key term Foucault uses to capture the emergence of
subjectivities (or subject-positions: particular spaces for being a subject)
is *assujettissement*. Variously translated as "subjectivation", "subjection"

or even "subjagation", the difficulties in rendering the word into English reflect the philosophical difficulties associated with its meaning. It describes a double process of the actions of power in relation to selves that is both negative and positive. First, *assujettissement* captures the idea that we are subjected or oppressed by relations of power. When a norm (which Foucault understands as a standard to which individuals are held as well as by which populations are defined) imposes itself on us, we are pressed to follow it. In this sense *assujettissement* describes a process of constraint and limitation. For example, "homosexuals" are constrained by the oppressive beliefs and practices of those who discriminate against them. In these moments, power serves its more familiar repressive function, holding back the capacities of those individuals against whom it acts. In many political theories of oppression, power plays only this negative role, and must be out-manoeuvred if we are to become free. For Foucault, however, power always also plays a positive role: it enables certain subject-positions (or certain actions or capacities for the individual). Thus at the same time as "homosexuals" are discriminated against, the invocation of this very label (which Foucault believes is a historically specific and contingent possibility, rather than simply the truth about a pre-existing group of people) itself permits political mobilization, solidarity, mutual identification, the creation of social spaces, and so on. Without homosexuals there would be no homophobia and no gay-bashing, but there would also be no gay bars or gay pride marches.

Many alternative political theoretical models of the individual assume that we – individuals – are *ontologically prior* to the exercise of power. That is, human beings have certain universal qualities that are then exercised, suppressed, or otherwise moulded by the exercise of power. Indeed, many of us commonly think of power as something that acts upon us – an outside force to which we may succumb or not, but never as something that made us who we are. "Be yourself" is a popular injunction in Western cultures, where the self one is supposed to be can be identified, eventually, or just in theory, as an object that is not determined by relations of power (where power is also often understood as a repressive force). This model of the self has been used for many progressive purposes: for example, feminism has urged women to look beyond male dominance to find the true selves patriarchy has denied and suppressed. Foucault, however, famously argued that power is not only repressive, and nor does it act only upon the already formed subject. Rather power enables the identities we claim at the same time as it represses or limits us – and these two actions ultimately cannot be separated. If this is the nutshell version (and perhaps the most philosophically controversial aspect) of Foucault's account of *assujet-tissement*, let us look very briefly at how he reaches this conclusion.

"The Subject" and *Assujettissement*

In *Discipline and Punish: The Birth of the Prison* (*Surveillir et Punir: Naissance de la Prison*, first published in French in 1975) Foucault rather indirectly sets out his account of power through a historical account of state punishment (Foucault 1979). What could a history of punishment and the prison – specifically, a history of how the French state enacted punishment between 1757 and 1837 – tell us about how subjects come into being?[2] The mechanisms of penality that "the carceral" comes to use are like those that permeate society more broadly; the "disciplinary" power developed in the context of the prison is continuous with educational, psychological and medical contexts. In particular,

> the activity of judging has increased precisely to the extent that the normalizing power has spread. Borne along by the omnipresence of the mechanisms of discipline, basing itself on all the carceral apparatuses, it has become one of the major functions of our society ... The carceral network, in its compact or disseminated forms, with its systems of insertion, distribution, surveillance, observation, has been the greatest support, in modern society, of the normalizing power. (*Ibid.*: 304)

Not only does the prison "support" the new form of power that concerns Foucault, but it also creates a way of thinking about subjectivity. He proclaims that:

> by an analysis of penal leniency as a technique of power, one might understand both how man, the soul, the normal or abnormal individual have come to duplicate crime as objects of penal intervention; and in what way a specific mode of *assujettissement* was able to give birth to man as an object of knowledge. (*Ibid.*: 24)

How did this come about? Foucault famously opens *Discipline and Punish* with a graphic and brutal account of the public torture and execution of Damiens, the man who in 1757 attempted to kill King Louis XV. Here "the body of the condemned" is made into a spectacle. The sovereign enacts through public extreme violence the retribution that will befall the body of anyone who makes an attempt on his life.

Suddenly this narrative stops, and Foucault jumps forward eighty years, to an 1838 text in which Léon Faucher describes the daily timetable of a Paris prison (*ibid.*: 3–7). The prisoners' waking hours are closely divided into periods for prayer, work, eating, recreation and education, and their activities (such as receiving instruction, or prayer) are constructive as much as they are overtly punitive. Furthermore, Foucault suggests that the body of the prisoner is a fundamentally different kind of object in each example: Damiens' suffering is a public spectacle. His passive body manifests the power of the sovereign, against his will. The prisoners of Faucher, by contrast, live their own bodies, and discipline themselves according to the timetable constructed to mould them into certain kinds of persons; they exercise, they engage in recreation.

What emerges for Foucault as the eighteenth century unfolds, then, is a new set of methods for controlling the operations of bodies. Prisoners must be rendered obedient in order to be *managed*, but this management must come at least in part from their own actions. This new form of power, which acts without the guidance of a central sovereign upon bodies to make certain kinds of persons, Foucault labels "disciplinary power". Although I will not elaborate here on Foucault's important distinction between sovereign and disciplinary power (see e.g. Allen 1999: 31–7), it is central to the kind of *assujettissement* that Foucault argues characterizes modernity. Disciplines create a subject who is self-monitoring, developmental, the object at the intersection of numerous vectors of management and coercion and, most of all, *useful*, productive. Not only prisons, but the military, medicine, education and the emerging human sciences all play a role in the development of this new kind of subject, using four key mechanisms (Foucault 1979: 149–69). In brief, first, the relation of the individual to *space* is redefined, through novel forms of architecture (most famously, the Panoptic prison) and mechanisms of population management; second, the individual's *activity* is exhaustively controlled and monitored and his body incorporated into that process (as, for example, in the precise drilling of soldiers); third, *time* is organized and monitored much more closely, and comes to be understood as both progressive (one of Foucault's examples is incremental examinations for the advancing school pupil) and minutely (even infinitely) divisible; finally, the composition of *forces* is restructured to maximize the productive effects of people working together, organizing bodies according to their relative position and mutual effects, and redirecting attention to efficient "tactics".

Foucault distils three techniques that cut across these four mechanisms to consolidate modern subjectivity (*ibid.*: 170–94). Hierarchical observation functions by making subjects constantly visible and knowable, through a single gaze that sees everything constantly. In the Panopticon this is a literal mechanism, but Foucault treats this kind of visibility as a metaphor for how power works on subjects more broadly. Second, normalizing judgement is enacted through the micromanagement of behaviour in areas of social life from which penality had previously been absent. Although in the orphanage or barracks there are explicit regulations, the order imposed through discipline legislates "natural and observable processes" to ensure greater conformity to a norm. For this reason punishment is not only retaliatory but also corrective (*ibid.*: 179): from beating the child who errs, for example, the teacher moves to assigning "lines": a repetitive exercise that serves as both punishment and training. "Through this micro-economy of a perpetual penality operates a differentiation that is not one of acts, but of individuals themselves, of their nature, their potentialities, their level or their value" (*ibid.*: 181). The third technique of disciplinary power is the *examination* (an instrument that combines hierarchical observation and normalizing judgement). In ritualized form, examination techniques incorporate the normalizing gaze as a mechanism of differentiation and evaluation, and Foucault's examples include the physician's rounds, the school exam and army inspections. Disciplinary power is itself invisible yet renders its subjects hyper-visible in order to tighten its grip: "it is the fact of being constantly seen, of being able always to be seen, that maintains the disciplined individual in his subjection" (*ibid.*: 187).

In short, discipline creates a novel subject-position: the *individual*. This individual is a conformist, docile, self-monitoring person, who is expected (including by emergent models in the biological and human sciences) to develop in particular ways and is subject to much closer yet more seemingly benign forms of management. At the same time (and, paradoxically, through many of the same mechanisms) we are told that we each have our own distinctive biography (worthy of investigation and representation) and that we are marked by qualities internal to ourselves (not only by a generic social status as members of kinship networks or socioeconomic classes). This discourse of the distinctiveness and authenticity of the individual is for other political philosophers a boon of modernity, which marks the emergence of democracy, egalitarian citizenship and autonomy. Foucault's attitude is more ambivalent, and he is critical of narratives of historical progress that see the increase in autonomy for the individual only as liberating her from relations of power. Instead, he thinks, what we consider an increase in autonomy is complicated by a concomitant intensification of our subjection to discipline (Foucault 1997e). For many political philosophers, human beings simply are, foundationally, individuals with certain definitive qualities (perhaps rationality, or certain capabilities), where this claim is not seen as historically contingent or dependent on any particular cultural frame of reference. Human progress then consists in the gradual realization of this individuality, through, perhaps, the acquisition of rights, or economic frameworks that permit the development of capabilities. Foucault, by contrast, insists that the idea of the individual is historically specific (indeed, embedded within a particular "genealogical" understanding of what history is [see Gutting 2005: 43–53]) and that the rise of individualism does not mark the unqualified realization of our human potential. Rather, it represents the emergence of some new capacities, and the intensification of our subjection to power; we become different kinds of subject, but not necessary "better" subjects than we were.

In Volume I of *The History of Sexuality* (first published in French in 1976), his next major work after *Discipline and Punish*, Foucault elaborates his account of *assujettissement* (1990a). Our typical historical account of sexuality, he argues, leans heavily on what he famously calls "the repressive hypothesis". We tend to think, that is, that the nineteenth century is marked by a growing discomfort with public discussion of sexuality. Sexuality happened only to those peripheral deviants, the "other Victorians", such as prostitutes, pimps and perverts. For the bourgeois classes, goes the popular historical perception, sexuality was taboo. The notion that the Victorian era marked a distinctively repressive origin in the history of sexuality enables a narrative extrapolation through the struggles of psychoanalysis with repression to the sexual liberation movements of the 1960s and 1970s and beyond: our problem is (and has always been) that we are uptight about sex, and we need to challenge our own silences and shame in order to liberate ourselves (*ibid.*: 3–7).

Near the beginning of *History of Sexuality*, Foucault tells us sardonically that his:

> aim is to examine the case of a society which has been loudly castigating itself for its hypocrisy for more than a century, which speaks verbosely of its own silence, takes great pains to relate in detail the things it does not say, denounces the powers it exercises, and promises to liberate itself from the very laws that have made it function … The question I would like to pose is not, Why are we repressed? but rather, Why do we say, with so much passion and so much resentment against our most recent past, against our present, and against ourselves, that we are repressed?
>
> (*Ibid.*: 7–8)

He has three main doubts about the repressive hypothesis. First, a historical doubt: is repression such an incontrovertible fact about the history of sexuality? Second, a theoretical doubt: does power in fact always work through repression (does it always say "no"?), as the hypothesis seems to assume? And third, a political qualm: is the "anti-repression" discourse of sexual liberationists actually all that different from the very discourse of repression that it claims to expose? Foucault answers these questions, as he does in *Discipline and Punish*, through a set of historical examples dating from the seventeenth through nineteenth centuries (mostly) in France. In the chapter "The Incitement to Discourse", Foucault identifies an explosion of ways of talking about sex in the late seventeenth century, key to which is the institution of the Christian confession. Just as the functioning of power in the prison becomes a metaphor and model for disciplinary power writ large, Foucault suggests, the idea of approaching a pastoral authority and revealing the hitherto concealed truth about one's sexual transgressions comes to represent a key mechanism in all of the disciplines of sexual knowledge. As the eighteenth century rolls around, sex becomes, he argues, a central object of political, economic and technical administration, through, for example, the study of population (birth control, population growth, reproductive statistics etc.), a fascination with the sexuality of children (especially analysing and preventing masturbation), the growth of psychiatry and its study and treatment of sexual disorders, and the criminalization of certain sexual practices (*ibid.*: 25–31). Perhaps most important for Foucault's account of *assujettissement*, in Chapter 3, "Scientia Sexualis", he argues that the new science of sex produces its truth through endless incitement and confession. We are constantly urged to reveal our sexual desires, perversions and "identities", in a variety of practices that cause us to be made into "case studies" for the quasi-medical, scientific discourses that now surround sexual truth.

Foucault provides two primary examples of sexual individuals in *History of Sexuality*.[3] The first is his controversial story of Jouy, a "simple-minded" farmhand who, in 1867, enticed local young girls into "caresses". Jouy, Foucault implies, is on the cusp of the historical moment when such behaviour is met not with a smack in the face, or indifferent refusal, or viewed as "inconsequential bucolic pleasures" from which both parties can walk away without any particular conclusion being drawn about their status as "sexual victim" or "pervert".[4] His behaviour attracts the attention of a girl's parents, and thence further authorities; Jouy was physically assessed and interviewed, and then incarcerated without being convicted of any crime as a "pure object of medicine and knowledge" (*ibid.*: 32). Indeed, Foucault's interpretation comes from the published "case study" of an early example of what we would now call a "paedophile". In a second example, Foucault argues that in this crucial historical period the idea that some people are essentially "homosexuals" is posited by sexology:

> As defined by the ancient civil or canonical codes, sodomy was a category of forbidden acts; their perpetrator was nothing more than the juridical subject of them. The nineteenth-century homosexual became a personage, a past, a case history, and a childhood, in addition to being a type of life, a life form, and a morphology, with an indiscreet anatomy and possibly a mysterious physiology.
> (1990a: 43)

His arrival is announced with Foucault's most quoted line, "the sodomite had been a temporary aberration [*relaps*]; the homosexual was now a species [*espèce*]" (*ibid.*). Discovering this identity becomes a personal as well as a legislative project, in which the individual deciphers the truth of the self as homosexual, or (later) heterosexual, or another taxonomic possibility, even as, Foucault argues, these are not natural kinds of human being only now being "discovered" or "understood" but rather historically contingent forms of *assujettissement*.

Discipline and Punish and the first volume of *The History of Sexuality*, then, are the texts in which Foucault shows us most clearly how power creates subjects. They tackle different historical case studies, but their underlying philosophical arguments are closely connected. Each shows that by learning something about how a particular institution functions we can learn something about how power functions to create certain kinds of individual; each aims to use historical enquiry to make the present less familiar (to unsettle our assumptions that prisons are, among other things, humanitarian institutions with no implications for "our" subjectivity, and that we are repressed about sexuality and talking about it is liberating and transgressive, respectively). Each also argues that this process of defamiliarization will actually invert our common-sense understanding of subjectivity: we discover that criminal justice in fact creates criminals rather than simply punishing them, and that throwing off the repression of our sexuality in fact places us in thrall to a new kind of discursive control.

Objections

Critics have suggested that Foucault's historical accounts are one-sided, simplistic, or plain wrong (e.g. Alford 2000; Taylor 1984: esp. 163–5). Foucault's writing is undoubtedly allusive and elliptical, sometimes tracking very large themes and theses in ways suspiciously like the grand historical narratives he disdains, and at other times for no apparent reason picking on a particular "scene" or exemplary text to make his philosophical point. In Nietzschean spirit, he claims to be offering only descriptive accounts of the emergence of subjectivity after discipline, and rejecting the endorsement of particular values, but there are hints of political allegiance and aspiration in his writing. Foucault was actively involved in the anti-prison movement in France, as well as being a prominent openly gay intellectual, and commentators have wondered just how his actions fit with his words in this regard (see Enns 2007: 73–98). Critics charge that Foucault posits the theoretical necessity of resistance within any account of power (Foucault 1990a: 95) but fails to provide concrete examples of what resistance looks like in practice (Hartsock 1990).

Here I will focus on just two philosophical objections that are specifically directed toward Foucault's account of *assujettissement*. First, critics charge that Foucault's subject of power lacks agency, and hence the capacity to resist the effects of disciplinary power Foucault describes (e.g. Fraser 1989). Mainstream philosophical understandings of resistance to oppressive power typically require that one stand outside the system of power (at least in theory) to push back against it. *Agency*, on this more familiar view, is the capacity to act on one's own behalf, drawing on beliefs and desires that are properly one's own, yet if these beliefs and desires are the product of the power one also wants to oppose, agency (of this kind) may be impossible. As Linda Alcoff says, "Foucault's demotion of subjectivity to an analytic position posterior to power results in a conception of subjectivity deprived of agency ... In the absence of agency ... resistance to domination is impossible and even conceptually incoherent" (1992: 73–4; see also Taylor 1984). Because disciplinary power emanates from everywhere and nowhere, there is no sovereign against whom resistance can be enacted. Damiens was executed for attempting to kill the king. His case is a literal instantiation of the more metaphorical point Foucault's critics make: in the absence of a clear locus of power that can be challenged, and with the insistence that we are all part of the networks of power that both form us and limit us, it is not clear how to act, or whom to act against, especially if one is interested in advancing social justice.

At one point in his work Foucault does suggest that domination is a particular limit-case of power, in which relations are "blocked, frozen" so that no resistance is possible (1997e: 283). To deny agency only in such extreme situations, however, does not help to justify claims about the illegitimacy of those relations of power that are less than complete domination, but nonetheless politically troubling. Foucault seems to be right that increasingly the forms of power that citizens of liberal democracies need to understand are not limited to abuses of sovereign power but rather include more subtle instantiations of disciplinary power that promise greater freedom without stipulating their own price. But if all his genealogies do is to describe, then he cannot be committed to making value-judgements about which relations of power are the more oppressive, damaging, or unjust. Thus, in a second closely related objection, Foucault has often been charged with having no way of making normative claims, choosing among competing values, or with any grounds on which to argue for social change. For some critics this charge is advanced a step further: perhaps Foucault does make tacit appeal to values, but he denies this appeal while depending on it for the coherence of his position (Taylor 1984). This is often referred to as the charge of *crypto-normativity*, a term typically used in the Foucault–Habermas debates by those who wish to highlight Foucault's implicit appeal to humanist, objective values in his genealogical texts (see, for example, Habermas's own formulation of the problem [Habermas 1994: 94–8]).

That Foucault had political opinions (and reasons for holding them) seems beyond doubt. Both these objections share the sense that without positing an exterior to disciplinary power (a place where a stronger kind of agency is possible, or from which we might appeal to better values to effect social change) we are stuck in the modes of *assujettissement* Foucault describes, without control of our fate. Defenders of Foucault have responded to both these objections by pointing out that his genealogical project is to unseat a humanist theory of the subject, without thereby replacing it with some new foundational account. Foucault wants to show us that our common perceptions of our own increasing autonomy, our overcoming of repression, our gradual march toward liberation, are all ways of thinking about our subjectivity that have historical roots and are guided by a particular configuration of power. Of course some things are enabled by this configuration and others are precluded, but as Foucault famously said in an interview:

> My point is not that everything is bad, but that everything is dangerous, which is not exactly the same as bad. If everything is

dangerous, then we always have something to do. So my position leads not to apathy but to a hyper- and pessimistic activism
... I think that the ethico-political choice we have to make every
day is to determine which is the main danger.

(Foucault 1997f: 256)

So what *is* "the main danger"? I see two primary avenues of response
for Foucault's defenders. The first simply sidesteps this question. In
Foucault's practice of critique we are not told what to criticize in
advance of its appearance; because he considers any account of human
nature to be an exercise of power within a regime of truth, we cannot
list the particular modes of *assujettissement* that would make us unfree
versus those that are liberatory. Instead, Foucault provides us with a
practice by which the subject takes on the right to "desubjectivize" himself: "critique will be the art of voluntary insubordination [*inservitude
volontaire*], that of reflective indocility [*indocilitié réfléchie*]" (1990e:
39). Thus there is no specific content to critique, only a method in
which we alert ourselves to what our current subjectivity allows or
limits (see Butler 2002). As Paul Patton argues, autonomy (understood
as the capacity to govern one's own actions) will always be held back
by situations that approach domination, and will always lead to opposition: "it is not a question of advocating such resistance, of praising
autonomy or blaming domination as respective exemplars of a good
and evil for all, but simply of understanding why such resistance does
occur" (Patton 1998: 73).

The second kind of response may be more satisfying to those
critics who, like Charles Taylor, argue that we simply cannot make
sense of Foucault's Nietzschean account of power without some non-
Nietzschean concepts of freedom and truth. As Thomas Flynn argues,
the kind of genealogical critique Foucault offers *always* appeals to its
audience's shared values – of freedom as autonomy in particular – while
showing that a particular practice of power fails to live up to them in
ways we have not recognized (Flynn 1989: 196–7). This is the only
foundation available: the realization that our cares and commitments,
on the one hand, and our ability to make sense of ourselves, on the
other, are at odds in ways that make us ineffective as the very kinds of
agents we aspire to be (see Owen 2003). Foucault consistently resists
any theory of the subject in favour of a pragmatic recognition that
making power more flexible and multivalent will open up new possibilities for thinking and acting: a project we are already tacitly inclined
to consider politically valuable, albeit for reasons that are very much
contingent to our historical and political location.

Weighty subjects

Thus Foucault argues that new subjectivities have become available to us that are both ways to be an individual – to be distinctive – and to be subject to the control of a range of extra-legal mechanisms. For some scholars, Foucault's example of homosexuality has been implausible: this may be for historical reasons (some critics argue that in fact the idea of "the homosexual" pre-dates Foucault's account) or scientific reasons (some think that biological explanations for homosexuality can be adduced). But for many less opinionated readers the suggestion that homosexuality is historically specific just does not feel convincing: even if Foucault were right, so much time has passed since the emergence of the homosexual "species", and the practices that consolidate the contemporary identity of "being" a homosexual have so much of a grip, that we cannot imagine things being otherwise. By contrast, the idea that one's weight might define a subject-position is, I have argued, much more recent, and still in the process of being sedimented in a variety of institutions and practices. Let me conclude with this example, then, to show how Foucault's account of *assujettissement* might play out in practice. Any process of *assujettissement* happens at two levels: the management of the social body, and the disciplinary forces acting on the individual's body. At the level of population, obesity is now decried as a marker of corruption in the body politic (Herndon 2005) and a public health catastrophe. The strident, compulsive nature of public anti-obesity discourse is enabled by seemingly infinite statistical parsing and public policy strategizing about the population's "obesity epidemic". The very ability to construct such statistical and policy information of course depends on a range of disciplinary institutions and practices, from public health nurses who record the weight of schoolchildren to actuaries who analyse death rates. Of particular historical significance, the standard height/weight tables that were produced in the 1950s (based on actuarial rather than strictly medical evidence) provide a technique for analysing the population (how many more people are now "overweight" or "obese"?) as well as a way for individuals to define their body mass index and weight status (Heyes 2007: 67–71; Gaesser 2002).

Thus at the level of the individual, weight is turned from an incidental feature of a person into an identity. Being "overweight" becomes a numerically defined status as well as a marker of individual failure to regulate the body appropriately. This is made possible not just by the "disciplines" of public health and medicine, but also by endless confessional narratives detailing the consumption pattern, weight, fat distribution, cholesterol level, caloric expenditure, exercise habits, and so forth, of each person. Some dieting internet discussion boards feature profiles introducing each person through opaque abbreviations that actually identify starting weight, current weight and goal weight; dieters discuss the minutiae of calorie-counting, carbohydrates and exercise options with reference to the weight deviations stipulated on the screen, invoking norms such as body mass index. The web is littered with video blogs of "my weight loss journey", in which ordinary people make of their biography an object worthy of representation, while also confessing the truth of their weighty selves, often dwelling on parts of their lives that might seem only tangentially related to dieting. Increasingly the identity "dieter" becomes as real as "homosexual". This consolidation of a subject-position requires that everything about a person be dragged within the remit of weight loss; the subject-position "dieter" becomes the lens through which personal identity is revealed (Heyes 2007). True to Foucault's predictions, the practice of dieting is not simply repressive (if it were, it would not be so popular) but is also enabling: people feel better about themselves (if only for a short time), learn new information (about nutrition, for example) and develop new skills (such as how to describe and manage their personal "weaknesses"), at the same time as they are drawn ever deeper into a disciplinary system that can then exercise its control and management.

In this brief discussion I hope to have shown why Foucault believes that the modern individual is not just a fact of our humanity but is rather a historical product of disciplinary power in its overall form as well as in the specifics of the subject-positions we have inherited. My own analysis of discourses of weight has struggled with the two objections I identified: what kinds of value-judgements are justified by a genealogical reading of dieting, and how can oppressed dieters fight back? In the end, I adopt both of the strategies I mentioned. I engage largely in practices of critique, showing how the intensification of power relations and the consolidation of subjectivity accompany a discourse that most of us assume simply aspires to increase our autonomy and liberate us from the demon fat. But I also show that our "cares and commitments" are in some ways at odds with the kind of subjectivity that dieting promotes, and that this gap between the kinds of people we aspire to be and those that our practices sediment can be exploited to ethical and political purpose.

Notes

1. "Il faut rappeler que le pouvoir n'est pas un ensemble de mécanismes de négation, de refus, d'exclusion. Mais il produit effectivement. Il produit vraisemblable-

ment jusqu'aux individus eux-mêmes. L'individualité, l'identité individuelle sont des produits du pouvoir ..." (Michel Foucault, "Je suis un artificier" ["I am an artisan"], 1975 interview with Roger-Pol Droit, available online in French at http://foucault.info/documents/foucault.entretien1975.fr.html [accessed August 2010]).

2. Foucault admits the specificity of his history to the French penal system (see 1979: 309 n.3). His translator Alan Sheridan also notes the distinctiveness of "*supplice*" – "the public torture and execution of criminals that provided one of the most popular spectacles of eighteenth-century France" (*ibid.*: "Translator's Note").

3. A third example is Foucault's reading of the memoir of Herculine Barbin, "a nineteenth century French hermaphrodite" (Foucault 1980b).

4. Feminist critics have suggested that in his haste to see Jouy as exemplary of a historical moment Foucault is too quick to characterize the power relations in which he participates as benign. See Alcoff (1996).

TWELVE

Practices of the self

Dianna Taylor

Previous chapters have illustrated that for Foucault subjectivity is not a state we occupy but rather an activity we perform. Moreover, it is an activity that always takes place within a context of constraint. We constitute ourselves as subjects (we are enabled) by way of various "practices of the self", which include activities like writing, diet, exercise and truth-telling. At the same time, we are constituted (we are constrained) in so far as the way in which we undertake these practices is shaped by institutions such as schools, courts of law, hospitals and the state security apparatus, as well as by the more general prevailing norms and values of the society in which we live.

Put differently, subjectivity is not distinct from but is rather formed in and through relations of power. There are not emancipatory institutions and norms that enable us, on the one hand, and oppressive or normalizing institutions and norms that constrain us, on the other; rather, we are simultaneously enabled and constrained by the same institutions and norms. We therefore find ourselves confronted with the task of figuring out when and how we are enabled and when and how we are constrained, of determining ways in which existing practices have the potential to loosen constraints and thus resist normalization, and of employing those practices not only for that purpose, but also in order to develop new and different practices – new and different ways of relating to ourselves and others. We need, in other words, to be able to reflect critically on the very process of becoming a subject.

This critically reflective activity comprises a specific set of practices, which Foucault collectively refers to as "critique". In this chapter I provide an overview of Foucault's account of the origins of modern

Western subjectivity in early Christian practices of the self. These practices reflect an interconnection of power and truth, in the sense that
one comes to know the truth about oneself and also gains access to the
truth more broadly by way of a process of self-abnegation: subjectivity
is achieved only by way of a sacrifice of self. According to Foucault, this
element of self-sacrifice is retained within the modern hermeneutics of
the subject, where it comes to characterize techniques of governmentality. In the second part of the chapter, we will see how the practice of
critique functions as a Foucauldian response to the problem of the self-
sacrificing modern subject. As he conceives of it, critique may loosen
the relationship between truth and power that characterizes modern
subjectivation (the process of becoming a subject) and in doing so facilitate the development of new, emancipatory forms of subjectivity.

Subjectivity and self-sacrifice

Early Christian practices of the self were carried out within a relationship through which persons were guided toward salvation by another
or others to whom they subordinated themselves (Foucault 1997b).
Within a "salvation-oriented" relationship, the subordinate individual
must submit to certain externally generated truths, such as religious
doctrines and codes. But this acceptance is not merely passive; the
subordinate individual also participates in various kinds of practices,
"general rules, particular knowledge, precepts, methods of examination, confessions, [and] interviews" in order to access and reveal the
truth about her or himself (*ibid.*: 26). Through taking up these practices, then, the individual also constitutes him or herself as a subject.
Practices of the self thus possess a two-fold character: on the one hand
they are manifestations of the norms and values of the society in which
an individual lives and thus establish a relationship between the individual and others; on the other, in so far as the individual takes them
up and incorporates them into the construction of his or her own
subjectivity, these practices establish a relationship of the individual
to her or himself.

Foucault shows that early Christian practices of the self, like their
ancient and Hellenistic counterparts, entail a process of "conversion".
To obtain the right to access the truth about oneself and the world, the
subject must "be changed, transformed, shifted, and become, to some
extent and up to a certain point, other than himself" (2005a: 15). In
ancient and Hellenistic contexts, conversion takes the form of a "turning" within the self: a kind of self-reflective taking stock of oneself

through which one gains (a different) perspective. By contrast, early Christian conversion, *metanoia*, entails not a turning of but instead a break within the self; it is less a process and more an "upheaval", a single, sudden transition from one form of existence to another: "death to life", "mortality to immortality", "darkness to light", "the reign of the devil to that of God" (*ibid.*: 211).

The break that occurs in *metanoia* is thus a kind of renunciation or sacrifice of the self, of one's "old" self, in the name of truth and salvation (*ibid.*: 250). A process characterized by self-practices comes into play, therefore, primarily after conversion has taken place. Post-conversion, practices of the self function to "decipher" the self in order to ensure that its thoughts are pure and properly focused on the truth and the light. This deciphering therefore involves practices that are intended to demonstrate that the old self has been renounced; it in fact involves a repeated and public sacrifice of the old self. Foucault identifies two practices as being fundamental to this process of renunciation and sacrifice: confession and self-examination. In early Christianity, these practices look quite different from the modern sacraments of penance and the confession of sins (Foucault 1980h). Penitence is not a "determined act" but a status that involves the execution of a number of different practices which allow a person who has sinned to become reintegrated into the religious community (*ibid.*). It is a public demonstration on the body through, for example, wearing a hair shirt, covering the head in ashes, and fasting, of the authenticity or truth of one's repentance (*ibid.*). Hence the reference of the entire reintegration process as "exomologesis" or "manifesting the truth" (*ibid.*).

Confession functions as a similar manifestation. As is the case with penitence, in order to be authentic, to reveal and thereby provide access to the truth, confession must be expressed to another. It performs a kind of check on self-examination in the sense that through confessing, one's thoughts and the condition of one's soul are expressed to another person who possesses the authority to interpret them. Unlike penitence, however, to which there is an identifiable end, Foucault argues that confession, with its requirement that one perpetually put the contents of one's soul into words – that one ceaselessly verbalize – establishes a permanent relation of obedience to authority. But verbalization does not merely subjugate the speaker to the listener. According to Foucault, these particular acts of verbalization are simultaneously acts of self-sacrifice:

Verbalization is a way for ... conversion, for the rupture of the self. It is a way for the conversion to develop itself and take effect.

Since under the reign of Satan the human being was attached to himself, the verbalization as a movement towards God is a renunciation of Satan. It is for the same reason a renunciation of oneself. (*Ibid.*)

Thus, Foucault argues that both penitence and confession entail a "self-revelation which is at the same time a self-destruction" (*ibid.*). One comes to know and tell the truth within a power relation in which "[n]o truth about the self is without the sacrifice of the self" (*ibid.*). In illustrating his point, Foucault tells the story of a young monk who, when he became gravely ill, was forbidden by his master to die (1980h). The monk "lived a few weeks more", at which time, commanded by his master to die, he did so (*ibid.*). "Even when the monk is old," Foucault writes, "even when he is, at his turn, the master, he has to keep the spirit of obedience as a *permanent sacrifice of his own will*" (*ibid.*, emphasis added).

Self-sacrifice and governmentality

From Foucault's perspective, this same type of power relation – one in which access to truth is linked to the sacrifice of self – characterizes modern Western subjectivity. With the rise of modernity, practices that had once possessed solely religious applicability were adopted within secular contexts and thereby came to characterize modern societies more broadly. This generalization occurred in part as a result of the inadequacy of sovereign power in the face of the increasing complexities of modern life. Given the social, political and economic restructuring that resulted from the "state centralization" and "dispersion and religious dissidence" (specifically, the Reformation and Counter-Reformation) of the fifteenth and sixteenth centuries (Foucault 1991c: 88), Foucault asserts that "[f]ar too many things were escaping the old mechanism of the power of sovereignty, both at the top and at the bottom, both at the level of detail and at the mass level" (2003: 249). Hence the concern within early modern societies with what Foucault refers to as the problem of "government". For Foucault, government includes but is not limited to the administration of a state and its people by a ruler. It also exists as a more general concern about how to direct the conduct of oneself and others. Government as a "general problem" pertains to "the government of oneself ... the problem of personal conduct, the government of souls and lives" as well as to "the government of children" (1991c: 87), "beggars and the poor", "families" and "armies" (1997b: 27). Foucault argues that at this time one can observe a preoccupation with questions about "[h]ow to govern oneself, how to be governed, how to govern others, by whom the people will accept being governed, [and] how to become the best possible governor" (*ibid.*).

It is not difficult to see how the two types of modern power Foucault identifies could emerge within a context characterized by a concern with government and, therefore, how early Christian practices of the self develop into modern governmentalizing techniques. Foucault's descriptions of prisons, army training and schools in *Discipline and Punish*, for example, illustrate how governmentalizing techniques function in the service of disciplinary power. Within each of these contexts, particular types of efficient yet limited subjectivity (the delinquent, the soldier, the pupil) emerge. With respect to biopower, governmentalizing techniques take the form of, for example, analysis by state agencies of rates of transmission of infectious disease. Such analysis produces norms of normality (health) and abnormality (illness) and, hence, "normal" and "abnormal" subjects. A certain number of annual deaths from influenza, especially among certain segments of the population (the elderly, infants, persons with compromised immune systems), are expected and therefore considered normal; intervention into the population by health officials is intended less to prevent these deaths than to protect the "normal" or healthy segment of the population and, therefore, "defend" society as a whole (Foucault 2003).

A whole host of societal institutions reproduce these subject categories: prisons, schools, courts of law, hospitals, government agencies (i.e. the Centers for Disease Control and Prevention), social services agencies, and state and private mental health agencies and treatment centres. To the extent that individuals participate within or are subject to scrutiny by these institutions (and all of us, to greater and lesser extents, do and are), we also constitute ourselves in and through these same subject categories; in doing so we implicate ourselves more deeply in modern relations of disciplinary power and biopower. To be clear, even if we have not been diagnosed with, for example, some form of physical or mental illness, our constitution of ourselves as "healthy" takes place in and through broad categories of normality and abnormality that prevail within our culture. It is no coincidence that the techniques and practices we employ in such constitution include some of the same practices that characterized the Christian pastoral: physical exercise, self-reflection, self-writing and confession (whether to a priest, a therapist or a police officer).

Self-sacrifice and the Western philosophical tradition

Even though these modern practices of self-constitution are no longer linked specifically to a religious context, given their origins and the fact that they were for the most part uncritically adopted within secular contexts as modes of individual and collective conduct, Foucault argues that they retain their self-sacrificing character. This modern interconnection between subjectivation and self-sacrifice has presented Western cultures with the problem of how to "[save] the hermeneutics of the self and [get] rid of the necessity of sacrifice of self which [is] linked to this hermeneutics" (1980h). Hence the concerted and sustained efforts within Western philosophy to construct and substitute a positive notion of subjectivity (i.e. the autonomous subject) for the self-sacrificing subject (*ibid.*). Foucault has in common with the rest of the Western philosophical tradition the desire to break with the cycle of "unconditional obedience, uninterrupted examination and exhaustive confession" which underpins modern subjectivity (1999a: 157). Yet, unlike the tradition, Foucault wishes to move away from self-sacrifice not because it violates the subject's independence and autonomy, but rather because it cultivates a destructive and therefore harmful relationship of the self to itself (*ibid.*). For him, critique provides ways of negotiating modern relations of power that loosen the interconnection between truth and power that characterizes modern power relations and, hence, opens up possibilities for being constituted and constituting ourselves as subjects in ways that do not simply reproduce an abnegating self-relation.

Critique

Critique, Foucault argues, emerges in response and is inextricably linked to the spread of governmentalizing techniques: it reflects a concern with the question of "how not to be governed" (1997b: 28). Rather than presenting itself as a simple opposition to the art of governing, this question reflects a concern with how to navigate a context characterized by governmentality in ways that expand the field of possible courses of action and modes of thought. This response does not (nor does it aim to) avoid or release persons from governance. As Foucault makes clear, given the nature of modern power relations our aim is not to get outside of power, but rather to navigate those relations differently. Critique can be conceptualized as a different kind of "art", which Foucault refers to as the "art of not being governed quite o much" (*ibid.*: 29). It is an art, he explains, "[of not being governed] *like that*, by that, in the name of those principles, with such and such an objective in mind and by means of such procedures, not like that, not for that, not by them" (*ibid.*: 28). If governmentality is the "movement through which individuals are subjugated in the reality of a social practice through mechanisms of power that adhere to a truth", critique functions as the "movement by which the subject gives himself the right to question truth on its effects of power and question power on its discourses of truth" (*ibid.*: 32). As a response to governmentality, then, critique might be understood as an "art of navigating power relations". As one of those techniques and practices that challenge and thereby loosen the link between truth and power, critique characterizes and in turn promotes modes of subjectivity that likewise challenge self-sacrifice. It retains a critically (self-)reflective character and therefore possesses emancipatory potential.

Let us be clear about how this kind of negotiation of power relations is possible; that is, let us be clear that although we cannot completely extricate ourselves from relations of power, we are not simply determined by them: we are not doomed to uncritically reproduce the prevailing norms and values of our society. If we were determined in this way I would, for example, accept and reproduce prevailing views about what it means to be a woman in US society. I would subordinate myself to men; I would behave in a passive and accommodating manner; and I would accept primary if not sole responsibility for caring for my (male) spouse, children and home. But I do not in fact do any of these things: I assert my equal standing with men; I am not passive and accommodating but instead argue, for example, that I ought to be paid the same wage for doing the same work; I am involved in a heterosexual marriage but I do not have children, I have a career, and my husband and I both work at making our relationship as egalitarian as possible.[1] Moreover, I even go a step further: rather than settling for equal status within the existing gendered order of things, I call into question the fact that we as a society adhere to a system of gender at all, and contend that there are other ways of organizing our lives that do not entail dominance and subordination. I am able to adopt a critical perspective precisely because I am not merely constituted, but also constitute myself. I identify as a woman but, owing to my experiences constituting myself and being constituted in this way, I also identify myself as a feminist and constitute myself in ways that challenge prevailing gender norms: in so far as I am the one who takes up the norms and values of my society, I have the capacity to take them up differently, or not to take them up at all. As Foucault puts it:

It may be that the problem about the self does not have to do with discovering what it is, but maybe has to do with discovering that the self is nothing more than the correlate of technology built into our history. Then ... [m]aybe the problem now is to change those technologies, or maybe to get rid of those technologies, and then, to get rid of the sacrifice which is linked to those technologies. (1980h)

Here Foucault reiterates the point made at the outset of this chapter, that part of what constituting ourselves as modern subjects must entail is critical analysis of precisely how we do this constituting. But for such critical analysis to be possible, we have to recognize that we actively participate in our self-constitution and thus possess the capacity to engage in such analysis. Subjectivity is not a matter of uncovering our "true self", a process which requires us to adhere to some pre-given, external definition of who and what we are; rather, it is a matter of calling into question such an understanding of what it means to be a subject, of investigating the effects that such a notion has on our relationship to ourselves and others, and of exploring possible ways of thinking and acting differently.

Critique as an emancipatory practice

Bearing these points in mind, we are in a position to better understand Foucault's assertion that subjects "give themselves the right" to critique, a right that is, at the same time, always constrained and that is exercised within a context of constraint. Judith Butler articulates this point clearly and succinctly when she argues, "it is not the case that a subject is formed and then turns around and begins suddenly to form itself ... the subject is both crafted and crafting, and the line between how it is formed, and how it becomes a kind of forming, is not easily if ever drawn" (Butler 2002: 225). Even more to the point: "The self delimits itself and decides on the material for its self-making, but the delimitation that the self performs takes place through norms which are, indisputably, already in place" (*ibid.*). This conceptualization of critique is also consistent with Foucault's view of power and freedom as mutually constitutive. He conceives of freedom as the ability to navigate power relations in ways that mediate against and attempt to minimize constraints (such as direction and management) while maximizing capacities, rather than as the ability to extricate oneself from relations of power. My constitution of myself as a feminist does not

180

require that I extricate myself from the context that defines me as subordinate because I am a woman: just as critique emerges within a context of governmentality, so feminism emerged within a context of sexism. The fact that subjects are simultaneously enabled and constrained by the same norms and practices may complicate but does not destroy possibilities for either freedom or subjectivity.

Now that we have a sense of how critique can facilitate the negotiation of power relations, let us explore in a little more detail precisely what it means to put critique into practice, as well as how its practice counters the self-sacrificing character of modern subjectivity and facilitates new forms of self-constitution. We have seen that critique emerges from and responds to our present context, a context within which prevailing conditions present themselves as necessary conditions (gender is viewed not as a contingent sociopolitical system but as a description of women's and men's inherent natures), where our relationships to ourselves and others, as well as to knowledge and truth, are relationships of obedience to authority and, as such, are relations of power. Foucault refers to our stance relative to our present generally as an "attitude". For him, an attitude encompasses "thinking, speaking and acting", our relationships to "what exists, to what one knows, to what one does" – in other words, our relationship to ourselves – as well as "to society, to culture, and ... to others" (1997b: 24). Critique, or a "critical attitude", thus comprises a particular way of responding to the present; specifically, a critical attitude entails thought, speech, acts and modes of relating that reflect "insubordination" against prevailing conditions, which reveal those conditions as contingent, and thus do not simply reproduce the same relationship between truth and power which leaves persons in a self-sacrificing relationship of obedience to the authority of prevailing norms (*ibid.*).

Taking into account these characteristics – critique is a practice that encompasses how we think, speak and act; critique establishes a way of relating to oneself and others within the context of one's present conditions; critique does not merely affirm and rearticulate those conditions – it is clear that Foucault, himself a cultivator of a critical attitude, is not simply going to tell us what a critical attitude looks like and how we need to go about practising it: to do this would be to undermine critique's insubordinate character and, therefore, its emancipatory potential. Nevertheless, Foucault does provide his readers with some clues or "tools" that we can utilize in ways that, given the challenges of our own present (which are not necessarily the same challenges of Foucault's), facilitate our insubordinate constitution of ourselves.

181

In a late interview, Foucault described himself as a "moralist", but he also made clear that he meant something very specific by this term. "In a sense, I am a moralist", Foucault explains:

> insofar as I believe that one of the meanings of human existence – the source of human freedom – is never to accept anything as definitive, untouchable, obvious, or immobile. No aspect of reality should be allowed to become a definitive and inhuman law for us. (Foucault 1980g)

What Foucault describes here bears a strong resemblance to the "insubordinate" character of critique, and his articulation of the specific "moral values" that underpin – and which he in turn seeks to articulate and practise through – his work gives us an idea of how he thought a critical attitude could be cultivated. The first value Foucault identifies is refusal – specifically, refusing "to accept as self-evident the things that are proposed to us" (*ibid.*). The second value is curiosity, which Foucault describes as "the need to analyze and to know, since we can accomplish nothing without reflection and knowledge" (*ibid.*). The third value is innovation: "to seek out in our reflection those things that have never been thought or imagined" (*ibid.*). While Foucault initially refers to refusal, curiosity and innovation as values, in the same interview he also refers to them as principles. Given their relevance to critique, and also taking into consideration that Foucault states that he both engages in and endeavours to promote them through his philosophical work, I think it is consistent with a Foucauldian perspective also to think of refusal, curiosity and innovation as techniques or practices.

Cultivating a critical attitude/countering self-sacrifice

The practices of refusal, curiosity and innovation illustrate that critique or a critical attitude opposes the self-sacrificing character of modern subjectivity. Self-sacrifice characterizes a mode of subjectivation that requires individuals to subjugate themselves to authority in order to gain access to truth. The first thing we notice about critique is that gaining such access is not central. Cultivating a critical attitude entails an oppositional or at least ambivalent stance relative to what is presented to us as true, as given, as necessary. It emphasizes reflection and knowledge, as opposed to truth, with the result that self-constitution is an ongoing and continually evolving process, not a linear development toward a pre-established goal. The non-linear nature of critique as a mode of self-constitution is further supported by the practice of innovation: critique functions in such a way as to develop new, different and unexpected modes of thought and existence; it does not move toward a pre-determined, identifiable end.

Considering a specific example from my own experience may help to illustrate how engaging in refusal, curiosity and innovation facilitates new modes of self-constitution – specifically, modes that do not entail self-sacrifice. A few years ago I began to experience physical pain that was unrelated to injury or, as far as I could tell, to illness. At an appointment with my primary care physician I described what I was experiencing. He made a diagnosis and prescribed medication. After a few days I was still in pain, and so went to the emergency room that weekend. The ER doctor said that the specific way in which I described the pain was puzzling to him, but given the area of the body in which the pain was present, he agreed with my primary care physician's diagnosis. He wrote me a new prescription and referred me to a specialist.

Two doctors had now suggested that my pain was stemming from a certain condition, despite the fact that the way in which I was describing the pain did not exactly coincide with the way in which that condition usually manifested itself. At this point, I began to doubt my own experience. Was I describing the pain incorrectly? Or did the pain in fact feel more like what the literature on this particular condition said it was supposed to? When I met with the specialist a few days later I could tell by the expression on his face that what I was describing was unfamiliar to him. I stopped mid-sentence and asked, "Haven't you ever heard things described in this way before by other patients?" He replied that he had not, and that he ought to examine me to see what was going on. I agreed to the examination and subsequently to a procedure he said would provide me with relief.

For the purposes of our discussion here, what matters about my experience is not the success of the procedure or the competence of my physicians. What requires our attention is rather how I constitute myself and am in turn constituted as a subject. Within the context of the health care system I constitute myself as a subject in order to gain access to the truth about myself by way of a set of practices that subordinate me to authority (not only that of physicians, but also of system and hospital administrators, insurance companies and the like). Within this system, in other words, I both constitute myself and am in turn constituted as a "patient" (and also as a "consumer"). Through this constitution, I sacrifice a part of myself, specifically, the insubordinate part, the part that "gives itself the right to question truth on its effects of power and question power on its discourses of truth" (Foucault 1997b: 32). Such sacrifice, in so far as it curtails my critical capacities, results in the reinscription of my own subordination. Sitting in physicians' offices and the emergency room, I questioned myself instead on what it was about my situation that was making me question myself. I agreed to treatment (medication and a procedure) even though I was uncertain about whether I was being properly diagnosed. I was inhibited from asking questions of my physician and taking a more active role in my own physical health and well-being.

As noted earlier, it is not the case that "good" doctors do not subordinate their patients and therefore promote self-sacrifice while "bad" doctors do: there are not beneficial norms I can utilize and harmful norms that I can avoid. As "the patient", I constitute myself (and am constituted) through norms and practices that subordinate me. Given the relationship I have illustrated between self-sacrifice and being a patient, we might be tempted at this point to fall back upon a sovereign notion of power, and say that doctors possess power which they then wield against their patients, thereby subjugating them. But we need to remember from earlier chapters Foucault's analysis of how modern power relations function; doing so, we see that doctors are also implicated in relations of power through which they are constituted and also constitute themselves in ways that promote self-sacrifice and inhibit critique. While it is true that "the doctor" is constituted as an authority figure who possesses knowledge that "the patient" does not, the doctor gains and maintains access to that knowledge only through adhering to accepted norms and practices within the health care system. She must, for example, conduct herself in a professional manner and treat patients in accordance with prevailing medical standards and protocols (as well as within the parameters set by insurance companies). This is not to say that doctors ought to adopt a casual attitude toward their patients' health, become overly friendly with them, or treat them with unapproved medical interventions. It is rather to encourage critical analysis of ways in which the (self-)constitution of "the doctor" *both enables and constrains* physicians' ability to effectively care for and promote the physical and mental health of their patients (and themselves, for that matter).

How might a critical attitude, characterized by the practices of refusal, curiosity and innovation, facilitate a new mode of self-constitution that does not entail such sacrifice on my part? My discussion in the previous paragraph, I think, constitutes refusal as Foucault conceives of it. In order to refuse particular norms that are presented to us as self-evident, we have to be able to see that prevailing modes of thought and xistence are not necessary modes; without such realization, refusal of particular norms and practices is not even conceivable, for how can I see as refusable what is simply inevitable? Once I see that I am in fact constituted as a patient within the health care system I can begin to take issue with particular aspects of how I am constituted and in doing so, begin to constitute myself differently. That is, having refused to accept that prevailing conditions are necessary conditions, I can become curious about my current situation. Recognizing that I constitute myself as obedient to authority within the context of the health care system in order to gain access to truth, I can begin to analyse what it is about the health care system that encourages me to behave in this manner, and analyse the effects of my current attitude. I can also begin to think about how I might act differently. For example, if I determine that part of the reason I defer to the authority of my doctor is because I do not want to appear disrespectful, I might consider why, within this particular context, I seem to be confusing respect with deference. Am I concerned with *appearing* respectful or with actually treating the physician with respect? I can then do some innovating by marking clear distinctions between respect and deference, beginning to experiment with conducting myself in a manner that is both respectful and assertive, and making sure that the physicians and others with whom I am dealing within the health care system are in fact worthy of my respect. If they are, I should treat them accordingly; if they are not, I shouldn't be concerned with appearances at all.

It is important to recognize that cultivating a critical attitude through the practices of refusal, curiosity and innovation does not get me outside of prevailing power relations. Even if I wanted to I could not become a medical doctor and treat myself to avoid being "the patient". I must rely up physicians for care, and I still have to navigate the system's bureaucracy: within the health care system I will be constituted as "the patient" or "the consumer", and my treatment within the system will be based on prevailing notions of what a patient or consumer is. But as Foucault makes clear, even though all self-constitution takes place within a context of constraint, I am not merely determined by those prevailing notions; I possess the capacity to constitute myself and I can do so differently by way of taking up existing norms and practices in new ways or rejecting them completely. While neither strategy is without its risks (my doctor may find me annoying if I ask too many questions or seek a second opinion) even negative consequences (being thought annoying) may open onto other possibilities: I can find a new doctor, engage in holistic practices like yoga that problematize the traditional Western separation of body and mind, explore alternative methods of alleviating pain (acupuncture, for example). Foucault's work thus provides us with the crucial insight that in so far as I constitute myself I can constitute myself differently. Equipped with this insight, I am able to take up practices that facilitate my negotiation of existing power relations in ways that maximize my critical and creative capacities thereby minimizing and working towards the eradication of subjectivity characterized by self-sacrifice.

Notes

1. In describing my own situation I am suggesting neither that marriage is unproblematic nor that feminists should not have children. Indeed, I believe that marriage as an institution is oppressive to women; I mention the fact that I do not have children simply in order to draw attention to the prevailing expectation that married women reproduce. From my perspective, my relationship to my own marriage is one way in which I endeavour to constitute myself differently.

Chronology

15 October 1926	Paul-Michel Foucault is born in Poitiers, France
1936–40	Attends Lycée Henri-IV, Poitiers
1940–45	Attends Collège Saint-Stanislaus, Poitiers
Autumn 1945	Enters Lycée Henri-IV, Paris (to study for *khâgne* – a year of special preparatory training for entry into the École Normale Supérieure); meets Jean Hyppolite
Autumn 1946	Enters École Normale Supérieure, Paris; meets Louis Althusser
August 1951	Achieves Agrégation de Philosophie; examined by Georges Canguilhem
Autumn 1951–Summer 1952	Fondation Thiers, Centre de recherches humanistes, Paris
June 1951	Earns a Diploma in Psychopathology from the Paris Institute of Psychology
1952–55	Assistant Lecturer at University of Lille
1955–58	Cultural Delegate to the University of Uppsala, Sweden; meets Georges Dumézil in March 1956
1958	Director of Center for French Civilization, Warsaw, Poland; teaches in the Romance Languages Institute at the University of Warsaw
1959	Director of French Cultural Institute, Hamburg, Germany; teaches in the Department of Romance Languages at the University of Hamburg
1960–66	Member of the Faculty of Letters and Human Sciences, University of Clermont-Ferrand; becomes a tenured professor in 1962 after successfully defending his thesis
1961	Publication of *Folie et déraison. Histoire de la folie à l'âge Classique* (*Madness and Civilization: A History of Insanity in the Age of Reason*)
1963	Publication of *Naissance de la Clinique. Une archéology du regard médical* (*The Birth of the Clinic: An Archaeology of Medical Perception*)
1966–68	Visiting Professor of Philosophy, University of Tunis, Tunisia

1966	Publication of *Les Mots et les choses. Une achéologie des sciences humaines* (*The Order of Things: An Archaeology of the Human Sciences*)
1968–69	Tenured Professor of Philosophy, University of Paris VIII, Vincennes
1969	Elected to the Collège de France; Publication of *L'Archéologie du savoir* (*The Archaeology of Knowledge*)
December 1970	Delivers inaugural lecture at the Collège de France, "L'Ordre du discours" (The Discourse on Language)
1971	Founds Groupe d'Information sur les Prisons (GIP)
1975	Publication of *Surveiller et punir. Naissance de la prison* (*Discipline and Punish: The Birth of the Prison*)
1976	Publication of *La Volonté de Savoir*: Volume I of *Histoire de la sexualité* (Volume I of *The History of Sexuality*)
1980	Visiting Professor at the University of California, Berkeley; delivers the Howison Lectures in October
Autumn 1982	Spends eight weeks at the University of Vermont
Autumn 1983	Visiting Professor at the University of California, Berkeley
1984	Publication of *L'Usage des plaisirs*: Volume II of *Histoire de la sexualité* (*The Use of Pleasure*: Volume II of *The History of Sexuality*)
1984	Publication of *Le Souci de soi*: Volume III of *Histoire de la sexualité* (*The Care of the Self*: Volume III of *The History of Sexuality*)
2 June 1984	Foucault collapses in his apartment; he is admitted to the Hôpital Salpêtrière on 9 June
25 June 1984	Foucault dies in the Hôpital Salpêtrière, Paris

All information comes from Eribon (1991).

Bibliography

Works by Michel Foucault

Foucault, M. 1972. *The Archaeology of Knowledge and the Discourse on Language*, A. M. Sheridan Smith (trans.). New York: Pantheon. Originally published as *L'Archéologie du savoir* (Paris: Gallimard, 1969).

Foucault, M. 1973. *The Order of Things*. New York: Vintage. Originally published as *Les Mots et les choses: Une achéologie des sciences humaines* (Paris: Gallimard, 1966).

Foucault, M. 1975. *The Birth of the Clinic: An Archaeology of Medical Perception*, A. M. Sheridan Smith (trans.). New York: Vintage. Originally published as *Naissance de la Clinique: Une archéology du regard medical* (Paris: PUF, 1963).

Foucault, M. 1976. *Histoire de la sexualité vol. 1: La volonté de savoir*. Paris: Gallimard.

Foucault, M. 1977. "Nietzsche, Genealogy, History". In *Language, Counter-Memory, and Practice: Selected Essays and Interviews*, D. F. Bouchard (ed.), 139–64. Ithaca, NY: Cornell University Press.

Foucault, M. 1979. *Discipline and Punish: The Birth of the Prison*, Alan Sheridan (trans.). New York: Vintage. Originally published as *Surveiller et punir: Naissance de la prison* (Paris: Gallimard, 1975).

Foucault, M. (ed.) 1980a. *Herculine Barbin, Being the Recently Discovered Memoirs of a Nineteenth-Century French Hermaphrodite*, Richard McDougall (trans.). Brighton: Harvester.

Foucault, M. 1980b. Introduction to *Herculine Barbin: Being the Recently Discovered Memoirs of a Nineteenth-Century French Hermaphrodite*. New York: Pantheon.

Foucault, M. 1980c. "Body/Power". In *Power/Knowledge: Selected Interviews and Other Writings 1972–1977*, C. Gordon (ed.), C. Gordon, L. Marshall, J. Mepham & K. Soper (trans.), 55–62. New York: Pantheon.

Foucault, M. 1980d. "Truth and Power". In *Power/Knowledge: Selected Interviews and Other Writings 1972–1977*, C. Gordon (ed.), C. Gordon, L. Marshall, J. Mepham & K. Soper (trans.), 109–33. New York: Pantheon.

Foucault, M. 1980e. "Power and Strategies". In *Power/Knowledge: Selected Interviews and Other Writings, 1972–1977*, C. Gordon (ed.), C. Gordon, L. Marshall, J. Mepham & K. Soper (trans.), 134–45. New York: Pantheon.

Foucault, M. 1980f. "The Politics of Health in the Eighteenth Century". In *Power/Knowledge: Selected Interviews and Other Writings 1972–1977*, C. Gordon (ed.), C. Gordon, L. Marshall, J. Mepham & K. Soper (trans.), 166–82. New York: Pantheon.

Foucault, M. 1980g. "Power, Moral Values, and the Intellectual". IMEC (Institut Mémoirs de l'Édition Contemporaine), Caen, France. Archival identification number FCL2. A02–06.

Foucault, M. 1980h. "Christianity and Confession". IMEC (Institut Mémoirs de l'Édition Contemporaine), Caen, France. Archival identification number FCL3.4, FCL2 A03–04.

Foucault, M. 1982a. "The Subject and Power". In *Michel Foucault: Beyond Structuralism and Hermeneutics*, H. Dreyfus & P. Rabinow (eds), 208–26. Chicago, IL: University of Chicago Press.

Foucault, M. 1982b. *I, Pierre Rivière, having slaughtered my mother, my sister, and my brother: A Case of Parricide in the 19th Century*. Lincoln, NE: University of Nebraska Press.

Foucault, M. 1984a. "What is Enlightenment?" In *The Foucault Reader*, P. Rabinow (ed.), 32–50. New York: Pantheon.

Foucault, M. 1984b. "Nietzsche, Genealogy, History". In *The Foucault Reader*, P. Rabinow (ed.), 76–100. New York: Pantheon.

Foucault, M. 1986. *The History of Sexuality, Volume III: The Care of the Self*, R. Hurley (trans.). New York: Pantheon. Originally published as *Histoire de la sexualité, vol. III: Le Souci de soi* (Paris: Gallimard, 1984).

Foucault, M. 1988. "Truth, Power, Self: An Interview with Michel Foucault". In *Technologies of the Self: A Seminar with Michel Foucault*, L. Martin, H. Gutman & P. Hutton (eds), 9–15. Amherst, MA: University of Massachusetts Press.

Foucault, M. 1990a. *The History of Sexuality, Volume I: An Introduction*, R. Hurley (trans.). New York: Vintage. Originally published as *Histoire de la sexualité, vol. I : La Volonté de savoir* (Paris: Gallimard, 1976).

Foucault, M. 1990b. *The History of Sexuality, Volume II: The Use of Pleasure*, R. Hurley (trans.). New York: Vintage. Originally published as *Histoire de la sexualité, vol. II: L'Usage des plaisirs* (Paris: Gallimard, 1984).

Foucault, M. 1990c. "Critical Theory/Intellectual History". In *Michel Foucault: Politics, Philosophy, Culture. Interviews and Other Writings 1977–1984*, L. Kritzman (ed.), A. Sheridan & others (trans.), 17–46. London: Routledge.

Foucault, M. 1990d. "Practicing Criticism". In *Michel Foucault: Politics, Philosophy, Culture. Interviews and Other Writings 1977–1984*, L. Kritzman (ed.), A. Sheridan & others (trans.), 152–6. London: Routledge.

Foucault, M. 1990e. "Qu'est-ce que la critique?" *Bulletin de la Société Française de Philosophie* 84(2): 35–63.

Foucault, M. 1991a. "How an 'Experience Book' is Born". In *Remarks on Marx*, R. J. Goldstein & J. Cascaito (trans.), 25–42. New York: Semiotext(e).

Foucault, M. 1991b. "Questions of Method". In *The Foucault Effect: Studies in Governmentality*, G. Burchell, C. Gordon & P. Miller (eds), 73–86. Chicago, IL: University of Chicago Press.

Foucault, M. 1991c. "Governmentality". In *The Foucault Effect: Studies in Governmentality*, G. Burchell, C. Gordon & P. Miller (eds), 87–104. Chicago, IL: University of Chicago Press.

Foucault, M. 1994. "The Ethics of Care for the Self as the Practice of Freedom". In *The Final Foucault*, J. W. Bernauer and D. Rasmussen (eds), 1–20. Cambridge, MA: MIT Press.

Foucault, M. 1996a. "The Ethics of the Concern for the Self as a Practice of Freedom". In *Foucault Live: Collected Interviews 1961–1984*, S. Lotringer (ed.), 432–49. New York: Semiotext(e).

Foucault, M. 1996b. "The Return of Morality". In *Foucault Live: Collected Interviews 1961–1984*, S. Lotringer (ed.), 465–73. New York: Semiotext(e).

Foucault, M. 1997a. *The Politics of Truth*, S. Lotringer & L. Hochroth (eds). New York: Semiotext(e).

Foucault, M. 1997b. "What is Critique?" In *The Politics of Truth*, S. Lotringer & L. Hochroth (eds), 23–82. New York: Semiotext(e).

Foucault, M. 1997c. *Ethics, Subjectivity and Truth: The Essential Works of Michel Foucault 1954–1984*, vol. 1, P. Rabinow (ed.). New York: New Press.

Foucault, M. 1997d. "Technologies of the Self". In *Ethics, Subjectivity and Truth: The Essential Works of Michel Foucault 1954–1984*, vol. 1, P. Rabinow (ed.), 223–51. New York: New Press.

Foucault, M. 1997e. "The Ethics of Concern for Self as a Practice of Freedom". In *Ethics, Subjectivity and Truth: The Essential Works of Michel Foucault 1954–1984*, vol. 1, P. Rabinow (ed.), 281–301. New York: New Press.

Foucault, M. 1997f. "On the Genealogy of Ethics: An Overview of Work in Progress". In *Ethics, Subjectivity and Truth: The Essential Works of Michel Foucault 1954–1984*, vol. 1, P. Rabinow (ed.), 253–80. New York: New Press.

Foucault, M. 1997g. "What is Enlightenment?" In *Ethics, Subjectivity and Truth: The Essential Works of Michel Foucault 1954–1984*, vol. 1, P. Rabinow (ed.), 303–19. New York: New Press.

Foucault, M. 1998. *Aesthetics, Method, and Epistemology: The Essential Works of Michel Foucault 1954–1984*, vol. 2, J. Faubion (ed.). New York: New Press.

Foucault, M. 1999a. "On the Government of the Living". In *Religion and Culture: Michel Foucault*, J. Carrette (ed.), 154–7. London: Routledge.

Foucault, M. 1999b. "The Debate on the Novel". In *Religion and Culture: Michel Foucault*, J. Carrette (ed.), 72–4. London: Routledge.

Foucault, M. 1999c. "Michel Foucault and Zen: A Stay in a Zen Temple". In *Religion and Culture: Michel Foucault*, J. Carrette (ed.), 110–14. London: Routledge.

Foucault, M. 2001. *Fearless Speech*, J. Pearson (ed.). New York: Semiotext(e).

Foucault, M. 2003. *Society Must Be Defended: Lectures at the Collège de France, 1975–1976*, M. Bertani & A. Fontana (eds), D. Macey (trans.). New York: Picador.

Foucault, M. 2005a. *The Hermeneutics of the Subject: Lectures at the Collège de France, 1981–1982*, F. Gros (ed.), G. Burchell (trans.). Basingstoke: Palgrave Macmillan.

Foucault, M. 2005b. "What Are the Iranians Dreaming About?" In *Foucault and the Iranian Revolution*, J. Afary & K. Anderson (eds), 203–9. Chicago, IL: University of Chicago Press.

Foucault, M. 2005c. "Iran: The Spirit of a World Without Spirit". In *Foucault and the Iranian Revolution*, J. Afary & K. Anderson (eds), 250–60. Chicago, IL: University of Chicago Press.

Foucault, M. 2005d. "Is It Useless to Revolt?" In *Foucault and the Iranian Revolution*, J. Afary & K. Anderson (eds), 263–7. Chicago, IL: University of Chicago Press.

Foucault, M. 2006a. *Psychiatric Power: Lectures at the Collège de France 1973–1974*, J. Lagrange (ed.), G. Burchell (trans.). Basingstoke: Palgrave Macmillan.

Foucault, M. 2006b. *History of Madness*. London: Routledge.

Foucault, M. 2007. *Security, Territory, Population: Lectures at the Collège de France 1977–1978*, M. Senellart (ed.), G. Burchell (trans.). Basingstoke: Palgrave Macmillan.

Foucault, M. 2008a. *Introduction to Kant's Anthropology*, Roberto Nigro and Kate Briggs (trans.). New York: Semiotext(e).

Foucault, M. 2008b. *Le gouvernement de soi de des autres: Cours au Collège de France, 1982–1983*. Paris: Seuil/Gallimard.

Foucault, M. 2008c. *The Birth of Biopolitics: Lectures at the Collège de France, 1978–79*, G. Burchell (trans.). Basingstoke: Palgrave Macmillan.

Foucault, M. 2009. *Le courage de la vérité: Le gouvernement de soi et des autres II. Cours au Collège de France, 1984*. Paris: Seuil/Gallimard.

Other works

Afary, J. & K. B. Anderson 2005. *Foucault and the Iranian Revolution: Gender and the Seductions of Islamism*. Chicago, IL: University of Chicago Press.

Alcoff, L. 1992. "Feminist Politics and Foucault: The Limits to a Collaboration". In *Crises in Continental Philosophy*, Arleen B. Dallery and Charles E. Scott with P. Holley Roberts (eds.), 69–86. Albany, NY: SUNY Press.

Alcoff, L. 1996. "Dangerous Pleasures: Foucault and the Politics of Pedophilia". In *Feminist Interpretations of Michel Foucault*, S. Hekman (ed.), 99–135. University Park, PA: Penn State University Press.

Alford, C. F. 2000. "What Would it Matter if Everything Foucault Said About Prison Were Wrong? *Discipline and Punish* After Twenty Years". *Theory and Society* **29**: 125–46.

Allen, A. 1999. *The Power of Feminist Theory: Domination, Resistance, Solidarity*. Amsterdam: SWP Publishers.

Arendt, H. 1985. *The Origins of Totalitarianism*. New York: Harvest Books.

Augustine 1991. *The Confessions*, H. Chadwick (trans.). New York: Oxford University Press.

Augustine 1993. *On Free Choice of the Will*, T. Williams (trans.). Indianapolis, IN: Hackett.

Bartky, S. 1988. "Foucault, Femininity and the Modernization of Patriarchal Power". In *Feminism and Foucault: Reflections on Resistance*, I. Diamond & L. Quinby (eds), 61–86. Boston, MA: Northeastern University Press.

Bayer, R. 1981. *Homosexuality and American Psychiatry: The Politics of Diagnosis*. Princeton, NJ: Princeton University Press.

Bernauer, J. W. 2004. "Michel Foucault's Philosophy of Religion: An Introduction to the Non-Fascist Life". In *Michel Foucault and Theology: The Politics of Religious Experience*, J. Bernauer & J. Carrette (eds), 77–98. Aldershot: Ashgate.

Bernauer, J. W. & M. Mahon 1994. "Michel Foucault's Ethical Imagination". In *The Cambridge Companion to Foucault*, G. Gutting (ed.), 141–58. Cambridge: Cambridge University Press.

Bigwood, C. 1991. "Renaturalizing the Body". *Hypatia* **6**(3): 54–72.

Black, E. 2004. *War Against the Weak: Eugenics and America's Campaign to Create a Master Race*. New York: Four Walls Eight Windows.

Bordo, S. 1989. "The Body and the Reproduction of Femininity: A Feminist Appropriation of Foucault". In *Gender/Body/Knowledge*, A. Jaggar & S. Bordo (eds), 13–33. New Brunswick, NJ: Rutgers University Press.

Bordo, S. 1993. "Feminism, Foucault and the Politics of the Body". In *Up Against Foucault*, C. Ramazanoglu (ed.), 179–203. London: Routledge.

Bordo, S. 2003. *Unbearable Weight*. Berkeley, CA: University of California Press.

Bradley, S. J. & K. J. Zucker 1990. "Gender Identity Disorder and Psychosexual Problems in Children and Adolescents". *Canadian Journal of Psychiatry* **35**: 477–86.

Braidotti, R. 1991. *Patterns of Dissonance: A Study of Women in Contemporary Philosophy*. Cambridge: Polity.

Butler, J. 1990. *Gender Trouble: Feminism and the Subversion of Identity*. London: Routledge.

Butler, J. 1997. *The Psychic Life of Power, Theories in Subjection*. Palo Alto, CA: Stanford University Press.

Butler, J. 2002. "What is Critique? An Essay on Foucault's Virtue". In *The Political: Readings in Continental Philosophy*, D. Ingram (ed.), 212–26. Oxford: Blackwell.

Carrette, J. 2000. *Foucault and Religion*. London: Routledge.

Childs, D. J. 2001. *Modernism and Eugenics: Woolf, Eliot, Yeats, and the Culture of Degeneration*. Cambridge: Cambridge University Press.

Coates, S. 1990. "Ontogenesis of Boyhood Gender Identity Disorder". *Journal of American Academy of Psychoanalysis* **18**(3): 414–38.

Davidson, A. 1994. "Ethics as Aesthetics: Foucault, the History of Ethics, and Ancient Thought". In *The Cambridge Companion to Foucault*, G. Gutting (ed.), 115–40. Cambridge: Cambridge University Press.

Deleuze, G. 1995. "Postscript on Control Societies". In *Negotiations*, Martin Joughin (trans.), 177–82. New York: Columbia University Press.

Dubel, I. & K. Vintges (eds) 2007. *Women, Feminism and Fundamentalism*. Amsterdam: SWP Publishers.

Enns, D. 2007. *Speaking of Freedom: Philosophy, Politics, and the Struggle for Liberation*. Palo Alto, CA: Stanford University Press.

Eribon, D. 1991. *Michel Foucault*. B. Wing (trans.). Cambridge, MA: Harvard University Press.

Feder, E. 1996. "Disciplining the Family: The Case of Gender Identity Disorder". *Philosophical Studies* **85**: 195–211.

Feder, E. 2007. *Family Bonds: Genealogies of Race and Gender*. Oxford: Oxford University Press.

Fine, M. & A. Asch 1988. "Disability Beyond Stigma: Social Interaction, Discrimination, and Stigma". *Journal of Social Issues* **44**(1): 3–21.

Flynn, T. R. 1989. "Foucault and the Politics of Postmodernity". *Noûs* **23**(2): 187–98.

Flynn, T. R. 1997. *Sartre, Foucault and Historical Reason, vol. 2: A Poststructuralist Mapping of History*. Chicago, IL: University of Chicago Press.

Fraser, N. 1989. *Unruly Practices: Power, Discourse and Gender in Contemporary Social Theory*. Cambridge: Polity.

Fraser, N. 1994. "Michel Foucault: A 'Young Conservative?'" In *Critique and Power: Recasting the Foucault/Habermas Debate*, M. Kelly (ed.), 185–210. Cambridge, MA: MIT Press.

Gaesser, G. A. 2002. *Big Fat Lies: The Truth About Your Weight and Your Health*. Carlsbad, CA: Gürze Books.

Grosz, E. 1994. *Volatile Bodies: Toward a Corporeal Feminism*. Indianapolis, IN: Indiana University Press.

Gutting, G. 1994. "Introduction: Michel Foucault: A User's Manual". In *The Cambridge Companion to Foucault*, G. Gutting (ed.), 1–27. Cambridge: Cambridge University Press.

Gutting, G. 2005. *Foucault: A Very Short Introduction*. Oxford: Oxford University Press.

Habermas, J. 1986. "Taking Aim at the Heart of the Present". In *Foucault: A Critical Reader*, D. C. Hoy (ed.), 103–8. Oxford: Blackwell.

Habermas, J. 1994. "Some Questions Concerning the Theory of Power: Foucault Again". In *Critique and Power: Recasting the Foucault/Habermas Debates*, M. Kelly (ed.), 79–107. Cambridge, MA: MIT Press.

Hadot, P. 1995. *Philosophy as a Way of Life: Spiritual Exercises from Socrates to Plato*, M. Chase (trans.). Oxford: Blackwell.

Halperin, D. M. 1995. *Saint Foucault: Towards a Gay Hagiography*. Oxford: Oxford University Press.

Hartsock, N. 1990. "Foucault on Power: A Theory for Women?" In *Feminism/Postmodernism*, L. Nicholson (ed.), 157–75. London: Routledge.

Heidegger, M. 1977. *The Question Concerning Technology and Other Essays*. W. Lovitt (trans.). New York: Harper Torchbooks.

Heidegger, M. 1996. *Being and Time*. J. Stambaugh (trans.). Albany, NY: SUNY Press.

Herndon, A. 2005. "Collateral Damage from Friendly Fire?: Race, Nation, Class and the 'War Against Obesity'". *Social Semiotics* 15(2): 127–41.

Heyes, C. J. 2006. "Foucault Goes to Weight Watchers". *Hypatia* 21(2): 126–49.

Heyes, C. J. 2007. *Self-Transformations: Foucault, Ethics, and Normalized Bodies*. New York: Oxford University Press.

Hobbes, T. 1986. *Leviathan*. New York: Penguin.

Honig, B. 2008. "What Foucault Saw at the Revolution". *Political Theory* 36(2): 301–12.

Kant, I. 2006. *Toward Perpetual Peace and Other Writings on Politics, Peace, and History*. D. L. Colclasure (trans.). New Haven, CT: Yale University Press.

Katz, J. N. 1995. *The Invention of Heterosexuality*. New York: Dutton.

Kukla, R. 2005. *Mass Hysteria: Medicine, Culture and Mothers' Bodies*. Lanham, MD: Rowman & Littlefield.

Liebmann Schaub, U. 1989. "Foucault's Oriental Subtext". *PMLA* 104: 306–16.

Lynch, R. A. 1998. "Is Power All There Is? Michel Foucault and the 'Omnipresence' of Power Relations". *Philosophy Today* 42(1): 65–70.

Lynch, R. A. 2009. "A New Architecture of Power: An Anticipation of Ethics". *Philosophy Today* 53 (SPEP Supplement): 263–7.

McNay, L. 1991. "The Foucauldian Body and the Exclusion of Experience". *Hypatia* 6(3): 125–40.

McNay, L. 1992. *Foucault and Feminism*. Cambridge: Polity.

McWhorter, L. 1999. *Bodies and Pleasures: Foucault and the Politics of Sexual Normalization*. Bloomington, IN: Indiana University Press.

McWhorter, L. 2009. *Racism and Sexual Oppression in Anglo-America: A Genealogy*. Bloomingon, IN: Indiana University Press.

Merleau-Ponty, M. 1962. *Phenomenology of Perception*. C. Smith (trans.). London: Routledge & Kegan Paul.

Nealon, J. 2008. *Foucault Beyond Foucault: Power and its Intensifications Since 1984*. Palo Alto, CA: Stanford University Press.

Okin, S. M. 1999. *Is Multiculturalism Bad for Women?* Princeton, NJ: Princeton University Press.

Oksala, J. 2005. *Foucault on Freedom*. Cambridge: Cambridge University Press.

Owen, D. 2003. "Genealogy as Perspicuous Representation". In *The Grammar of Politics: Wittgenstein and Political Philosophy*, C. J. Heyes (ed.), 82–96. Ithaca, NY: Cornell University Press.

Patterson, O. 1991. *Freedom in the Making of Western Culture*, vol. 1. New York: Basic Books.

Patton, P. 1998. "Foucault's Subject of Power". In *The Later Foucault: Politics and Philosophy*, J. Moss (ed.), 64–77. London: Sage.

Polanyi, K. 2001. *The Great Transformation: The Political and Economic Origins of Our Time*. Boston, MA: Beacon Press.

Rekers, G. A. & J. Varni. 1977. "Self-Regulation of Gender-Role Behaviors: A Case Study". *Journal of Behavior Therapy and Experimental Psychiatry* **8**(4): 427–32.

Rekers, G. A., P. M. Bentler, A. C. Rosen & O. Vivar Lovaas 1977. "Child Gender Disturbances: A Clinical Rationale for Intervention". *Psychotherapy: Theory, Research, and Practice* **14**(1): 2–11.

Sartre, J.-P. 1989. "Existentialism is a Humanism", Philip Mairet (trans.). In *Existentialism from Dostoyevsky to Sartre*, Walter Kaufman (ed.), 345–69. New York: Meridian.

Sawicki, J. 1991. *Disciplining Foucault: Feminism, Power and the Body*. London: Routledge.

Simons, J. 1995. *Foucault & the Political*. London: Routledge.

Soper, K. 1993. "Productive Contradictions". In *Up Against Foucault*, C. Ramazanoglu (ed.), 29–51. London: Routledge.

Spivak, G. C. 1993. "More on Power/Knowledge". In *Outside in the Teaching Machine*, 25–52. London: Routledge.

Taylor, C. 1984. "Foucault on Freedom and Truth". *Political Theory* **12**(2): 152–83.

Taylor, C. 1986. "Foucault on Freedom and Truth". In *Foucault: A Critical Reader*, D. C. Hoy (ed.), 67–102. Oxford: Blackwell.

Taylor, C. 1992. *The Ethics of Authenticity*. Cambridge, MA: Harvard University Press.

Taylor, F. W. 1967. *The Principles of Scientific Management*. New York: Norton.

Thompson, K. 2003. "Forms of Resistance: Foucault on Tactical Reversal and Self-Formation". *Continental Philosophy Review* **36**(2): 113–38.

Vintges, K. 2004. "Endorsing Practices of Freedom: Feminism in a Global Perspective". In *Feminism and the Final Foucault*, D. Taylor & K. Vintges (eds), 275–99. Chicago, IL: University of Illinois Press.

Vlastos, G. 1991. *Socrates, Ironist and Moral Philosopher*. Ithaca, NY: Cornell University Press.

White, M. & D. Epston. 1990. *Narrative Means to Therapeutic Ends*. New York: Norton.

White, S. 1996. *Political Theory and Postmodernism*. Cambridge: Cambridge University Press.

World Health Organization 2004. *International Classification of Diseases and Related Health Problems*, 10th rev., 2nd ed. (ICD-10). Geneva: World Health Organization.

Zucker, K. J. & S. J. Bradley 1999. *Gender Identity Disorder and Psychosexual Problems in Children and Adolescents*. New York: Guilford.

Index